Collaborating

Barbara Gray

Foreword by Eric Trist

Collaborating

Finding Common Ground
for Multiparty Problems

Jossey-Bass Publishers

San Francisco • Oxford • 1991

COLLABORATING
Finding Common Ground for Multiparty Problems
by Barbara Gray

Copyright © 1989 by: Jossey-Bass Inc., Publishers
350 Sansome Street
San Francisco, California 94104
&
Jossey-Bass Limited
Headington Hill Hall
Oxford OX3 0BW

Library of Congress Cataloging-in-Publication Data

Gray, Barbara, date.
    Collaborating : finding common ground for multiparty problems /
Barbara Gray ; foreword by Eric Trist. — 1st ed.
        p.   cm. — (Jossey-Bass management series) (Jossey-Bass
social and behavioral science series)
    Bibliography: p.
    Includes index.
    ISBN 1-55542-159-8 (alk. paper)
    1. Problem solving. 2. Interorganizational relations. I. Title.
II. Series. III. Series: Jossey-Bass social and behavioral science
series.
HD30.29.G73   1989
658.4'03—dc19   88-46094
                                                                        CIP

Manufactured in the United States of America

The paper in this book meets the guidelines for
permanence and durability of the Committee on
Production Guidelines for Book Longevity of the
Council on Library Resources.

JACKET DESIGN BY WILLI BAUM

FIRST EDITION
HB Printing   10 9 8 7 6 5 4 3
Code 8933

A Joint Publication in
The Jossey-Bass Management Series
and
The Jossey-Bass Social and Behavioral Science Series

Contents

Tables and Figures

Chapter Eight

Chapter Nine

Chapter Ten

Chapter Eleven

Chapter Twelve

Foreword

As one long preoccupied with the issue of collaboration, its crucial significance for our times, and the difficulties of securing enough of it, I welcome Barbara Gray's path-breaking book. By combining the perspectives of organizational behavior and political science she has fashioned a new process-oriented approach to the study of collaboration. This approach incorporates two interrelated processes: conflict resolution and the advancement of shared visions. The first process involves working through emotionally charged issues to achieve negotiated settlements; the second involves the discovery of common values that can give direction to the development of social domains. When the first process is embedded in the second, powerful results may be obtained.

Barbara Gray's book offers by far the most comprehensive and systematic treatment yet to be attempted of the whole set of issues in the field of collaboration. Her book will, in my view, fundamentally influence the field's future in both theory and practice. This is high praise, but I believe most readers who seriously study this book will agree with me, whatever their criticisms or reservations.

The world has become so interdependent, the rate of change so rapid, that to go on fighting and competing with one another as we have been doing, especially since the industrial revolution, will not provide societal modes capable of seeing us through to any desirable future. No organization now is large or powerful enough to go it alone in what my Australian colleague, Fred Emery, and I have called the *turbulent environment*—and the turbulence is steadily increasing. The sane alternative is collaboration. But shall we be able to collaborate on a sufficient scale and at an efficient pace to avert serious disasters that may soon begin to overwhelm us? At present this is an open question. However, the richness and variety of Gray's empirical material, which discloses the amount of collaboration currently going on at all levels of society—most of it little noticed and certainly never before correlated—has made me, a rather pessimistic soul, more cautiously optimistic than I was before reading her book.

My own realization that the need for collaboration was becoming critical began some thirty years ago when Emery and I were examining the meaning of a new type of project being brought to the Tavistock Institute. This type of project presented complex problems involving interorganizational relations. The solution required envisioning a better future through establishing a common value base and resolving conflict to a degree not usually attempted. At that time we did not, of course, have the benefit of Gray's conceptualizations. A paper we read on collaboration at the 1963 International Psychology Congress in Washington was not well understood, because few of our colleagues in organizational behavior were then working experientially on interorganizational problems and were not confronted with the need for organizing efforts at this level. I say this to emphasize that the need to look for a new theory was forced on us, as on many others, by the practical dilemmas we were encountering in the field—not by our musings in the "ivory tower."

Some years later ideas about collaboration within large-scale social systems began to be taken up by researchers in several countries—some influenced by us, others proceeding from their own premises. In still another few years these ideas began to enter the language of certain leading individuals in industry and government. Let us note here that the need for collaboration was anticipated long before by Jean Monnet, the architect of the Iron and Steel Community, the French Planning Commission, and the European Economic Community.

Now, in the late 1980s, the recognition has become wide-spread that we are entering a new era in which collaboration, rather than competition, will in all likelihood become the leading or governing value in interorganizational relations. Competition, though still important, will play a subordinate role.

Our inherited value structure is against this reversal. The transition will be profoundly resisted at both conscious and unconscious levels. Though Barbara Gray has noted this, I am not sure that she has taken sufficient account of the extent of the psycho- and sociodynamic problems we shall have to confront. We may not get through them—at least, not in time to prevent a number of destructive regressions.

Although much progress toward the recognition of the value of collaboration has been made at the appreciative level (e.g., recognizing the value of collaboration), too little has been made at the practical level. This book offers for the first time a map of the main issues likely to arise in concrete collaborative undertakings. We now know what these issues are, how they relate to one another, and what strategies and methods we need to deal with them. In fact, Gray includes a "how to" handbook within the larger scholarly and conceptual text. We learn about *problem-* and *agenda-setting* and the special importance of the mediator's role. In reading about designing projects concerned with shared values, we learn about *search conferences*—a relatively new methodology. In the section on designing projects concerned with conflict resolution, we learn about *policy dialogues* and *negotiated rulemaking*.

Gray's overall goal is nothing less than to set society moving toward a negotiated order. I very much like her use of the plural forms *collaborations* and *orders*, because what we undertake is specific collaborations resulting in specific negotiated orders. These specific collaborations may lead in time—albeit a long time—to a new social norm of collaboration and a new organizational principle of negotiated order as a basis for evolving a changed structure for society.

Gray gives us specific sets of conditions for when and when not to collaborate. Her theory is that collaboration is a new way of organizing in which all stakeholders surrender some sovereignty while retaining some power. The result envisaged is a political system different from pluralism, elitism, or control of consciousness.

All this and more is packed into this book. In place of a rather vague and aspirational idea of collaboration, I now have a road map and a tool kit with which to undertake my next collaborative venture. I shall have more hope than before that there may emerge both the commitment and the skill to secure a concrete negotiated order satisfying to all stakeholders.

April 1989   Eric Trist
Emeritus Professor of Social Systems Sciences
The Wharton School, University of Pennsylvania

Preface

Collaborating: Finding Common Ground for Multiparty Problems describes a process for solving the complex problems we face as a society. What the future holds in store depends in large measure on how we as a society begin to tackle problems that continually press for answers: acid rain, unsatisfactory toxic waste disposal, contamination of groundwater, decaying of urban infrastructures, racial tensions, tort liability, questionable use of biotechnology, illiteracy, and many others. The answers to pressing societal problems such as these often seem illusory. Frequently, proposed solutions are characterized as unfeasible because they are believed to be financially impossible or technologically out of reach. Often no solutions are forthcoming because the decision makers are polarized, hopelessly deadlocked in political battles, or stuck in protracted legal wranglings. Inaction or repeated failures to arrive at a solution can be costly to the parties involved and to society as a whole.

This book proposes a way to confront these impasses. Many of our problems appear insoluble because our limited conceptions about how to manage in an increasingly interconnected world are limited. Our current problem-solving models frequently position participants as adversaries, pit them against one another, and leave them to operate with an incomplete appreciation of the problem and a restricted vision of what is possible.

The impasses are typically characterized as technical or

economic. I argue in this book that the roadblocks are as much conceptual and organizational as they are technical and economic. Many of our problems are unsolvable because our systems of organizing are not geared for a highly interdependent environment.

Finding creative solutions in a world of growing interdependence requires envisioning problems from perspectives outside our own. We need to redesign our problem-solving processes to include the different parties that have a stake in the issue. Achieving creative and viable solutions to these problems requires new strategies for managing interdependence.

Collaboration offers such a viable strategy. It essentially provides a framework for approaching problems and searching for solutions. However, collaboration itself is not the solution. To put it simply, collaboration is a process in which those parties with a stake in the problem actively seek a mutually determined solution. They join forces, pool information, knock heads, construct alternative solutions, and forge an agreement. Many examples of successful collaboration are examined in this book. They range from settling local disputes over fishing rights to conducting international negotiations about protecting the ozone layer. The parties involved include public-private partnerships for coping with urban problems and multifirm consortia that promote cutting edge research. Not all attempts at collaboration have been successful, but our examples provide the grist for analysis of what works and what we still have to learn in order to collaborate successfully.

This book focuses on collaboration as a method for solving interorganizational problems. Such problems generally involve the interests of multiple parties and often cut across several sectors of society. Frequently, constructive resolution of these dilemmas will benefit society as a whole as well as the parties involved.

In *Collaborating* I draw on organization theory to explain why collaborative alliances between businesses, government, labor, and communities are necessary and warranted at this time. It is my aim to provide specific insights into how collaborations are conducted and critical evidence from practice about the realities of collaborating.

Because of the burgeoning interest in collaboration in every sector of society, this book is written for managers, public officials, scientists, lawyers, planners, dispute resolution practitioners, and other professionals and citizens—all of whom may be potential partners in collaboration in the days to come.

The book is organized into four parts. Part One establishes the need for collaboration. Chapter One explains how collaboration incorporates multiple perspectives to solve societal problems. It provides a detailed definition of collaboration and enumerates the potential benefits to be gained from collaborating. The chapter also includes a case illustrating how controversial differences in perceptions about community safety were reconciled using a collaborative approach.

Chapter Two is more analytical in nature. It explains why collaborative initiatives are increasing and specifically identifies six contextual incentives that are creating an impetus to collaborate.

In Part Two I delve into the dynamics of collaborating. In Chapter Three I describe the three-phase process by which collaborations unfold. Key issues that surface during each phase of collaboration are enumerated and illustrated with case examples. A comprehensive case study in Chapter Four demonstrates how this sequential process of collaborating was used successfully to resolve a dispute between citizens and lenders over investment in a community.

Students of organizations, political scientists and managers from public- and private-sector organizations, and dispute resolution practitioners should find Chapters Five and Six particularly interesting because these reveal the political dynamics associated with collaboration. The case of the National Coal Policy Project illustrates how political issues shaped the outcome of a classic collaboration between business and environmental groups.

Parties in a collaboration often seek the assistance of a mediator. Chapter Seven considers the role of a mediator in collaboration and outlines the various tasks that mediators can perform to move the collaboration toward constructive outcomes.

In Part Three I explore different designs for collaborating. Chapter Eight begins with a framework for classifying collaborative designs into four general types. Then several designs for collaboration currently used when parties share a common vision of a problem are introduced. In Chapter Nine collaborative designs for resolving conflicts are investigated in detail. This chapter contains extensive treatment of regulatory negotiations and site-specific disputes dealing with environmental hazards.

Part Four describes the challenge of collaborating from both conceptual and practical perspectives. In Chapter Ten I examine collaboration from the perspective of organization theory, assailing traditional theories of interorganizational relations for their failure to capture the dynamic, emergent aspect of these relations, and I propose a reconceptualization based on negotiated order theory. Collaborations are depicted as dynamic processes for changing problem domains. This chapter will appeal particularly to behavioral scientists interested in theories of organization.

A much more practical orientation to organizing a successful collaboration is offered in Chapter Eleven. Those interested in initiating a collaborative venture should find this chapter particularly helpful. In it I take a realistic look at the difficulties of putting collaboration into practice and when and how to overcome them.

Chapter Twelve introduces the theme of shared stewardship and examines the challenges of developing the capacity to exercise it in the 1990s. The chapter closes with predictions about the transformative potential that collaboration affords us for coping with critical local, national, and international problems.

Warriors Mark, Pennsylvania　　　　　　　　　　Barbara Gray
April 1989

Acknowledgments

This book is the culmination of many years of work. The questions that initially compelled me to embark on this research grew out of my work as director of an inner-city alternative high school in Cleveland, Ohio. My question then was a fairly simple one: How can low-power groups influence more powerful ones (for example, a big-city school system)? My continuing interest in community politics during the middle and late 1970s helped to expand and refine my research questions and to expose me firsthand to arenas in which conflict and collaboration were at work. I am indebted to Tom Bier and Lana Cowell, two compatriots from that era whose commitments to action have left a lasting imprint on my work.

My first serious answers to my questions were shaped under the tutelage of my mentor David Brown. In Dave I found a kindred spirit whose curiosity about the dynamics of interorganizational relations was then and continues to be a source of inspiration. I am most indebted to Dave for modeling how values shape one's research agenda and how to merge personal and academic integrity in one's work. Dave's influence is undoubtedly present in subtle and not so subtle ways throughout this manuscript.

I have also been greatly persuaded by the work of Eric Trist, who has influenced my basic theoretical orientation. I fondly recall how moved I was, shortly after receiving my Ph.D.

degree, listening to Eric deliver the Academy of Management's Distinguished Lecture in August 1979. I have profited immensely from his counsel over the years.

Special thanks are due to my colleague Joe McCann, with whom the plan to write this book was originally conceived. Although a coauthored version never emerged, the seeds of many ideas contained herein were planted during extended conversations between Joe and me during 1983-1985.

As my commitment to write a book began to solidify, I had many conversations with friends, students, and colleagues, who made important contributions to the argument. Often their ideas were incorporated directly as examples or supporting arguments. Many of these people critiqued early drafts of the manuscript and helped to tease out of me what I really meant to say. My thanks to Chris Argyris, Graham Astley, John Bagby, John Dunlop, Wendy Emrich, John Flynn, Patricia Greenfield, Christopher Moore, Udo Staber, Eileen Steif, Lawrence Susskind, Donna Wood, and a few anonymous reviewers. There are others, I am sure, whose contributions I have neglected to mention. I hope they will take heart in seeing their influence in the printed word and gently point out my omission to me.

I am also grateful to the Program on Negotiation (PON) at the Harvard Law School for allowing me the privilege of being a visiting scholar during 1987-88, while I was devoting my energies to this project. The opportunity to work in an intellectual community devoted to research on the theory and practice of negotiation provided both an intellectual and an emotional boost to forge ahead with my work. In particular, I wish to thank Deborah Kolb and Jeffrey Rubin, who helped make my stay a profitable one. To Debbie also go special thanks for her thorough and constructive review. I also express my gratitude to the support staff at PON.

I need to acknowledge two other organizations that have supported my research intellectually, philosophically, and financially. The Institute for Development Research (David Brown, Jane Covey, and March Leach) continues to present new opportunities for learning about collaboration. So, too, do Peggy Dulany and Bruce Sherer, at Synergos Institute, who seem like fellow pilgrims on this journey.

Collaborative endeavors with several of my students have undoubtedly improved this work. Many of the data for the National Coal Policy Project case were collected and organized by Tina Hay. Robin Allen, Anne Donnellon, Dan Greening, and Aimin Yan have also provided the appropriate mix of respect and challenge for these ideas. In addition, the latter two have provided much needed last-minute help in preparing the manuscript.

One individual who deserves a medal for her contribution to this book is Judy Sartore of the Research Publications Center at Pennsylvania State University's College of Business Administration. I marvel at how she transformed endless revisions into a polished manuscript overnight. I am deeply indebted to Judy for her outstanding commitment to the project and her forbearance under adverse conditions and short deadlines. Her staff, particularly Barbara Apaliski, Carmella Dunn, and Barbara Lippincott, also deserve praise for jobs well done.

In addition to those already mentioned, a few people have provided encouragement and personal support throughout this project. It was to them that I turned when I began to question the wisdom of my endeavor. I am deeply grateful to Anne Donnellon, Elaine Johnson, Mark Kriger, Ed Ottensmeyer, Linda Smircich, and Maurine Myoon Stuart for just being there.

Finally, my deepest appreciation goes to my husband, Ray, and my daughter, Lara, who have borne up under my physical and emotional absence over this past year. Their patience and generosity, in loving me at a distance when I needed to be left alone and cheering me on from the wings, have been immensely important.

B.G.

To my father,
Clayton A. Gray

The Author

Barbara Gray is an associate professor of organizational behavior at Pennsylvania State University, where she has been on the faculty since 1979. She received a B.S. degree (1968) in chemistry from the University of Dayton and a Ph.D. degree (1979) in organizational behavior from Case Western Reserve University.

Gray is an associate director of the Center for Research in Conflict and Negotiation at Penn State and has been studying multiparty collaboration for over twelve years. Her work has been published in a number of professional journals, including *Administrative Science Quarterly, Human Relations,* the *Academy of Management Review,* and the *Journal of Applied Behavioral Science.* She has served as a consultant to many public- and private-sector organizations and as a facilitator for several multiparty conflicts. She is a trained mediator and teaches conflict management and negotiating skills in Penn State's executive programs.

Gray spent 1987–88 as a visiting scholar at the Program on Negotiation at the Harvard Law School. She is a member of the Academy of Management and the Society of Professionals in Dispute Resolution and is part of the professional training staff of the NTL Institute. She has also been a high school director and a research chemist for Glidden-Durkee, a division of SCM Corporation.

Collaborating

1

Collaboration:
The Constructive Management
of Differences

The world must be kept safe for differences.
—Clyde Kuckholn

The Need to Manage Differences

Our society is at a critical juncture. Constructive approaches for confronting difficult societal problems are essential to managing our global future. The pace at which new problems are generated is rapid, and individual organizations are hard pressed to make effective or timely responses. As a result, problems are piling up; new problems are cropping up daily, while yesterday's problems often go unsolved. Problems range in scope from local (such as allocating water rights for local development) to global (such as preventing deterioration of the ozone layer, which shields our planet from ultraviolet radiation).

This pileup of problems and the inability of organizations to contend with them reflects the turbulence of our environment. Under turbulent conditions organizations become highly interdependent with others in indirect but consequential ways (Emery and Trist, 1965, 1972; Trist, 1977). Under these circumstances it is difficult for individual organizations to act unilaterally to solve problems without creating unwanted consequences for other parties and without encountering constraints imposed by others. Because of this interdependence, the range of interests associated with any particular problem is wide and usually controversial.

1

Consider the situation in Franklin Township, rural community adjacent to a growing midwestern university town.

In 1970 Franklin Township was a thriving farming community comprising many large family farms. Over the next fifteen years Franklin Township's population increased from 759 to 975 residents as a few scattered tracts of farmland were sold for development. By the mid 1980s, developers began eying the township as a potential bedroom community. When an eighty-acre tract of farmland was sold to a local farmer whose family had lived in the area since 1830, township residents breathed a sigh of relief. Development had been coming too fast, creating traffic and excessive demands on the local water system operated by the township's water company.

Local residents were shocked a few months later when the farmer submitted plans to the township supervisors for a development of eighty one-acre lots. The community mobilized quickly, and fifty-seven people showed up at the supervisors' meeting to protest the development. Many residents expressed concerns about overtaxing an already inadequate water supply. They carried a petition demanding the supervisors oppose the development and threatened to sue the water company and the township if they did not. The previous summer these residents had gone without water on several occasions during dry spells, and they feared the situation would worsen when eighty additional faucets were turned on.

A second group of residents, dubbed the "horse people," complained that the development would block their access to the riding trails in the state game lands that abutted the proposed development. These residents requested an easement for public access to the game lands. Objections also came from the residents whose private road was to become the gateway to the new homes and from the fruit farmer whose irrigation system depended on private wells close to the proposed development.

Franklin Township is a simple illustration of a situation in which the interests of multiple parties have become intertwined. The parties in the Franklin Township scenario include a neighbor-turned-developer, part-time township supervisors, local interest groups such as the "horse people," water company authorities, a local commercial farmer, and ordinary citizens concerned about taxes, traffic, and so forth. From many of their perspectives, the solution to the problem seems black-and-white—either support or oppose the development. Yet, for the township supervisors, the problem is more complex. They are faced with several questions: How should the township supervisors handle the developer's request for permits? How should they respond to the opposition from homeowners? What is the developer's responsibility to the community? Are the residents' concerns legitimate? Is it prudent to expect the water system to accommodate the new level of demand? What if other farmers followed suit and similar developments were proposed?

The township supervisors have several options. One is the "ostrich approach." They can postpone making a decision for as long as possible and hope the problem will go away. That outcome is, of course, unlikely since township ordinances usually mandate a specific response period. A second option is to take sides with one or more of the parties. There are several possible consequences of this choice, including escalation of the conflict, as township supervisors in North Salem, New York, recently discovered (Foderaro, 1988). In North Salem a developer sued the supervisors, charging that a new zoning ordinance was exclusionary. Dissension among the supervisors over development also caused one to resign and another to lose a bid for reelection.

Other options are available to the supervisors in Franklin Township. They can adopt a "hands off, let the experts decide" approach in which they rely on legal or engineering advisers to make the decisions for them. A fourth option, the traditional approach, involves holding public hearings in which interested parties can vent their concerns. These, however, frequently churn up issues and raise community expectations, often well beyond what responsible public officials can reasonably deliver. Though well intended, both of these options also often lead to less than satisfactory solutions.

One reason the solutions are unsatisfactory is that they are often not accepted by the public. For highly controversial issues, it is likely at least some of the public will not accept the decision of public officials, even when these officials decide only after conscientiously gathering and weighing information from all interested parties. Often, these officials must spend countless future hours justifying their decision after the fact. This problem occurs because parties who gave input do not know if or how their interests were considered during decision making (Delbecq, 1974; Wondolleck, 1985). Because parties are not privy to the process by which their interests and those of others are evaluated, those who gave input initially often feel betrayed when the final solution does not satisfy their requests (Carpenter and Kennedy, 1988). The problem of acceptance increases if the decision threatens basic values or creates a situation of high perceived risks for some stakeholders (Klein, 1976).

Seasoned public officials often become thick skinned, shrugging off the conflict with the adage "you can't please everyone." Unfortunately, heated issues do not die easily and often reemerge in an escalated form.

Additionally, there is growing evidence that for complex problems of this type, individual and collective efforts to solve them are often suboptimal because even well-intended decision makers do not really understand the interests they are trying to reconcile (Fisher and Ury, 1981; Wondolleck, 1985; Lax and Sebenius, 1986). Research has shown, for example, that it is often possible to improve on an agreement through a procedure called postsettlement settlement (Raiffa, 1985). In this procedure, parties reach a preliminary agreement and then invite a third party to review it and recommend improvements that benefit all of the parties. Often these opportunities for joint gains lie in trade-offs that the parties were unable to recognize for themselves (Lax and Sebenius, 1986). Procedures that encourage parties to search for these joint gains have the potential to produce better agreements and to prevent escalation.

In light of this, consider a fifth option available to the Franklin Township supervisors. They can assemble a representative sample of the stakeholders (those with a stake in the problem) and let them work out an agreement among themselves. The stakeholders in this case include the developer, the commercial fruit farmer, the township supervisors, the "horse people," the water company board, the homeowners concerned about water, and the homeowners concerned about traffic. This option has the advantage of dealing with interrelated issues in the same forum, since the township supervisors do not have jurisdiction over the water company but do have authority to approve or disapprove the rest of the development plan. Getting all the stakeholders together to explore their concerns in a constructive way allows them to search for a solution they can all accept and averts the potential for escalation of the conflict. Additionally, the supervisors do not abdicate their responsibility, because they must agree to any decision that is reached. This approach is called collaboration.

Collaboration as an Alternative

Collaboration is a process through which parties who see different aspects of a problem can constructively explore their differences and search for solutions that go beyond their own limited vision of what is possible. Collaboration is based on the simple adages that "two heads are better than one" and that one by itself is simply not good enough! Those parties with an interest in the problem are termed stakeholders. Stakeholders include all individuals, groups, or organizations that are directly influenced by actions others take to solve the problem. Each stakeholder has a unique appreciation of the problem. The objective of collaboration is to create a richer, more comprehensive appreciation of the problem among the stakeholders than any one of them could construct alone. The term *problem domain* will be used here to refer to the way a problem is conceptualized by the stakeholders (Trist, 1983).

A kaleidoscope is a useful image to envision what joint appreciation of a domain is all about. As the kaleidoscope is rotated, different configurations of the same collection of colored shapes appear. Collaboration involves building a common understanding of how these images appear from their respective points of view. This understanding forms the basis for choosing a collective course of action.

Collaboration is not really a new concept. It is not unlike

the town meeting concept, which is a cornerstone of the democratic process. Town meetings turn on the principles of local participation and ownership of decisions. Collaboration reflects a resurgence of interest in those fundamental principles. Any one of the stakeholders in Franklin Township could suggest that they try collaboration. Because of their responsibility for rendering a permit decision, however, the township supervisors are in the best position to initiate a collaborative dialogue. Their role in such a process would be to help the parties articulate their interests and to facilitate a reconciliation.

Questions like those facing the supervisors and residents of Franklin Township are being asked in communities around the world. In some, like Franklin Township, the issues are controversial. In other cases, such as those concerning the cleanup of toxic dumps or the destruction of the ozone layer, the issues are scientifically and politically complex, involve many interested parties, and are often hotly contested.

Not all occasions for collaboration are conflict induced. In some cases, parties may have a shared interest in solving a problem that none of them alone can address. The opportunity for collaborating arises because stakeholders recognize the potential advantages of working together. They may need each other to execute a vision that they all share. Managing a joint business venture is a good example. Addressing the problem of illiteracy in a community is another. Parties come together because each needs the others to advance their individual interests. Opportunities for collaborating are arising in countless arenas in which business, government, labor, and communities are finding their actions interconnected with those of other stakeholders. In the next section, several public- and private-sector opportunities for constructive collaboration are considered.

Opportunities for Collaborating

Situations that provide opportunities for collaborating are many and varied. They include joint ventures among selected businesses, settlement of local neighborhood or environmental disputes, revitalization of economically depressed cities, and resolution of major international problems. These opportunities can be classified into two general categories: resolving conflicts and advancing shared visions.

Resolving Conflict

Collaboration can be used effectively to settle disputes between the parties in multiparty conflict. Collaboration transforms adversarial interaction into a mutual search for information and for solutions that allow all those participating to insure that their interests are represented. Often, parties in conflict are motivated to try collaboration only as a last-ditch effort when other approaches have reached impasse or have produced less than acceptable outcomes. Parties will try collaboration only if they believe they have something to gain from it. In protracted stalemates, for example, the cost to all parties of inaction may be a sufficient incentive to induce collaboration.

Collaboration has been used to settle hundreds of site-specific environmental disputes (Bingham, 1986), important product liability cases, intergovernmental disputes, and many other community controversies involving transportation, housing, and mortgage lending. Within the environmental area, Bingham (1986) has identified six broad categories within which collaborative solutions to disputes have been sought: land use, natural resource management and public land use, water resources, energy, air quality, and toxics.

The potential for collaboration in international affairs also appears promising. Within the last year a number of major political conflicts have moved from stalemate to early dialogue, signaling a growing potential to search for alternatives to violence. In addition, the list of major global issues in which the interests of several nation-states, nongovernmental organizations (NGOs), and multinational corporations intersect continues to grow. Salient issues include a variety of property rights issues related to the use of the seas and exploration in Antarctica, global environmental issues such as the future of rain forests and control of acid rain, and transnational technology issues such as the management of international telecommunications. For problems of this scope, international collaboration is essential for finding solutions.

The chlorofluorocarbons treaty reached in Montreal in March 1987 provides one model of successful international collaboration. The treaty is historical because it is the first international agreement designed to avert a global disaster (Benedick, 1988). The treaty restricts the production of chemicals (chlorofluorocarbons and others) that erode the stratospheric ozone layer, which protects the earth from the sun's damaging ultraviolet rays. Stakeholders included chlorofluorocarbon producers in several countries, NGOs such as environmental groups and the United Nations Environment Program, members of the scientific community, and governments from the North and the South. Forty-eight countries have signed the treaty, and it is awaiting formal ratification by the countries involved. In addition to the freeze on production, the treaty paves the way for discussions of longer-term strategies to preserve the ozone layer.

Advancing Shared Visions

Collaborations induced by shared visions are intended to advance the collective good of the stakeholders involved. Some are designed to address socioeconomic issues such as illiteracy, youth unemployment, housing, or homelessness, which cut across public- and private-sector interests. Collaborating is also becoming increasingly crucial to successful business management, as companies see advantages in sharing research and development costs (Dimancescu and Botkin, 1986) and exploring new markets through joint ventures (Perlmutter and Heenan, 1986). The proliferation of joint ventures in the auto industry alone has surprised analysts, who a decade ago were predicting a major shakeout in that industry would force many automakers to go out of business (Holusha, 1988).

Public-private partnerships that have sprung up to address deteriorating conditions in U.S. cities are illustrative of collaborative efforts across sectors to advance shared visions. In these partnerships, public and private interests pool their resources and undertake joint planning to tackle economic redevelopment, education, housing, and other protracted problems that have plagued their communities. In the area of education, for example, representatives of industry, labor, and schools have teamed up to deal with youth unemployment and juvenile crime (Elsman and The National Institute for Work and Learning, 1981). These and other partnerships such as the Boston Compact, the Greater Baltimore Committee, the Newark Collaboration, and the Whittier Alliance in Minneapolis began with stakeholders articulating a desirable future they collectively wanted to pursue.

Successfully advancing a shared vision, whether in the public or the private sector, requires identification and coordination of a diverse set of stakeholders, each of whom holds some but not all of the necessary resources. To be successful, coordination must be accomplished laterally without the hierarchical authority to which most managers are accustomed. These circumstances require a radically different approach to organizing and managing, especially for international joint ventures.

> The challenge of managing these coalitions is staggering, given the complexity of the stakeholder network that often involves at least two foreign governments. As a result, interorganizational relations must be carefully worked through in order to gain the advantages of such a union [Heenan and Perlmutter, 1979, p. 82].

Even when parties agree initially on a shared vision, collaboration among them is not necessarily free of conflict. Conflicts inevitably ensue over plans for how the vision should be carried out. And further problems typically arise when stakeholders try to implement their agreements. Overcoming the barriers created by different institutional cultures is frequently a formidable task. Getting the business community and a major urban school district to work together on problems of youth employment, for example, requires considerable adaptation on the part of each. Similar obstacles must be overcome by Japanese and American managers who are trying to implement a management system for a new joint venture (Holusha, 1988).

Nature of Collaborative Problems

It should be clear by now that there is no shortage of problems for which collaboration offers a decided advantage over other methods of decision making. The characteristics of these problems can be described generally as follows:

- The problems are ill defined, or there is disagreement about how they should be defined.
- Several stakeholders have a vested interest in the problems and are interdependent.
- These stakeholders are not necessarily identified a priori or organized in any systematic way.
- There may be a disparity of power and/or resources for dealing with the problems among the stakeholders.
- Stakeholders may have different levels of expertise and different access to information about the problems.
- The problems are often characterized by technical complexity and scientific uncertainty.
- Differing perspectives on the problems often lead to adversarial relationships among the stakeholders.
- Incremental or unilateral efforts to deal with the problems typically produce less than satisfactory solutions.
- Existing processes for addressing the problems have proved insufficient and may even exacerbate them.

Problems with these characteristics have been dubbed "messes" (Ackoff, 1974) or metaproblems (Chevalier, 1966). What is needed to deal constructively with problems of this type is an alternative model of how to organize to solve them. This book proposes a model of organizing based on collaboration among the parties rather than on competition, hierarchy, or incremental planning (Trist, 1977). This book offers a comprehensive treatment of collaborative dynamics in the hope that potential parties will appreciate how they can use collaboration to successfully address multiparty problems. Let us turn now to an in-depth look at what collaborating entails.

Dynamics of Collaboration

Collaboration involves a process of joint decision making among key stakeholders of a problem domain about the future of that domain. Five features are critical to the process: (1) the stakeholders are interdependent, (2) solutions emerge by dealing constructively with differences, (3) joint ownership of decisions is involved, (4) stakeholders assume collective responsibility for the future direction of the domain, and (5) collaboration is an emergent process.

Collaboration Implies Interdependence

Collaboration establishes a give and take among the stakeholders that is designed to produce solutions that none of them working independently could achieve. Therefore, an important ingredient of collaboration is interdependence among the stakeholders. Initially, the extent of interdependence may not be fully appreciated by all the parties. Therefore, the initial phase of any collaboration usually involves calling attention to the ways in which the stakeholders' concerns are intertwined and the reasons why they need each other to solve the problem. Parties in conflict especially lose sight of their underlying interdependence. Heightening parties' awareness of their interdependence often kindles renewed willingness to search for trade-offs that could produce a mutually beneficial solution. In the collaborations investigated in this book, external events often propel reexamination of taken-for-granted interdependencies.

Solutions Emerge by Dealing Constructively with Differences

Respect for differences is an easy virtue to champion verbally and a much more difficult one to put into practice in our day-to-day affairs. Yet differences are often the source of immense creative potential. Learning to harness that potential is what collaboration is all about.

Consider the parable of the elephant and the blind men. Several blind men walking through the jungle come upon an elephant. Each approaches the elephant from a different angle and comes into contact with a different part of the elephant's anatomy. The blind man who contacts the elephant's leg declares, "Oh, an elephant is like a tree trunk." Another, who apprehends the elephant's tail, objects to the first's description, exclaiming, "Oh, no, the elephant is like a rope." A third, grasping the elephant's large, floppy ear, insists, "You are both wrong; the elephant is like a fan." Clearly, each man, from his vantage point, has apprehended something important and genuine about the elephant. Each one's perception of elephant is accurate, albeit limited. None of the blind men, through his own inquiries, has a comprehensive understanding of the phenomenon called "elephant." Together, however, they have a much richer and more complete perspective.

Like the blind men, most of us routinely make a number of assumptions that limit our ability to capitalize on this creative potential. One assumption that we frequently make is that our way of viewing a problem is the best. Best to us may mean the most rational, the fairest, the most intelligent, or even the only way. No matter what the basis, we arrive at the conclusion that our way is superior to any other. Thus we lose sight of the possibility that multiple approaches to the elephant yield multiple perceptions about what is possible and what is desirable.

Even if we grant that multiple perceptions are possible, we can easily fall prey to another common assumption; that is, we conclude that different interpretations are, by definition, opposing interpretations. But here we need to distinguish between interpretations that differ from each other and those that are truly opposed. As Fisher and Ury have aptly pointed out, "Agreement is possible precisely because interests differ" (1981, p. 44). Without differing interests, the range of possible exchanges between parties would be nonexistent. Because parties' interests do vary, as do the resources and skills they have to solve a problem, they are able to arrange trade-offs and to forge mutually beneficial alliances.

It is also frequently the case that as we strive to articulate our differences, we discover that our underlying concerns are fundamentally the same. These shared concerns may have been masked by the different ways we described or framed the problem or may have been obscured by strong emotions that deafened us to the messages coming from the other parties. Parties in conflict are known to engage in selective listening and to pay more attention to information that confirms their preconceived stereotypes of their opponents. Stereotypes cause us to discount the legitimacy of the other's point of view and cause both sides to ignore data that disconfirm their stereotypes (Sherif, 1958). Stereotypes also restrict the flow of information between the parties. Without this exchange of information, the parties cannot discover clues about their shared or differing interests that may contain the seeds of an agreement.

Stereotyping figures prominently in the type of complex multiparty disputes addressed in this book. Frequently the parties have had a long history of interaction, fighting out their differences in legislative and judicial arenas. Working on opposite sides in these arenas allows the parties to continually reconfirm their stereotypic impressions with hard evidence (about the other side's motives, values, and willingness to reach accommodation). Collaboration operates on the premise that the assumptions that disputants have about the other side and about the nature of the issues themselves are worth testing. The premise is that testing these assumptions and allowing a constructive confrontation of differences may unlock heretofore disguised creative potential. Through such exploration stakeholders may discover new options that permit constructive mergers of interests previously unimagined or judged infeasible.

Collaboration Involves Joint Ownership of Decisions

Joint ownership means that the participants in a collaboration are directly responsible for reaching agreement on a solution. Unlike litigation or regulation, in which intermediaries (courts, regulatory agencies, legislators) devise solutions that are imposed on the stakeholders, in collaborative agreements the parties impose decisions on themselves. They set the agenda; they decide what issues will be addressed; they decide what the terms will be. Any agreements that are reached may be free-standing contracts, or they may serve as input to a legal or a public policy process that ratifies, codifies, or in some other way incorporates the agreements. Clearly where matters of public policy are under consideration, collaboration cannot serve as a substitute for constitutional decision-making processes. However, it can "provide a sense of direction, smooth social conflict, and speed formal processes" (Dunlop, 1986, p. 24).

When collaboration occurs, the various stakeholders bring their idiosyncratic perceptions of the problem to the negotiations. Each holds assumptions, beliefs, and viewpoints that are consistent with their independent efforts to confront the problem. Through collaboration these multiple perspectives are aired and debated, and gradually a more complete appreciation of the complexity of the problem is constructed. This more complete appreciation forms the basis for envisioning new alternatives that take into account the stakeholders' multiple interests. Thus, the outcome of collaboration is a weaving together of multiple and diverse viewpoints into a mosaic replete with new insights and directions for action agreed on by all the stakeholders. Three key steps in reaching a joint decision include (1) the joint search for information about the problem, (2) the invention of a mutually agreed upon solution about the pattern of future exchanges between stakeholders, and (3) ratification of the agreement and plans for implementing it.

Stakeholders Assume Collective Responsibility
for Future Direction of the Domain

One outcome of collaboration is a set of agreements governing future interactions among the stakeholders. Trist (1983) refers to this as self-regulation of the domain. During collaboration a new set of relationships among the stakeholders is negotiated as they address the problem at hand. The process of collaborating essentially restructures the socially accepted rules for dealing with problems of this type. The negotiations may also restructure the rules governing how stakeholders will interact with respect to the problem in the future. That is, formal or informal contracts about the nature of subsequent exchanges among the stakeholders are forged during collaboration. Collaboration may lead to increased coordination among the stakeholders, although that is not a necessary outcome of the process.

Collaboration Is an Emergent Process

Collaboration is essentially an emergent process rather than a prescribed state of organization. By viewing collaboration as a process, it becomes possible to describe its origins and development as well as how its organization changes over time. Hence, collaboration can be thought of as a temporary and evolving forum for addressing a problem. Typically, collaborations progress from "underorganized systems" in which individual stakeholders act independently, if at all, with respect to the problem (Brown, 1980) to more tightly organized relationships characterized by concerted decision making among the stakeholders.

Collaboration as it is defined here should be distinguished from the terms *cooperation* and *coordination* as used by Mulford and Rogers (1982). They use these terms to classify static patterns of interorganizational relations. Coordination refers to formal institutionalized relationships among existing networks of organizations, while cooperation is "characterized by informal trade-offs and by attempts to establish reciprocity in the absence of rules" (Mulford and Rogers, 1982, p. 13). While these distinctions may be useful for distinguishing formal and informal relationships, they do not capture the dynamic evolutionary character of the phenomenon described in this book. To presume that the parties in a collaborative effort are already part of an organized relationship underrepresents the developmental character of the process and ignores the delicate prenegotiations that are often necessary to bring stakeholders together initially.

Both cooperation and coordination often occur as part of the process of collaborating. The process by which reciprocity is established informally in the absence of rules is as important to collaboration as the formal coordination agreements that eventually emerge. Skillful management of early interactions is often crucial to continued collaboration, since these informal interactions lay the groundwork for subsequent formal interactions.

Once initiated, collaboration creates a temporary forum within which consensus about the problem can be sought, mutually agreeable solutions can be invented, and collective actions to implement the solutions can be taken. Understanding how this process unfolds is critical to successfully managing the kinds of multiparty and multiorganizational relations described earlier in the chapter.

Envisioning interorganizational relations as processes rather than as outcomes in which stakeholders assume decision-making responsibility for their collective future permits investigation of how innovation and change in currently unsatisfactory exchange relationships can occur. If collaboration is successful, new solutions emerge that no single party could have envisioned or enacted. A successful example can best illustrate the dynamics of collaboration.

Successful Collaboration

Pernicious stereotypes and misinformation precipitated a major conflict between government agencies and citizens in the community surrounding Three Mile Island Nuclear Reactor. The conflict surfaced over plans for cleanup of the reactor, which was badly damaged during a catastrophic accident in 1979. Through an unprecedented intervention, called the Citizens' Radiation Monitoring Program, local residents and the federal and state governments collaboratively generated credible information to assuage residents' fears about radiation exposure during the initial phase of the cleanup (see Gricar and Baratta [1983] for a more detailed description).

Citizens' Radiation Monitoring Program

The accident at Three Mile Island (TMI) in March 1979 released small but significant levels of radioactivity into the atmosphere, exposing residents of the area surrounding TMI to a maximum radiation dosage twice that of average yearly background levels.

Despite reports of no immediate or long-term health affects from the accident, many residents were concerned about the risks associated with radiation exposure. These concerns were heightened when Metropolitan Edison (the operator of Three Mile Island) proposed releasing low levels of radioactive krypton gas into the atmosphere as the first step in the proposed cleanup of the reactor. The full extent of damage to the reactor could not be determined until the gas it contained was removed. The staff of the Nuclear Regulatory Commission (NRC) had determined that the purge would not endanger the health and safety of the public (TMI Support Staff, 1980).

At the time public trust in Met Ed and the NRC was seriously eroded because of the widespread belief that these agencies had deliberately misled the public about radiation levels during the accident. The NRC's own special inquiry into the accident attributed what it called "public misconceptions about risks" to "a failure to convey credible information regarding the actual risks in an understandable fashion to the public" (Rogovin, 1980). This mistrust prompted several communities to appeal to the governor and to the President for independent sources of information about radiation levels. Concern about the risks grew to extreme proportions in March 1980 during public meetings on the environmental impact of the purge. Public opposition to the proposed purge was so fierce that it drowned out the NRC's announcement that a community monitoring program was under way.

In February, the U.S. Department of Energy (DOE) assembled a team of representatives (called the Technical Working Group) from the Environmental Protection Agency, the Pennsylvania Department of Environmental Resources (DER), the Pennsylvania State University, and EG&G Idaho (a technical consultant to Met Ed) to design and implement the Citizens' Radiation Monitoring Program. The program's purpose was to ensure that citizens in the vicinity of TMI received accurate and credible information about radiation levels during the purge. The program was based on the premise that citizens were more likely to believe information generated by themselves or by their neighbors than by government officials, whose credibility they considered questionable. Through the program, local citizens conducted routine monitoring of radiation levels using equipment provided by the Department of Energy.

The Technical Working Group (TWG) sought input on the design of the program from officials of three counties and twelve municipalities that fell within a five-mile radius of TMI. Each community nominated four citizens to serve as monitors. The monitors included teachers, secretaries, engineers, housewives, police officers, and retirees. They ranged in age from early twenties to senior citizens. Their political persuasions about nuclear power ran the gamut from pro- to antinuclear. The monitors were given an intensive "crash course" on radiation and its effects and detection methods, and were given hands-on training so that they could operate the monitoring equipment and interpret the measurements for their fellow citizens.

Each participating community drew up its own monitoring schedule and selected the locations for its monitoring equipment. The citizen monitors posted daily results of the monitoring in the townships, and the TWG disseminated the results to the local media and to the participating agencies.

The Citizen's Radiation Monitoring Program represents a dramatic departure from typical government efforts to communicate with the public. In this case, traditional efforts by government agencies to disseminate public information were grossly ineffective and only increased public mistrust of the agencies. Following months of technical review of Met Ed's proposal for the purge, the NRC tried at public meetings to present a rational argument in support of the purge. Both the meetings and the environmental assessment itself focused exclusively on the technical aspects of reactor decontamination. Rational arguments, however, meant little to citizens whose calculation of the risks involved was much more personal. The accident clearly had left social and psychological scars on the community (Scranton, 1980; Kemeny, 1979; Brunn, Johnson, and Ziegler, 1979) and had created widespread uncertainty about safety. Because of general unfamiliarity with radiation and its effects, the lack of credible information, and the imperceptible nature of radiation itself, the public had little basis for judging either the level of danger or its seriousness. With no precedents to consider, it is not surprising that public fears about potential risks were running high.

Perceptions by public officials that those who resisted were troublemakers or fanatics only fueled the controversy. By underestimating the degree to which emotional concerns for safety shaped public attitudes, these officials reduced their own credibility and further escalated public mistrust.

Collaboration in this case occurred among the Department of Energy, the other agencies involved in the Technical Working Group, and the local municipalities and counties.

Let us examine this case with respect to the five features of collaboration described above. First, how were the stakeholders interdependent? The stakeholders in this case were interdependent because neither Met Ed nor the community could afford not to begin cleanup of the reactor. Leaving the krypton gas inside the reactor posed an unknown risk to the public and prevented Met Ed from determining the extent of damage from the accident. Thus safe but timely decontamination of the reactor was critical.

Second, how were differences handled? Initially in this case there were very different perceptions about safety and about the credibility of those agencies disseminating safety information. Prior to the monitoring program, Met Ed and the government agencies had relied on a rational, technocratic approach to educate the public and had dismissed the citizens' concerns as irrational. The monitoring program was an acknowledgment that these differing perceptions of risk needed to be addressed, not ignored. Enlisting local citizens as monitors was a novel and unprecedented step by these agencies, which typically relied on narrow, technically oriented solutions.

Third, were the stakeholders jointly involved in decision making? The initial proposal for citizen monitoring came from the mayor of one of the affected communities. Exploratory meetings involved several, but not all, stakeholder groups. Once the DOE made the decision to go ahead, decision making was shared among several agencies in the TWG, and, to a lesser ex-

tent, the local communities and their citizen monitors participated in making decisions about the execution of the program.
Met Ed, a key stakeholder, was purposely excluded from the
group because its participation would likely have damaged the
credibility of the entire effort. Thus, this process did not provide for full participation by all the stakeholders, but it did incorporate widespread representation in the overall planning.

Fourth, who assumed responsibility for the future direction of the domain? This case graphically illustrates how responsibility for ensuring that credible information about radiation
levels was available to the communities surrounding TMI was
shared among the stakeholders. The DOE supplied the financial
resources; EG&G Idaho, the EPA, and the DER contributed
technical expertise and staff; the university designed the equipment and provided training and organizational expertise; and
the citizens donated their time and talent to carry out the monitoring.

Finally, to what extent was the collaboration emergent?
The process of collaborating grew out of a major public controversy. At the outset, mechanisms for managing the differing interests and coordinating a viable plan of action were underdeveloped. The Citizens' Radiation Monitoring Program emerged
through a series of steps. It began with the citizens' opposition
to the venting and their plea for credible information. This was
followed by the formation of the TWG, involvement of the
communities, creation of the training program, and, finally, the
monitoring itself. Because of the urgency of the situation, the
entire collaborative process lasted only five months.

The consequences of this collaborative effort are summarized below:

- Met Ed was allowed to execute a critical first step in the
  reactor cleanup process.
- Residents in the community received information they could
  trust to judge their own levels of radiation exposure. A survey conducted before and after the training indicated a significant increase in the monitors' belief that they could get
  accurate information about radiation levels and that they

had sufficient information to make a judgment about their own safety (Gricar and Baratta, 1983).

• Residents who participated as monitors gained a deeper appreciation for the technical issues associated with nuclear power and engaged in rational dialogue and debate with each other on contested topics during the training program.

In addition to the above outcomes, the Citizens' Radiation Monitoring Program demonstrated that government, communities and the private sector often hold very different perceptions about a problem. Without a frank and open dialogue characterized by reason and respect, these perceptions cannot be examined. Had the NRC proceeded with the purge without community guarantees about credible information, the conflict would only have escalated, probably to the level of violence.

Benefits of Collaborating

When collaboration is used to address multiparty problems, several benefits are possible (see Table 1).

First, collaboration increases the quality of solutions con-

Table 1.   The Benefits of Collaboration.

• Broad comprehensive analysis of the problem domain improves the quality of solutions.
• Response capability is more diversified.
• It is useful for reopening deadlocked negotiations.
• The risk of impasse is minimized.
• The process ensures that each stakeholder's interests are considered in any agreement.
• Parties retain ownership of the solution.
• Parties most familiar with the problem, not their agents, invent the solutions.
• Participation enhances acceptance of solution and willingness to implement it.
• The potential to discover novel, innovative solutions is enhanced.
• Relations between the stakeholders improve.
• Costs associated with other methods are avoided.
• Mechanisms for coordinating future actions among the stakeholders can be established.

sidered by the parties because solutions are based on a broad, comprehensive analysis of the problem. The collective capacity to respond to the problem is also increased as stakeholders apply a variety of complementary resources to solving it. Collaboration also offers a way to reopen negotiations when impasse imperils more traditional processes. More important, use of collaboration early in a multiparty conflict can minimize the possibility that impasse will occur.

The process of collaborating builds in certain guarantees that each party's interests will be protected. It does so by continually remanding ownership of the process and any decisions reached to the parties themselves. Parties often assume that by collaborating they will lose any individual leverage they have over the problem. This concern about loss of control is deceptive, however. It is rare in any multiparty conflict that any party satisfies 100 percent of their interests and incurs no costs while the other parties gain nothing. Collaborative processes protect each party's interests by guaranteeing that they are heard and understood. In addition, the processes are structured to ensure that ownership of the solution remains with the participants since ratification hinges on their reaching agreement among themselves.

> Instead of trying to restrict participation, a common
> tactic, the professional manager gains more control over
> the situation by ensuring that all the necessary parties
> are there at the table, recognizing that parties in a dispute
> often engage in adversarial behavior because no other
> approach is available to protect their interests [Carpenter
> and Kennedy, 1988, p. 26].

Parties retain control during collaboration precisely because *they* must be the ones to adopt or reject the final agreement.

Ownership of the process and of the outcomes generates two additional benefits. The parties themselves, who are most familiar with the problem, not their agents, fashion the solution. Additionally, commitment to the solution is generally high as a result of collaboration. Investment in a process of building a comprehensive appreciation of the problem and designing a solution jointly enhances the parties' acceptance of the solution and their commitment to carry it out (Delbecq, 1974).

By focusing on interests and encouraging the exploration of differences, the potential to discover novel, innovative solutions like the Citizens' Radiation Monitoring Program is enhanced. Even when parties are unable to reach closure through collaboration, some benefits from collaborating are still possible. Collaborating usually leaves parties with a clearer understanding of their differences and an improved working relationship. These outcomes permit the parties to amicably "agree to disagree" or to accept a decision imposed by a traditional dispute resolution forum in lieu of reaching a collaborative agreement. Sometimes parties reach agreement on all but one or two areas and turn to a judicial or administrative agency to resolve the remaining disagreements.

Collaboration also has the potential to reduce the costs parties incur from acting alone or the costs associated with protracted conflict among the stakeholders. Although it is difficult to make reliable comparisons (of the cost of collaborating versus not doing so), it is reasonable to assume that collaboration can reduce the cost of hiring intermediaries (such as attorneys in legal disputes), the cost of research and development (R&D) expenditures for partners in R&D consortia, and a myriad of social costs stemming from protracted inaction on critical social and international problems.

Finally, through collaboration stakeholders can develop mechanisms to coordinate their future interactions. Through this coordination, stakeholders take concerted rather than disconnected actions to manage the problem domain, and interdependencies become more predictable.

Realities of Collaborating

Just as it is important to articulate the benefits of collaborating, it is equally important to dispel the notion that collaboration is a cure for all evils. There are many circumstances in which stakeholders are unable or unwilling to engage each other in this way. Collaboration is not always an appropriate alternative. For example, when one party has unchallenged power to influence a domain, collaboration does not make sense. Circumstances in which collaboration is not warranted are explored in Chapter Eleven.

Nor is collaboration an idealistic panacea. Realistically, collaboration involves difficult issues that have often eluded simple solutions in the past. Many multiparty problems are political in nature because they involve "distributional" issues. In distributional disputes the stakeholders are concerned about the allocation of funds, the setting of standards, or the siting of facilities. Groups in distributional disputes are contesting "a specific allocation of gains and losses" (Susskind and Cruikshank, 1987, p. 19). Allocating gains and losses, however, involves the allocation of risks that, as the Three Mile Island case illustrated, are perceived very differently by different stakeholders. Moreover, perceptions of risk often have deep psychological and emotional roots. Dealing with these emotional attachments is a tricky business. Success depends as much on the process of legitimizing parties' interests as on the substantive outcomes. The design of meetings between stakeholders is crucial to success. Many well-intended efforts to involve the public in government decisions, for example, are exercises in frustration and often exacerbate rather than improve the situation because careful attention to the process of managing differences is neglected (Wondolleck, 1985; Carpenter and Kennedy, 1988).

Thus, solving complex multiparty problems requires more than sound economic policies and technological breakthroughs. It also demands careful attention to the process of making decisions. Successful collaborations are not achieved without considerable effort on the part of the participating stakeholders and usually not without the skill and forbearance of a convening organization and/or a skilled third party. Often parties perceive real risks to collaborating, if only because the process is unfamiliar and the outcomes are uncertain. Unless issues like these and more serious ones such as concerns about cooptation or lack of fairness are dispelled up front, attempts at collaboration will not succeed. It is often the convener or third party who initially proposes the possibility of collaborating and who then shepherds the parties through a collaborative process. Hence, for collaboration to occur, someone must introduce a mind set, a vision, a belief in the creative potential of managing differences, and must couple this mind set with a constructive process for designing creative solutions to complex multiparty problems.

Before moving on to Chapter Two, it is important to clarify how the terms *negotiation, consensus building,* and *mediation* will be used throughout this book. Negotiation is not used here to denote specific tactics of positional bargaining, which are often associated with collective bargaining or buyer-seller transactions. Instead, negotiation is used in the broader sociological sense used by Strauss (1978). Through their talk, stakeholders try to arrive at collective interpretations of how they see the world. These interpretations form the basis for actions. Negotiation, therefore, refers to conversational interactions among collaborating parties as they try to define a problem, agree on recommendations, or design action steps. In this way they create a negotiated order. For an elaboration of this theoretical perspective on collaboration, see Chapter Ten.

Not all collaborations lead to agreements for action, but when agreements are reached, they are arrived at by consensus. Consensus is achieved when each of the stakeholders agrees they can live with a proposed solution, even though it may not be their most preferred solution. Both consensus building and negotiation will be used throughout the book to refer to the process of constructing agreements among the stakeholders.

Collaboration can occur with or without the assistance of a third party who serves as a mediator or facilitator. The task of the third party is not to render a decision (in the way that a judge does, for instance) but to help structure a dialogue within which the parties can work out their differences. The term *mediator* will generally be used here to refer to this third-party role. A detailed description of the mediator's role is provided in Chapter Seven.

2

The Impetus
to Collaborate

*We cannot live only for ourselves. A thousand fibers connect
us with our fellow-men; and along those fibers, as sympa-
thetic threads our actions run as causes, and they come back
to us as effects.*

—Herman Melville

Growing Interest in Collaboration

Over the last fifteen years examples of collaboration have been
emerging in virtually every sector of society—business, government, labor, and communities. The incidence of collaboration
among businesses is becoming increasingly common. Especially
in the telecommunications, computer, automobile, aerospace,
robotics, and biotechnology industries, international joint ventures represent critical additions to firms' portfolios. Evidence
of labor-management cooperation is increasing in the labor
arena, and some scholars believe a major transformation of industrial relations is under way (Kochan, Katz, and McKersie,
1987; Katz, 1985; Schuster, 1985).

Since the early 1970s, numerous public-sector and environmental disputes have been successfully resolved using collaborative processes, often with the assistance of a mediator
(Carpenter and Kennedy, 1988; Susskind and Cruikshank,
1987). These cases range from local development disputes, such
as Franklin Township, to major policy issues, such as oil-drilling
rights in the Bering Sea (Redford, 1987). Several federal regulatory agencies are also using collaboration in selected rulemaking cases. In Canada, the Cabinet recently adopted a proposal for Volunteer Cooperative Community Planning for use in

siting hazardous waste facilities. The proposal provides for a facilitated dialogue between developers and communities interested in volunteering as development sites.

The judicial system is also turning to collaboration to settle complex multiparty cases (Brazil, 1986; McGovern, 1986; Goldberg, Green, and Sander, 1985). Civil courts and administrative law boards cannot cope with the proliferation of cases before them, and many of these institutions are augmenting traditional adjudication with alternative dispute resolution processes. Interest in alternative mechanisms (ranging from revolving-door courthouses, minitrials, and private mediation services to complex environmental policy dialogues) is increasing, and so is the cadre of professionals interested and willing to serve as third parties.

The remainder of the chapter analyzes the reasons for this growing interest in collaboration. The analysis is presented in two parts. First I argue that collaboration is a necessary response to turbulent conditions. Then I review in detail six specific contextual factors that are creating specific incentives to collaborate.

Collaboration as a Response to Turbulence

Organization theorists posit that collaboration is a logical and necessary response to turbulent conditions (Emery and Trist, 1965; Trist, 1977; Astley and Fombrun, 1983; Wamsley and Zald, 1983). Under turbulent conditions organizations become highly interdependent with others in unexpected but consequential ways (Emery and Trist, 1965, 1972; Trist, 1977, 1983; Wildavsky, 1979). There is ample evidence that turbulent conditions prevail at this time. Numerous accounts of economic, social, and political trends point to the rapidly changing character of our global environment (Ackoff, 1974; Bell, 1979; Naisbett, 1982; Schön, 1980) and to the increased interconnections among organizational actions (Luke, 1984; Rosenau, 1980; Wildavsky, 1979). Turbulence is a result of these rapid changes and the uncertainty generated by them.

Turbulence cannot be managed individually because disruptions and their causes cannot be adequately anticipated or averted by unilateral action. In the face of turbulence, the ability of any single organization to accurately plan for its future is limited by the unpredictable consequences of actions taken by seemingly unrelated organizations. Organizations facing turbulent environments find that unilateral strategic actions taken to control environmental exigencies are often ineffective. The limits of unilateral action can be better understood by picturing a finite field in which many organizations are making independent decisions.

> Large numbers of large organizations, all acting independently in many diverse directions, produce unanticipated dissonant consequences in the overall societal environment, which mount as the common field becomes more densely occupied. Especially when further limited by a finite resource base drawn on by all, the corporation can no longer act simply as an individual entity but must accept a certain surrender of sovereignty much as the nation-state [Perlmutter and Trist, 1986, p. 9].

Thus, individual attempts at adaptation are severely constrained because all stakeholders vie for the same limited resources and block each other's attempts at adaptation.

A recent case provides a vivid illustration of how turbulence impacts organizations. Consider how economic changes provoked by deregulation of the banking industry created unexpected deflation in the price of British oil stocks (Mitroff, 1987). A minor Ohio savings and loan association closed when a government securities dealer, in which the savings and loan had one-third of its assets invested, filed for bankruptcy. Within a week the value of British oil inventories in the North Sea plummeted in response to major devaluation of the U.S. dollar against the British pound. The devaluation was triggered by a loss of confidence in U.S. banks, created in part by the collapse of the Ohio savings and loan.

Collaboration offers an antidote to turbulence by building a collective capacity to reduce these unintended consequences. By building collective appreciations and sharing resources, organizations increase variety in their repertoire of responses to environmental change (Trist, 1983). Researcher have found that system change is associated with the capacity to absorb external variety (Rittel and Webber, 1973; Prigogine, 1976; Jantsch, 1979). Successful adaption means matching external variation with comparable variation in internal response capability (Ashby, 1960; Meyer and Scott, 1983; Scott and Meyer, 1987). Collaborative alliances represent one critical mode of adaptation to turbulent conditions.

Contextual Incentives to Collaborate

Examined individually, collaborative initiatives may appear to be unique, situationally motivated dynamics. Given the multiple arenas in which these initiatives are emerging, however, it seems reasonable to ask if these various initiatives are haphazard occurrences or if they are indicative of a larger trend in society. Are they adaptive responses to environmental turbulence? Or, stated another way, are there features of the current milieu in which organizations function that are creating incentives to collaborate?

Six contextual factors are associated with increased environmental turbulence and are creating powerful incentives to collaborate:

- rapid economic and technological change
- declining productivity growth and increasing competitive pressures
- global interdependence
- blurring of boundaries between business, government, and labor
- shrinking federal revenues for social programs
- dissatisfaction with the judicial process for solving problems

As the definition of turbulence implies, many of these factors are interconnected. Indeed, some may be partial causes or consequences of others. The objective of this analysis, however, is not to sort out these causal relationships but instead to examine their collective impact on interorganizational interactions. What follows is a discussion of each of these factors and the incentives for collaboration they create.

Economic and Technological Change

The rapidity with which economic and technological changes have been bombarding organizations has increased at an alarming rate. Fluctuations in economic conditions and new developments in technology command daily attention from organizations. The frequency and unforeseen character of these changes leave many organizations struggling to adapt. Countless resources are spent in environmental scanning and in designing strategic adaptations to changing environments. The ability of a single organization to plan in the face of these changes, however, is becoming increasingly constrained.

Fast-paced technological changes (for example, in electronics, communications, biotechnology, and materials research) have the potential to make older technologies obsolete virtually overnight. The speed of international communication shortens the technology gap by quickening the rate of technology diffusion and shortening product life cycles. This reduced technology gap compels firms to turn research designs into finished products very quickly to maintain competitive advantage (Arndt and Bouton, 1987).

With respect to technological change, the United States has lost its competitive edge in many industries. This loss of competitiveness is due in part to decreasing R&D expenditures (Scherer, 1983, 1984; Lichtenberg and Siegel, 1987; Baily and Chakrabarti, 1988) and to the shortening of product life cycles (Arndt and Bouton, 1987).

> The quickening pace of innovation and of imitation, the latter made possible by the greater speed with which knowledge and information are disseminated around the globe, is shortening the life cycles of many products. Some products mature and become standardized faster, others are replicated faster, and in either case the competitive advantages that accrue to the innovator are

eroded faster than in the past [Arndt and Bouton, 1987, pp. 33–34].

The collective impact of economic and technological change has forced a dramatic overhaul of many industries in the United States. General Motors (GM), one of the most successful U.S. businesses for decades, vividly exemplifies the collective impact of these changes. According to O'Toole (1983), the composite of external events that occurred between 1970 and 1980 challenged all of GM's core business assumptions, which for years had served as pillars of GM's business strategy. The events (such as the Arab oil embargo and growing consumer preference for small cars) eventually forced GM to reexamine and radically alter or abandon each of these assumptions. Like many of the other U.S. automakers, GM was unprepared for such fundamental attacks, lulled by years of success that had reinforced adherence to GM's core assumptions and insulated it from critical examination of their inappropriateness for GM's current competitive environment. Core business assumptions such as stable environments and the superiority of high-volume, standardized mass production, which have characterized what Robert Reich calls "the management era" for the last fifty years, are now being challenged. Stagnant growth rates for American business and the onslaught of products from foreign competitors have rendered these fundamental assumptions of the management era obsolete and have thrown American business into turmoil. According to Reich:

> The shift has been slow and painful because America is simply not organized for economic change. Its organizations are based on stability rather than adaptability. The extraordinary success of high-volume, standardized production during the half century of the management era has left America a legacy of economic inflexibility. The institutional heritage of our past success now imperils our future [1983, p. 139].

Traditionally, when faced with environmental change, individual organizations rely on strategic adaptation at the firm level to maintain competitive advantage. Firms scan their environments, predict changes, and devise corporate- and business-level strategies to capture and preserve market niches. However, these strategies are maladaptive in a turbulent environment. In order to cope with turbulence associated with economic and technological change, an increasing number of firms are resorting to what Astley and Fombrun (1983) call "collective strategies." Many are initiating joint ventures or participating in research and development consortia with universities and other firms.

Participation in these collective strategies offers several hedges against increasingly turbulent business environments and allows firms to compensate for their inability to keep pace with technological changes. This occurs in several ways.

First, joint ventures stimulate innovation by distributing the risks of investing in new-technology development across several firms. R&D consortia, for example, enable firms to pursue state-of-the-art research designed to enhance their long-term competitive advantage while shouldering only a percentage of the total cost of initiating such research. One example of this form of collaboration is the Semiconductor Research Corporation (SRC), an R&D consortium among twenty companies organized by IBM in 1982 to shore up the sagging U.S. semiconductor industry. By pooling and channeling corporate funds for university research, SRC provides an infusion of new scientific research into the participating companies (Dimancescu and Botkin, 1986).

In the aerospace industry, in particular, the cost savings from joint ventures can be substantial, since the initial investments for a single new project may exceed the net worth of the company (Moxon and Geringer, 1985). Joint ventures also provide a hedge against market-based uncertainties associated with the protracted development time for new aircraft.

High launch costs and significant uncertainties lead to a high level of risk facing manufacturers contemplating new aircraft or engine projects. Not surprisingly, many projects and companies have been unsuccessful. The formation of multination partnerships is in part an attempt by industry participants to limit these economic risks [Moxon and Geringer, 1985, p. 57].

Collaborations also reduce the experience curve for entering new markets and minimize the costs of introducing new process innovations by transferring technological know-how from partners who have already successfully implemented these innovations. Thus, collaborative ventures ensure a more steady stream of both product and process innovations, the ingredients necessary for sustaining a competitive advantage (Manufacturing Studies Board, 1986).

Expanded access to markets and reduction of competition are other likely outcomes of collaborative ventures. "Multinational joint ventures can provide preferred access to export markets at a lower cost. Bringing companies from several nations together can assure access to all their national markets" (Moxon and Geringer, 1985, p. 58). Expanded markets permit the necessary economies of scale needed for production efficiencies, and having foreign partners reduces the political concessions often demanded in exchange for access to national markets. Teaming up with actual or potential competitors also serves to reduce the field of competitors overall and to enhance the likelihood of success for the jointly sponsored product (Moxon and Geringer, 1985).

In addition to alliances among business, economic and technological change has also promoted collaboration across sectors to cope with economic change in an entire region. A novel partnership between a union, local social service agencies, a university, and a manufacturing firm was created to ease the transition of 850 workers who were to be laid off when a firm shut down a plant. The MN Community Services Council was formed to provide a coordinated response to the multiple social, psychological, and economic needs of the unemployed workers (Taber, Walsh, and Cooke, 1979).

One of the most well known and successful examples of stakeholders collaborating in the face of changing economic conditions is the Jamestown Area Labor Management Committee (JALMC), formed in Jamestown, New York, in 1972. Jamestown, like scores of other northern cities, was suffering from a severe erosion of its industrial base as many of local manufacturing firms relocated in the South. The town also has a reputation for poor labor relations. JALMC was created to revitalize the remaining industries through improved labor/management relations and collaborative efforts between local corporations and local government to improve the business climate. In the period from 1972 to 1981, JALMC is credited with saving 824 jobs in the community and attracting another 1413. In addition, a substantial improvement in the labor relations climate can be attributed to the formation of many labor-management committees at the plant level (Hanlon and Williams, 1982). Jamestown is clearly emblematic of how collaborative adaptation to turbulence associated with economic decline and increased competition can succeed.

The collaborative responses and their intended impacts that result from economic and technological change are summarized in Table 2, along with the impact of the other five incentives to collaborate.

Declining Productivity Growth and Increasing Competitive Pressures

A second related factor promoting partnerships among organizations is the recent decline in productivity growth and the pressure of foreign competition. This decrease in productivity growth has been especially severe for the United States, although major U.S. competitors, such as France, Germany, Japan, Britain, and Italy, have also suffered losses in productivity growth (Committee for Economic Development, 1983; Baily and Chakrabarti, 1988). Comparatively, however, for the period from 1973 to 1986, labor productivity growth (measured as output per hour of work) in the private business sector in the United States dropped from an average yearly increase of 3.3 percent (for 1946 to 1965) to 1.4 percent (for 1965 to 1985). Despite modest increases in the last few years, U.S. productivity growth generally remains substantially lower than that of several other industrialized nations (Committee for Economic Development,

Table 2. Impact of Incentives to Collaborate.

Incentive	Collaborative Response	Intended Impact
Economic and technological change	Interfirm joint ventures	Stimulate innovation Minimize risk
	Business-university consortia	Exchange expertise Expand market access Reduce competition
	Public-private partnerships	Cope with economic decline Stimulate socioeconomic revitalization
Declining productivity	Labor-management committees	Improve productivity Increase worker input into planning
	Interfunctional collaboration	Facilitate introduction of new-technology/new-product designs
Global interdependence	Multilateral collaboration (nations/NGOs/multinationals)	Facilitate world preservation Facilitate global management of resources/technology Prevent violence
Blurred boundaries	Labor-management committees	Create broader collective bargaining agenda Increase worker input into planning
	Policy dialogues (business/government/communities/interest groups)	Resolve policy disputes Develop broad consensus on new policies
	Intergovernmental collaboration	Resolve policy disputes Speed decisions
Shrinking federal revenues	Public-private partnerships	Cope with economic decline Stimulate socioeconomic revitalization
Dissatisfaction with courts	Policy dialogues Regulatory negotiation Mediated site-specific disputes	Overcome impasse Settle conflicts Improve solutions

1983; Baily and Chakrabarti, 1988). This decline in the average annual rate of change in total factor productivity was registered for all the major economic sectors except communications, agriculture, and service industries (American Productivity Center, 1982). For the period from 1973 to 1979, primary metals, petroleum, construction, and mining suffered the most noticeable drops in productivity growth, and these industries continued to experience negative growth trends during 1979 to 1985 (American Productivity Center, 1986).

While some improvement in productivity was seen in the statistics for manufacturing generally between 1983 and 1985, multifactor productivity for the nonfarm nonmanufacturing sector (including construction, mining, finance, and service industries) maintained a steady decline from 1973 through 1985 (American Productivity Center, 1986). Moreover, the increase in manufacturing productivity has been partly attributed to a temporary surge of organizational restructuring, downsizing, and mergers that is unlikely to be repeated (Baily and Chakrabarti, 1988; Pennar, 1988). Also, productivity growth in the computer industry accounts for much of the aggregate increases in manufacturing productivity between 1979 and 1985 (Bailey and Chakrabarti, 1988).

Declines in productivity growth relative to other industrialized nations contribute to a loss of competitive advantage. This has been especially true for U.S. firms. In certain industries, such as steel, machine tools, automobiles, clothing, and semiconductors, foreign competition for American products skyrocketed during the 1970s. By 1980, America was importing 25 percent of its cars, 25 percent of its steel, 60 percent of its calculators, 27 percent of its metal-forming machine tools, 35 percent of its textile machine tools, and 53 percent of its numerically controlled machine tools. In 1986 imports captured 47 percent of the U.S. market for machine tools, while the U.S. share plummeted to 4 percent (down from 46 percent in 1964 ["Can America Compete?" 1987]). A global indicator of the threat to U.S. competitiveness is the U.S. trade balance, which steadily declined between 1975 and 1986.

This onslaught of foreign competition has left many U.S.

businesses at the starting block in the race for market share. The forces have been sufficiently jarring to fundamentally alter the economic infrastructure of American business (Astley and Brahm, 1988; Reich, 1983). In an effort to remain competitive (or to regain competitive advantage), many American businesses have restructured their assets, closed factories, jettisoned entire business units, added environmental scanning departments, and redesigned basic production processes. Accompanying many of these changes are proposals for new alliances. As we have seen in the previous section, alliances *among* businesses are becoming commonplace. Additionally, competitive pressures are also stimulating new alliances within firms.

Competitive pressures are forcing many firms to undertake fundamental overhauls of shop-floor management practices and to establish more participative forms of management. Firms are striving to create more flexible structures so that they can reorganize themselves on short notice (Ackoff, 1981; Hedberg, Nystrom, and Starbuck, 1977; Toffler, 1985). Proposals for more flexible organization designs and creative problem-solving techniques are receiving increasing attention (Mitroff, 1987; Peters, 1988). For example, Peters (1988, p. 108) describes the "fleet-of-foot organization of the future" in which traditional organizational boundaries become more permeable, flexibility is paramount, and partnerships are encouraged. "The movement from adversarial to new non-adversarial partnership relations with outsiders of all stripes is one of the biggest shifts required of American firms" (Peters, 1988, p. 108).

In order to stay competitive, many manufacturing firms are introducing computer-integrated manufacturing into their operations. To capture the full benefits to productivity that these computer-based technologies offer, more collaborative ways of incorporating the contributions of various functional areas are needed. Specifically, expertise from many functional areas (such as manufacturing and marketing) is now required in the early stages of planning for new-product development. To achieve this up-front involvement (and the goal of improved production efficiency), new patterns of interaction among functional units must be created (Dean and Susman, 1989). Thus,

new designs for collaboration among functional areas within
business are being explored to address the changes introduced
by computer-integrated manufacturing.

Declining productivity has also spawned a number of experiments in cooperation between unions and management.
In a speech delivered at Chautauqua Institute in July 1986,
Douglas Fraser, former president of the United Auto Workers,
heralded what he called "a greater spirit of labor/management
cooperation" brought about by the economic decline of the
early 1980s (Fraser, 1986). In particular, Fraser pointed to the
"new ventures program" written into union contracts and to
GM's Saturn project as illustrations of this cooperative spirit. In
the Saturn project, union and management undertook a joint
experiment to redesign one of GM's manufacturing plants with
the latest automated technology and a radically different "rule
by consensus" management style. Numerous collaborative initiatives including quality circles, labor-management committees
and gain-sharing plans as well as some changes in the collective
bargaining system itself have been introduced. The primary motivations for such changes are the need to improve productivity
and a desire for improved labor relations generally (Schuster,
1985; Dunlop, 1986).

Data on these alterations in union-management relationships point to some success. Traditional ideological differences
between unions and management do not die easily (Levitan and
Werneke, 1984), but where collaborative efforts are successful,
fundamental changes in the parties' relationship have occurred
(Scobel, 1982; Schuster, 1985; Kochan, Katz, and McKersie,
1987). In those cases, labor and management engaged in more
rational examination of issues and spent more time addressing
productivity and less time addressing grievances and concerns
about management rights (Schuster, 1985). The most successful
quality-of-work-life projects are those that link workplace issues
with changes in the strategic affairs of the company, including
layoffs and competition from cheaper labor pools (Kochan,
Katz, and McKersie, 1987).

Extralocal cross-sectoral alliances among organizations
have also formed in response to declining productivity. Forums

for union-management dialogue at regional and national levels have been established. One such effort begun in 1976 is the Labor-Management Group, which comprises AFL-CIO leaders and business roundtable chief executive officers (CEOs) concerned with such topics as economic policies and health care (Dunlop and Salter, 1987). Within Pennsylvania, the legislature created the MILRITE Council, which sponsors the development of regional labor-management committees in the state.

Problems of productivity are intimately tied to changes in the global economy, which are also creating incentives to collaborate. These are discussed next.

Global Interdependence

The advent of new communications technologies and increased international trade have virtually shrunk the size of the earth and created a fundamentally new pattern of relationships among societies across the globe (Bell, 1979; Rosenau, 1980). These developments have heightened the interdependence of local communities on national and international issues and have elevated local political issues to global importance. Societies are now linked economically, politically, and socially in ways that were unsuspected a decade or two ago.

> Microeconomic interdependence exists where global decisions impact individual markets, regions or firms. Macroeconomic interdependence results, for example, from international trade impacting economic aggregates such as employment levels, rates of growth, and money supply [Luke, 1984, p. 4].

With this interdependence have come new global tensions as the balance of trade shifts, currency values fluctuate, and multinational corporations reshape competition in the world market.

Classical theories of international relations depict nation-states as the primary actors, but now the pattern of interactions is much more complex and includes many nongovernmental actors (Rosenau, 1980). Virtually all nations are dependent on resources from outside their boundaries, but the new patterns of interdependence also include vertical relations between nation-states and the global private sector. As multinational businesses diversify geographically and in terms of products, they are gradually shaping a world economy that transcends the traditional boundaries of nation-states. Many multinationals have adopted global strategies in which assets are coordinated worldwide and operations are strategically relocated to take advantage of cheap labor pools or natural resources. Coordination of such diverse activities worldwide requires immense flexibility by multinationals in deploying and removing assets to capture new market opportunities. "Multinationals were thus faced with the task of devising organizational systems for orchestrating both local objectives and worldwide objectives as part of coherent global strategy" (Astley and Brahm, 1988, p. 32). These global strategies create a complex matrix of interdependencies between multinationals and the host countries in which they operate.

John F. Welsh, chairman and chief executive officer of General Electric Company, talking to an audience at the Harvard Business School, predicted that "cooperative alliances, designed to achieve global scale and strong positions for both companies involved in the transaction," will become increasingly common (Van Bever, 1987, p. 5). He urged students to develop skills to work in such alliances (Van Bever, 1987).

As noted in Chapter One, the need for alliances extends beyond just private-sector interests. Indeed, collaboration is an essential tool for addressing problems that involve public, private, and nongovernmental organizations worldwide. The Third Club of Rome, conducted by Nobel laureate Jan Tinbergen, offered as one of its major conclusions:

> What is required is a new international order in which all benefit from change. What is required are fundamental institutional reforms, based upon a recognition of a common interest and mutual concerns, in an increasingly interdependent world [Tinbergen, 1976, pp. 7–8].

Clearly, we cannot underestimate our role as planetary partners when it comes to negotiating arms reductions and issues of global survival. It is also clear that collaboration around issues of this magnitude involves high stakes for individual parties as well. Fundamental issues of representation and resource distribution are potentially explosive ones and will demand considerable sensitivity to differences, forbearance, and even humility to craft workable multinational agreements.

Blurring of Boundaries Between Business, Labor, and Government

The interdependence of economic, resource, and political sectors globally is also reflected in the interpenetration of these sectors domestically. Business decisions increasingly have social and political ramifications; local, state, and federal governments have intervened to limit business discretion when exercise of that discretion runs contrary to "the public good." Global competition is also forcing a redefinition of the roles of labor and management and is raising questions about the role of government in protecting domestic labor from layoffs and from foreign immigration. Finally, relations between one level of government and another are becoming increasingly interwoven: state, federal, and local authorities share jurisdiction over taxes, environmental protection, and trade and commerce; federal programs are dependent on implementation by state and local governments; and state and local governments are dependent on the federal government for policy guidelines and fiscal resources (Luke, 1984). These interpenetrating relationships have created considerable controversy over roles and have led to a blurring of the traditional boundaries between business, government, and labor (Smith, 1983; Bozeman, 1984). The extent of this blurring will be examined in more detail below.

The *Union-Management Relationship.* Productivity decline and competitive pressures from abroad have forced many American businesses to close and others to lay off substantial portions of their work force. As a result, union membership has decreased steadily since 1979, dropping from 24.1 percent to 17.5 percent in 1986. Also, unions in some industries have been forced to abandon the standard wage formulas and in some cases to accept substantial reductions in real wages and fringe benefit packages to shore up corporate economic performance during recent hard times. These erosions in the status of unions coupled with new human resource management practices and the unique differences in labor forces across the world have raised questions about the future of unions and their role in global competition (Kochan, Katz, and McKersie, 1987).

While unions have been consolidating their ranks, management has also had to reconsider the extent of its authority. Cooperative ventures with the union require power sharing with respect to some areas of decision making previously the sole prerogative of management. The collective bargaining agenda for the 1980s has broadened beyond economic issues to include health and safety, plant closings, and job security.

The Business-Government Relationship. Managerial discretion has also been challenged by the increased role of government in corporate affairs, which began with the introduction of a new wave of "social regulation" in the late 1960s and early 1970s (Lilly and Miller, 1977). This wave of federal regulations, along with an increasing array of state and local laws, has fundamentally altered the nature of the economic enterprise. Government efforts to counteract market failures and to minimize externalities (negative consequences to third parties, such as pollution or discrimination resulting from market activities) are now a fundamental factor with which managers must contend (Millstein and Katsh, 1981). And, despite the push for deregulation, indications are that government presence has not diminished during the 1980s (Bucholtz, 1988). Especially in the area of managing the economy, governments have played an increasingly preeminent role—through fiscal policies at the federal level and through economic development incentives at the state and local levels (Kirlin, 1982; Luke, 1984).

At the same time, evidence of business influence over government is visible. Ongoing deliberations in Congress over trade barriers to protect American industries from foreign competitors is one prominent example. Other areas in which business and government are tussling for influence include protective parities for agriculture, federal plant-closing legislation, tax incentives and abatements, and environmental regulations of all kinds. Government is also dependent on business for delivery of goods and services, including defense and space research, computer services, and perhaps even postal delivery in the near future.

Intergovernmental Relations. Interlocal disputes among government agencies are increasing in frequency as state, local, and federal levels of government share jurisdiction over an increasing number of issues. State and local agencies impose their own regulations for environmental protection, for example, and these often create inconsistent and conflicting requirements for regulatees. Agencies are also dependent on each other for information, resources, and policy decisions, making it impossible for any agency to act unilaterally. This tight network of interdependent relations, known as "fused federalism," is a vestige of the Great Society era, in which over one hundred categorical grant programs were launched by the federal government. Luke (1984) also notes a blurring of the historical separation of legislative, judicial, and administrative functions (for example, agencies develop alliances with constituency groups, which then exert political influence on legislators).

How does this blurring of roles among sectors create incentives for collaboration? Several connections are noteworthy. First, the interpenetration of government and business agendas requires cooperation between these sectors in searching for solutions that balance many interests simultaneously. Many regulatory issues involve complex technical information and projections. Often information about the consequences of various regulatory choices is distributed in varying degrees among the private sector, public interest groups, and one or more government agencies. In these circumstances, it behooves the agency to involve these stakeholders in inventing a solution rather than to pursue an incremental decision process in which agency efforts to internalize and reconcile all the conflicting interests fail to satisfy any of the parties (Rittel and Webber, 1973; Gricar and Baratta, 1983; Wondolleck, 1985; Carpenter and Kennedy, 1988). At the local level, too, planners, city commissioners, and other local authorities need to take leadership roles in convening stakeholders and in initiating collaborative processes for issues on which community, business, and governmental interests conflict.

Second, the edicts of various government agencies often create conflicting priorities. For example, proposals to stimulate productivity call for a reduction in non-cost-effective regulations and increased use of programs that allow management more discretion and greater flexibility in choosing the most cost-effective responses to regulations. The details of how programs like these will actually be implemented need input and cooperation from all the stakeholders if they are to satisfy these diverse agenda. For example, mediated negotiations among parties (patterned after regulatory negotiations already in use) offer considerable potential for ironing out guidelines for programs such as the Environmental Protection Agency's (EPA's) "bubble concept." The bubble concept is a program in which the agency grants greater discretion to industry to tailor compliance programs so that firms are not crippled by high compliance costs. This eases the burden of regulatory compliance and allows firms to stay competitive.

Third, a report on federal assistance management by the Office of Management and Budget underscores the need for collaborative processes among governmental units.

> Thus these recommendations stress processes. Some processes are to prevent or resolve conflicts at the policy level. Others are to speed resolution of unavoidable conflicts at the recipient level. Much stress is placed on improved cooperation and coordination, both among agencies and with recipients. Strong emphasis is placed on clarifying relationships and expectations [Executive Office of the President, 1980, p. 15].

Intergovernmental negotiations among the relevant government agencies have already been used effectively to iron out conflicting statutory authority (Richman, 1985; Agranoff and Lindsay, 1983).

Fourth, despite arguments to improve productivity by reducing regulations, serious environmental problems looming large on the environmental policy horizon will not just go away. Problems such as acid rain, groundwater contamination, hazardous waste disposal, and biotechnology all require some legislative and regulatory attention. Given the simultaneous national goals of addressing these fundamental resource issues, of stimulating economic productivity, and of improving U.S. competitiveness, balancing these agenda will necessitate careful, deliberate planning by all concerned. Thus, as roles become more blurred, the incentive for business, government, and unions to jointly negotiate such plans increases.

Fifth, policy dialogues offer promising avenues for forging preliminary consensus in particularly controversial areas in which legislation or regulation may be needed. Efforts to promote deliberations of this kind in the preliminary stages of planning are being fostered in several private and public forums. For example, in 1986 the Keystone Center began a policy dialogue on strategies for managing hazardous waste. More than fifty stakeholders, including officials from the American Paper Institute, Eastman Kodak Company, the Gulf Coast Fisherman's Environmental Defense Fund, the Sierra Club, Waste Management Inc., and the U.S. Environmental Protection Agency agreed to participate. The dialogue is still under way, and some preliminary recommendations were disseminated during 1987. Similar dialogues on other issues have been initiated by several intermediary organizations. For example, the Illinois Environmental Consensus Forum sponsored a dialogue about agricultural land use in Illinois. The Institute for Resource Management brought environmentalists and business representatives together to discuss oil and gas development in the outer continental shelf off the California coast.

Shrinking Federal Revenues for Social Problems

A fifth factor contributing to the formation of collaborative alliances is the decline in federal funds for social programs. During the 1960s and early 1970s, major incursions of federal dollars flowed into local communities. Between 1960 and 1970 federal aid to state and local governments jumped from $7 billion to $24 billion; by 1980 the figure was almost $91 billion. These funds were designed to address a myriad of social ills (such as poverty, urban decay, unemployment, crime, and inferior education) particularly endemic to large urban areas. After a decade of experience, it became clear that these expenditures were grossly insufficient and largely ineffective in addressing increasingly intractable problems. As a result, since 1978 fewer and fewer federal funds have been made available. In the first six years of the Reagan administration, across-the-board cuts in funds for social programs became a common theme. In the wake of these cutbacks, social programs struggling to stay alive began to look to each other and to private enterprises and local initiatives for assistance.

As federal funds to aid cities evaporated, in some cities public-private partnerships began to emerge to fill the void. These partnerships between social agencies, local governments, and the private sector have addressed issues of economic redevelopment, education, housing, employment, and adult literacy (Fosler and Berger, 1982; Brooks, Liebman, and Schelling, 1984; Davis, 1986).

Initial inspiration for collaboration between public and private sectors to counteract growing social and economic problems of urban areas was articulated in the President's Urban and Regional Group Report ("A New Partnership . . . ," 1978). This report presented a national urban policy with public-private partnerships as one plank. These partnerships were proposed not as wholesale replacements for waning federal initiatives but to advance specific economic revitalization projects closely connected to business interests (Lyall, 1986). The thrust of these partnerships was public-sector leverage of opportunities for private-sector investment in declining urban areas.

> Most importantly, we must recognize that urban problems cannot be solved by the federal government alone. A successful urban policy must incorporate a philosophy of partnership among the federal government, state and

local governments, private businesses, neighborhood
groups, voluntary organizations and urban residents
["A New Partnership . . . ," 1978, pp. 6-7].

This theme of leveraging private investment was reiterated a few
years later by the National Research Council (1982).

During the Reagan administration, stimulus for public-
private partnerships was provided at least symbolically through
the President's Task Force on Private Sector Initiatives. The
task force was never conceived as a policy office, and, while
it served primarily as a clearinghouse for information on partnerships across the country, it also utilized peer persuasion to
"entice" business participation in local partnerships (Berger,
1986). As a result, many local partnerships began to spring up.

Public-private partnerships have served as the vehicle for
major downtown redevelopment efforts in cities such as Baltimore, Pittsburgh, Minneapolis–St. Paul, Portland, Dallas, and
others (Fosler and Berger, 1982; Brooks, Liebman, and Schelling,
1984). While such partnerships do not all operate as smoothly
or produce as dramatic results as those in the cities listed above,
they currently afford a viable avenue for marrying private-sector
funds and expertise with local community needs. In the eight
years since the national urban policy was introduced, there appears to be a gradually increasing awareness that business partnership with public and not-for-profit organizations is essential
to the future of viable urban centers (Lyall, 1986; Levine and
Trachtman, 1985).

Local partnerships have begun to address more intractable social problems in addition to economic redevelopment,
recognizing that it is in their own interest to do so. With respect
to education, for example, "the relationship between the stability and vitality of the immediate community and its schools
and the economic well-being of local business has become a central concern to business" (Otterbourg and Timpane, 1986, p.
61). Even if federal revenues were again suddenly available, past
experiences with Model Cities, CETA, and other centralized federal programs suggest that local initiatives may hold far greater
promise because the problems now touch multiple stakeholders

for whom resolution is increasingly critical. Despite increased
incentives for collaboration, however, collaborative initiatives
across these culturally diverse sectors pose considerable challenges for all the players (Berger, 1986).

Dissatisfaction with Court-Initiated Solutions

A final factor contributing to the search for collaborative alternatives is dissatisfaction with decisions rendered by our legal
system. A growing philosophy of entitlements in America has
led to vigorous pursuit of litigation to resolve disputes (Lieberman, 1983). Concerns over rights of all kinds (such as the right
to privacy, to clean air, to equal employment opportunities, to
safe products, and so forth) have become part of our everyday
vocabulary. These rights form an expanded set of claims for
which people seek legal redress when they believe their rights
have been violated. As a result, new classes of plaintiffs have
emerged, court dockets have swelled, and backlogs have bal-
looned.

To illustrate, between 1967 and 1976 appeals in state
courts increased eight times as fast as the population (Woodcock, 1982). In 1983, 241,842 civil cases were filed in U.S. district courts. This represented a 74.3 percent increase over the
level of cases in 1978. Similarly, the court of appeals experienced a 56.6 percent increase in cases for the same time period
(Bingham, 1986). In the environmental protection area alone,
former EPA administrator William Ruckelshaus estimated that
more than 80 percent of EPA rules faced court challenges
(Ruckelshaus, 1984).

In addition, the onslaught of social regulation in the 1970s
established a proliferation of agency rules. These rules are en-
forced through a parallel system of administrative adjudication
governed by the Administrative Procedure Act. This system, intended to provide more informed decision making than the civil
courts, has become increasingly complex and similar to litigation in time and expense (Bureau of National Affairs, 1985).
Rule-making processes themselves are extremely costly in terms
of time and resources for the agencies and for those parties who

choose to influence the process by challenging the proposed regulations through the required review-and-comment process.

The costs and long delays associated with litigation are frequently cited as major incentives for parties to search for alternative means of settling their differences. While it is difficult to compare the costs of litigation to the costs of reaching a settlement through alternative means, the costs of litigation in the United States are staggering, estimated to equal 2 percent of the gross national product (Woodcock, 1982). The length of time it takes to conclude a case varies considerably from jurisdiction to jurisdiction. In Los Angeles County, for example, 40,000 civil cases were awaiting trial or settlement in the superior court in 1985 (Chambers, 1986). Instead of waiting four to five years (the average time it takes to go to trial), some plaintiffs and defendants opted for a speedier resolution through California's private judicial system. In the private system, cases go before private justices (often retired judges) and are frequently settled in a matter of days. Backlog in the Franklin County court in Columbus, Ohio, prompted that court to initiate "settlement week." In an effort to trim the court docket of 6,885 civil cases, the court earmarked some 600 cases for mediation during a special week set aside for that purpose (Solomon, 1986).

A study of civil cases in U.S. district courts revealed that the median duration for those cases that went to trial was nineteen months. Some environmental cases took as long as sixty-seven months. These data lead Bingham (1986) to conclude that the threat of protracted litigation, rather than the average case length, induces the search for alternatives to litigation. The Center for Public Resources, which sponsored complex multiparty negotiations between asbestos producers and insurance companies over asbestos-exposure claims, estimates that twenty-five years of litigation were avoided by thirty months of mediation in that extremely complex case.

In addition to time and expense, several other limitations of adversarial legal processes have instigated a search for alternative means of settling multiparty disputes. Our propensity for litigating not only has greatly overburdened the judicial system but also has often failed to produce enduring solutions to the underlying disputes (Gellhorn, 1984). By their nature the rules of civil procedure position the parties as adversaries. Parties argue adamantly for positions, communication is restricted, information is used selectively to bolster arguments, and emotional appeals are invoked. As positions harden, polarization occurs, and each party typically develops hostility toward the other side. When these same parties meet repeatedly in court, battle lines are often drawn well before proceedings begin. These characteristics of adversarial conflict resolution are summarized in Table 3.

Table 3.   Characteristics of Adversarial and Collaborative Processes for Dispute Resolution.

Adversarial	Collaborative
Rules position parties as adversaries	Parties positioned as joint problem solvers
Third parties intervene before issues are mature	Issues can be identified before positions crystalize
Characterized by positional bargaining	Characterized by interest-based bargaining
Facts used to buttress positions	Joint search used to determine facts
Characterized by polarization of parties and issues	Characterized by search for underlying interests
Face-to-face contact restricted among contending parties	Face-to-face discussions encouraged among all parties
Seeks winning arguments	Seeks workable options
Yields all-or-nothing resolution of issues	Yields resolution by integrating interests
Narrows options quickly	Broadens field of options
Authority for decision rests with judge	Authority for decisions rests with parties
Characterized by suspicion and high emotion	Characterized by respect and application of reason
Parties often dissatisfied with outcome	Outcome must be satisfactory to all parties
Often fosters bitterness and long-term mistrust	Promotes trust and positive relationships

Source: Adopted from Center for Policy Negotiation, Inc., 1985.

The costs of such scenarios for multiparty disputes can be substantial. First, because court proceedings effectively preclude direct participation by the parties, important information about their interests (such as what is most important to them) is subordinated to presenting the best legal case possible. Through the legal process issues may be introduced in which the principals in the case have little or no interest. If left to solve the case in their own terms, the parties may well arrive at a very different solution than that of the court. Second, when relationships become embittered, future communications in or outside of court are inevitably impaired. Third, many multiparty conflicts involve complex technical issues. It is unrealistic to assume that the judiciary has the time or is competent to settle these technical issues or that an adversarial process can foster the exchange of information, joint analysis, and trading off of interests that lead to creative resolutions. Historically, the courts produce winners and losers. In these circumstances, often neither party leaves the proceedings feeling satisfied that the underlying issues in the dispute are resolved.

Fourth, the courts are frequently unable or unwilling to monitor the results of their decrees. The judiciary is not equipped to handle administrative functions and, because of heavy demands, is impatient with protracted litigation.

A final concern about court proceedings expressed by some is that not all parties who are likely to be affected by the decisions are represented in the proceedings. For some parties, access is precluded by the prohibitive costs of legal services. In other cases, parties have no way of knowing that a decision is being rendered and may have adverse consequences for them. Decisions forged between just a few stakeholders may or may not represent the wider common good and may allow some stakeholders to promote their values at the expense of others (Warren, 1967; Abel, 1982). These solutions are not optimal for the domain, and they are likely to be short-lived if they generate additional rounds of conflict provoked by those stakeholders who were adversely affected. Thus, for some problem domains, the process itself contributes to turbulence. Problems are inadequately solved and reappear at a later time in another forum or remain unsolved because of impasse. Consider, as a case in point, how such entanglements crippled the efforts of one region to improve water-pollution control for fourteen years until the deadlock was finally broken through mediated negotiation with the help of a court-appointed special master.

In 1972 the federal government created a regional sewage authority for a northeast community. Not long afterward, one irate municipality filed a lawsuit challenging the design and cost allocation structure of the sewage treatment facility proposed by the regional authority. Subsequently, other communities and interested parties also filed suits. Smaller communities refused to pay assessments, asserting that their waste disposal needs were adequately served by local septic systems. While the cases dragged on in court, little was done to maintain the existing disposal system and federal standards for water quality became increasingly more stringent. Meanwhile, the regional authority was accumulating a substantial debt, federal funds for the project had expired, and construction costs had skyrocketed. The number of stakeholders grew to include landowners and developers when, in the mid 1980s, a Superior Court judge banned all new sewer connections until the disputes were settled. Finally, the court appointed a "special master" to mediate among all the parties. By meeting individually with all the parties and through the use of a computer model to test the cost implications of various solutions, an acceptable agreement was eventually reached (Susskind, 1985).

Table 3 also presents a summary of characteristics associated with collaborative processes for dispute resolution. In contrast to adversarial processes, collaborative ones focus on interests rather than on positional bargaining (Fisher and Ury, 1981). Parties jointly search for complete explanations rather than using facts selectively to buttress their positions. Face-to-face contact is encouraged rather than discouraged. Because the parties retain authority over any decisions that are reached, they are much more likely to be satisfied with the outcome.

Clearly, court proceedings have their place, and advocates of alternative methods have never advocated wholesale replacement of due process with these alternatives. Instead, the proposals for alternatives offer avenues to reduce the burden on the courts and to enlarge our capacity to invent wise, just, and feasible agreements, particularly in cases in which the parties themselves are the most technically capable of making the decisions and must bear the responsibility for implementing them. Commitment to implementation of a decision is heightened by participation.

It is appropriate to note that some legal scholars have raised questions about the political consequences of extrajudicial, informal systems of justice (Abel, 1982; Galanter, 1979; Harrington, 1980). Abel (1982), for example, points out several contradictions in the role of informal justice in both extending and reducing state control over disputants. Despite these inherent contradictions, he concludes:

> It [informalism] is advocated by reformers and embraced by disputants precisely because it expresses values that deservedly elicit broad allegiance: the preference for harmony over conflict, for mechanisms that offer equal access to the many rather than unequal privilege to the few, that operate quickly and cheaply, that permit all citizens to participate in decision making rather than limiting authority to "professionals," that are familiar rather than esoteric, and that strive for and achieve substantive justice rather than frustrating it in the name of form [p. 310].

An Era of Collaboration

The incentives to collaborate vary from sector to sector, as do the forms that collaboration takes. As noted earlier, these are summarized in Table 1. Some incentives stimulate private-sector collaboration; some promote collaboration between governmental units; others generate cross-sectoral collaboration. Collectively, however, the trend is obvious. Increasing interdependence among stakeholders is forcing a reexamination of institutional relations from the local to the global level.

The environmental complexities of the organizations of today and tomorrow exist because of the diverse stakeholders who hold the solutions to international problems. No doubt, problems—international or domestic—require multiorganizational appreciation, collaborative planning, and cooperative interventions [Heenan and Perlmutter, 1979, p. 165].

Despite powerful incentives to collaborate, our capacity to do so is underdeveloped. As evidence in the following chapters will reveal, we have begun to develop the right instincts about the value of collaboration, but there are also compelling forces that cause those who try to collaborate to fall short.

The remainder of this book provides a realistic appraisal of collaborative efforts in a wide number of arenas. Overall, the potential for collaboration looks both promising and sobering. In order to capitalize on the potential, we need to understand much more about the fundamental assumptions underlying collaborative processes and the practical dynamics of how these processes unfold and can be managed. This will require some radical revisions in our thinking and expansion of our problem-solving skills as a society. Part Two provides an in-depth look at the dynamics of collaborating.

3

The Collaborative Process

*If we do not understand where we are in the negotiating
process, we may use the wrong instruments in trying to
move the process forward.*

—Saunders, 1985

This chapter examines the step-by-step process by which collaboration among multiple parties unfolds. While there is not a
clearly prescribed pattern that characterizes every collaboration,
there appear to be some common issues that crop up repeatedly
and conform to a general sequence independent of the specific
circumstances and content of the negotiations. Clearly the length,
the significance, and the difficulty of a particular phase may
vary considerably depending on whether the collaboration is
over a site-specific environmental dispute, a public-private partnership, or an interfirm research and development initiative.

One major difference, noted in Chapter One, depends on
whether the motivation to collaborate is induced by conflict or
by a shared vision concerning the problem. Presumably, in the
latter circumstances stakeholders may initially be more willing
to convene to look into some joint activity. That is, they may
have a greater readiness to collaborate than stakeholders starting
from an overt conflict. In the former situation, with no common definition of the problem, the parties must recognize the
need to search for one in order to begin collaborating. As Saunders (1985) points out with respect to the long-standing unresolved conflict among Arabs, Israelis, and Palestinians, an inability to reach agreement on the substance of the problem
prevents any negotiations from taking place. In many of the

cases described in this book, gaining agreement among the stakeholders to experiment with collaboration was as critical a step as the actual negotiations. Therefore, the early steps in which the convening stakeholders attempt to persuade others to explore the problem collaboratively may require careful timing, patience, and diplomacy.

A second factor that distinguishes collaborative processes is the intended outcome. Some collaborations are designed for information exchange among the stakeholders that may lead them to voluntarily correlate their actions in the future. Other collaborations produce more binding agreements, either in the form of recommendations to an agency authorized to implement them or a formal commitment among the stakeholders to authorize implementation.

Collaborative processes also differ with respect to the strength of convening power and the availability of an institutionalized arena within which discussions can be initiated. In mediated negotiations established by judicial mandate with a special master appointed to break the impasse, an arena is clearly designated and the convener's power is derived from the court. In those cases, getting the parties to the table is not the challenge. However, the consensus-building process in those cases may be delicate, laborious, and technically complex. The implementation phase, crucial to the success of collaboration, may also be protracted.

The three-phase model of collaboration introduced in this chapter is predicated on the assumption that although certain phases may be more significant for some collaborations than for others, there remains a fundamental set of issues that must be addressed in the course of any collaboration. The model presented is therefore a generic one that includes three major phases: problem setting, direction setting, and implementation. (Several authors have described generic phases of collaboration [McCann, 1983; Cummings, 1984; Gray, 1985; Saunders, 1985; Susskind and Madigan, 1984; Dunlop, 1987]. These descriptions of the process range from three- to five-step models. The differences are largely attributable to certain steps being subsumed under others. However, despite these differences, conceptually there is general agreement among scholars about what it takes to get to the table and to explore, reach, and implement an agreement.) Developing the necessary "process literacy" (Carpenter, 1988) to manage collaboratively entails understanding the steps within each of the three phases of collaboration and knowing how to engineer them successfully. The constructive management of each step is crucial to the outcome. Table 4 provides a list of the steps in each phase of the collaborative process.

Table 4.   The Collaborative Process.

Phase 1: Problem setting
- common definition of problem
- commitment to collaborate
- identification of stakeholders
- legitimacy of stakeholders
- convener characteristics
- identification of resources

Phase 2: Direction setting
- establishing ground rules
- agenda setting
- organizing subgroups
- joint information search
- exploring options
- reaching agreement and closing the deal

Phase 3: Implementation
- dealing with constituencies
- building external support
- structuring
- monitoring the agreement and ensuring compliance

Problem Setting

The problem-setting phase is concerned with getting to the table so that face-to-face dialogue can begin. Often this is the most difficult step. Problem setting requires identification of the stakeholders, mutual acknowledgment of the issues that join them, and building commitment to address these issues through face-to-face negotiations. This phase has also been referred to as prenegotiation. "The primary objective of problem-setting is to give the situation an explicit form or identity that allows stakeholders to communicate about it and eventually act upon it" (McCann, 1983, p. 18). Several issues are salient during the problem-setting phase.

Common Definition of Problem

Unless this step is satisfactorily undertaken, subsequent efforts to collaborate are unlikely to succeed. This depends on finding some overlap in how the parties define the major issues of concern. If a problem is defined to the satisfaction of some parties but not others, the latter will have little incentive to collaborate. Indeed, under those circumstances it may be in the latter's best interest to block the negotiations.

Delicate shuttle diplomacy by a third party or by the convening stakeholders is frequently necessary to decipher the obstacles to collaboration and to tease out a problem definition that is sufficiently broad or ambiguous to incorporate the agendas of multiple stakeholders. Sherif (1958) has called this a superordinate goal. In a recent regulatory negotiation convened by the U.S. Environmental Protection Agency to establish standards for deep-well injection of hazardous wastes, it took a mediator six weeks to help the parties agree on a problem definition. At issue was what constituted a "hazardous waste."

The common problem definition around which parties can unite is rooted in their interdependence. The recognition by stakeholders that their desired outcomes are inextricably linked to the actions of the other stakeholders is the fundamental basis for collaborating. Getting parties to the table is often accomplished by heightening their awareness of the forces that join them and of their collective ability to manage these forces. Skillful conveners are able to appreciate and to articulate these interdependencies (Sarason and Lorentz, 1979).

Furthermore, the acknowledgment of mutual dependence ensures that the participating parties each have some standing in the negotiations. In the accord between Egypt and Israel, a crucial factor in getting Israel to the table was Egyptian president Anwar Sadat's public acknowledgment of Israel's historic sovereignty as a state (Saunders, 1985).

Commitment to Collaborate

Sharing a common definition of the problem is often not a sufficient ingredient to get people to the table. There are five interrelated judgments that stakeholders weigh in deciding whether or not to collaborate (Schermerhorn, 1975; Gray, 1985; Saunders, 1985). These judgments include:

1. Does the present situation fail to serve my interests?
2. Will collaboration produce positive outcomes?
3. Is it possible to reach a fair agreement?
4. Is there parity among the stakeholders?
5. Will the other side agree to collaborate?

The stakeholders' commitment to collaborate is strengthened the more each stakeholder can answer "yes" to these questions.

1. *Does the present situation fail to serve my interests?* Generally, parties to a collaboration are dissatisfied with the status quo. They anticipate that, unless something is done by someone, the problems will remain the same or worsen, causing them to incur unwanted costs. In an effort to avert these costs, they turn to collaboration.

Impasse often induces parties to reconsider the possibility of collaborating, but often not until more traditional approaches (such as individual strategic initiatives or litigation) for handling the problems have proven unsuccessful (Fox, 1982b).

> When the failure of contending parties to reach an agreement promises to cost one or more of the parties more than the costs of reaching agreement, the chances for a negotiated settlement are remarkably enhanced. The fate of a major project may well depend on the perceptions of such costs—and the confidence of the parties in the strength of their positions. With the waning of confidence comes increased incentive to bargain [Bacow and Cohen, 1982, p. 44].

Mediators often make use of a stalemate to stimulate commitment. That is, stalement is used as leverage to induce subsequent agreement to submit to mediation (Touval and Zartman, 1985). Prolonging or worsening a stalemate may be a deliberate tactic to prevent parties from taking unilateral actions. "The stalemate must be seen by both parties as unbreakable, except in the direction of a bilateral agreement reached with the help of a mediator" (Touval and Zartman, 1985, p. 13).

The conveners' motivation to initiate the National Coal Policy Project (NCPP) was based on mutual dissatisfaction with years of litigation over environmental issues. Prior to the NCPP dialogue, interactions among industrialists and environmentalists concerned about coal use in the United States were character- ized by acrimony and outright hostility as their lawyers fought bitter battles in the courts. By the time the NCPP was proposed in 1977, stakeholders shared "a nearly unanimous dissatisfac- tion, often rising to the level of frustration, with the decisions rendered by the traditional system" (Murray and Curran, 1982, p. 27). Because this discontent was widely shared among stake- holders, the NCPP was able to convene. The discontent, how- ever, was not unanimous. Some environmental groups believed they were winning substantial victories in the courts. Thus, they were satisfied with the status quo, believed they had nothing to gain from negotiations, and refused to participate. Their behav- ior demonstrates that incentives to negotiate only occur if the leaders of each stakeholder group believe that the benefits of taking action exceed the costs of doing nothing (Davidson, 1976; Schmidt and Kochan, 1977).

2. *Will collaboration produce positive outcomes?* The stakeholders' commitment to collaborate hinges on their per- ception that the negotiations provide an enhanced opportunity to satisfy their interests. That is, before stakeholders agree to collaborate, they must believe that they can derive positive out- comes from doing so (Schermerhorn, 1975; Saunders, 1985). If it appears to them that their objectives are best served by pur- suing other alternatives (such as litigation) or by preventing an agreement, successful negotiations are unlikely. This was the case in the negotiated rulemaking over benzene sponsored by the Occupational Safety and Health Administration (OSHA). Although the agency was able to seat participants from labor

and industry, ultimately no agreement was reached because both sides had reasons to favor the traditional process. Labor was confident OSHA would independently promulgate a regulation favorable to them; industry participants were optimistic the standards would be blocked by subsequent litigation or by the Office of Management and Budget (OMB), which had to approve them. Thus, neither side had a strong incentive to collaborate, and OSHA's decision not to participate in the proceedings precluded the agency from taking steps to dispel these interpretations (Perritt, 1987).

For some stakeholders incentives may be needed to induce their participation. The incentives must be substantial enough to offset these stakeholders' perceptions that collaboration will not produce positive gain. One powerful source of incentives is cultural norms supporting collaboration (Schermerhorn, 1975). For example, the cultures of Japan and Sweden favor collaborative over adversarial approaches for addressing a variety of business and political decisions. It is interesting to note also that Minnesota (which has a strong Scandinavian heritage) is well known for collaborative projects initiated by its state and local governments. Another cultural norm may be community goodwill; that is, a group may not want to gain a reputation as "hard-nosed" or uncompromising bargainers because that might exclude them from subsequent opportunities to influence policy decisions through negotiations. In the case of national environmental groups, motivation to participate in a mediated settlement may depend on the issues the organization is currently championing and whether participation is expected to enhance or erode future financial contributions from constituents (McCarthy, 1984).

In some cases the stature and credibility of a third party will be sufficient to give stakeholders the assurances they need that their concerns will be addressed and that positive outcomes will be possible. This was the case in the negotiations over the proposed Storm King hydroelectric power plant on the Hudson River in New York State. After fifteen years of litigation and administrative hearings, Consolidated Edison and several environmental groups agreed to try to settle the dispute through mediation. Both sides agreed to the choice of former EPA administrator Russell Train, then president of the World Wildlife Fund, to serve as mediator. In addition to Train's credibility, the parties' long-standing inability to settle the dispute through litigation undoubtedly influenced their decision to resort to mediation. According to Bingham (1986), "The parties probably would not have agreed to mediation instead of litigation if the former has been available in the early 1960s. At the beginning of the dispute, the economic, environmental and legal interests of all the parties did not give those parties sufficient incentives to compromise" (pp. 129–130).

In a case involving a proposed forum on nuclear power, leaders of an antinuclear coalition were reluctant to divert resources to the dialogue and away from pursuit of legal action. They were concerned that the forum would drain already scarce resources and dilute their effectiveness in both settings. Believing that the costs did not outweigh the gains, they not only decided not to participate but also took steps to block funding for the forum.

3. *Is it possible to reach a fair agreement?* Reaching a fair settlement may be of particular concern when there is no previous history of negotiating among the stakeholders and there are no precedents to which to refer. Concerns about fairness may also be present when one of the parties has suffered substantial losses in previous interactions. Ensuring fairness may require both parties to lower their aspirations vis-à-vis the reality of achieving their demands.

4. *Is there parity among the stakeholders?* Taking steps to ensure that all stakeholders are relatively equal players in the negotiations may also be necessary. Achieving such balance may by accomplished by providing financial or technical assistance to resource-poor stakeholders. For example, in the regulatory negotiations sponsored by the EPA, environmentalists and consumer groups are offered assistance to ensure that they have access to the same level of technical or scientific support that their business counterparts can draw on.

5. *Will the other side agree to collaborate?* In deciding whether collaboration is possible, it is critical to acknowledge circumstances in which parties are not willing to negotiate.

It is instructive to look first at the conditions under which negotiations cannot occur. If one party to the dispute believes it can achieve a unilateral victory, it clearly will see no need to negotiate. Victory may be the ability to force continued delays of a project, it may reflect assurance of a favorable legal outcome, or an expectation that a political decision will be unequivocally positive. Mediation, as an aid to the regulatory process, explicitly presupposes that each interest group has some doubt about its ability to achieve all its objectives [McCarthy, 1984, p. 24].

In some disputes the interests of one or more parties may best be served by preventing a negotiated agreement. This is often the case in environmental disputes in which a business wishes to delay the imposition of pollution-control sanctions on its operations, or conversely, a local community group wants to prevent some new project from being developed. For example, Vermont's senator Patrick J. Leahy proposed a mediation over designation of wilderness areas in the state. Opponents of the wilderness areas nominally agreed to mediate but, in fact, preferred to keep the issue alive during an upcoming political campaign in which they hoped to unseat Senator Leahy (McCarthy, 1984).

Timing is often a critical issue in joint venture collaborations, too. Some parties may be playing several possible alliances against each other and may want to buy time to determine which alliance will be more favorable to their interests (Moxon and Geringer, 1985).

Often parties underestimate or are reluctant to acknowledge their interdependence on others. Nonetheless, if they know that other stakeholders are willing to explore jointly ·crafted solutions, their own commitment to collaborate is often increased, assuming that they are also motivated by some positive gain. Sometimes, a reluctant stakeholder's fear of being "left out" is sufficient to induce a commitment to try collaboration if all the other stakeholders are willing to proceed. In still other cases, one party may want to prevent another from substantially improving its relationship with a third and will agree to participate in order to prevent the other two from strengthening their alliance (Touval and Zartman, 1985).

Identification of Stakeholders

The question of who should participate in a collaborative negotiation is a very important one with serious implications for the outcome of the collaboration. For multiparty problems, multiple sources of information are necessary to foster as complete an understanding of the problem as possible. The collection of stakeholders should include those whose expertise is essential to constructing this comprehensive picture. A more comprehensive understanding of the problem is achieved as more stakeholders share their perceptions of the problem and how it impacts them (Vickers, 1965). Sufficient variety in the information gathered is needed to match the complexity inherent in the problem itself and to garner support from those who can prevent any agreement from being implemented. By building in this variety, the stakeholders gain a greater appreciation of the patterns of interdependence that underlie their actions with respect to one another (Friend and Jessop, 1969) and thus have an enhanced capacity to design an effective solution.

For example, it is unreasonable to expect the public sector and private citizens to clean up chemical dumps, since the chemical companies have the most expertise about how to handle the toxic materials involved; however, it is not desirable for chemical companies to act independently, since information about the exact nature of the consequences resides with members of the community, including residents, medical professionals, regulatory agencies, and the like. An added complication in these cleanup efforts, of course, is allocation of costs among businesses and government agencies.

The importance of having those stakeholders who will be responsible for implementing the solution present during the negotiations cannot be emphasized enough. Acceptance of any solution is enhanced when those who must abide by it are included in designing the solution (Delbecq, 1974). Additionally, those who must implement a decision often have vital information about the feasibility of alternative solutions. Failure to include them in the design stage only invites technical or political difficulties during implementation. According to Fox (1982b, p. 402), "Parties that are left out may disrupt the proceedings or ultimately challenge the outcome reached, while parties that stay out are implicitly challenging the effort as it begins." It has been suggested that identification and inclusion of additional labor unions may have improved the outcome of the benzene negotiations mentioned above.

> The representation problem in the benzene negotiation was not the exclusion of interests wishing to participate, but rather a more subtle one of failing to identify and include everyone who had the incentive and the power to block a negotiated resolution [Perritt, 1987, p. 917].

In a study of over 100 mediated environmental disputes in which agreement was reached, Bingham (1986) found that participation by those with authority to implement the decision significantly influenced the likelihood that the agreement was implemented. For site-specific disputes, implementation increased from 67 percent to 85 percent when someone with authority to implement the decision was involved in the negotiations from the beginning. When implementers were not present, modifications in the agreements were necessary before implementation could occur.

Stakeholders may be well defined and easily identifiable, or they may be relatively unknown. The former is true if the problem concerns already existing agencies who are part of a service delivery system (for example, social service agencies or hospitals). For other problems, such as the cleanup of a toxic waste dump (such as Love Canal, New York), identifying the stakeholders is much more difficult. In that situation neither the victims nor the chemical companies who had utilized the dump were readily identifiable. Establishing liability is extremely difficult for dumps that were used by multiple firms. Identifying victims is also problematic, since not all victims experience symptoms simultaneously. In addition, some mechanisms must be established to determine the legitimacy of those filing claims.

Legitimacy of Stakeholders

Part of the process of identifying stakeholders is determining which have a legitimate stake in the problem (Walton, 1972; McCann, 1980; Gricar, 1981).

> A legitimate stake means the perceived right and capacity to participate in the negotiations. Those actors with a right to participate are those impacted by the actions of other stakeholders. They become involved in order to moderate those impacts. However, to be perceived as legitimate, stakeholders must also have the capacity to participate. That is, they must possess resources and skills sufficient to justify their involvement. . . . Some stakeholders are perceived as legitimate because they have recognized expertise to bring to bear on the problem. Others control needed financial or informational resources. Still others wield the power to effectively veto an agreement reached either through direct action or by failing to carry out the agreements once they're negotiated [Gray, 1985, p. 922].

Disputes over Legitimacy. Often stakeholders will disagree about the legitimacy of other stakeholders. Perceptions of legitimacy will undoubtedly be colored by historical relationships among the stakeholders. For example, throughout the planning and execution of the Citizens' Radiation Monitoring Program discussed in Chapter One, both Metropolitan Edison and the Nuclear Regulatory Commission were purposely excluded. Despite their indisputable standing as stakeholders, their association with the program was perceived as a major liability, since the credibility of both organizations with the community at large was severely jeopardized at that time.

Particularly in heated conflicts where the parties have built up stereotypical impressions of their opponents, concerns about legitimacy may arise. For example, government officials may not perceive citizens as having a legitimate voice in a technical issue, even though the citizens will have to live with whatever solution is adopted. In constructing a forum to discuss nuclear energy in a community, questions of legitimacy were rampant among the stakeholders. Pronuclear stakeholders questioned whether stakeholders with antinuclear persuasions would listen to reason. The pronuclear group wanted up-front assurance that the antinuclear group would not stage protests during the negotiations. The antinuclear group expressed concern about token membership and insisted that there be a balance of pro- and antinuclear points of view. Local elected officials and some federal regulatory staff characterized some citizens as "irrational" and questioned the need to include citizens in the forum at all.

Similarly, in an effort to design a youth employment program for a major urban area, members of a public-private partnership excluded local community groups from the design phase of the project. Subsequently, when political pressure was needed to implement the plans, the community was not organized to support the proposals. One participant attributed the exclusion of the community groups to racism.

> There was a struggle to get other community organizations involved. They were stakeholders, but they represented a different racial mix than the partnership could handle. By not including them and the mechanisms to legitimate these individuals, the partnership undermined its own power. No one was waiting for what the partnership was going to say. Not including them limited the quality and the political force of the recommendations and drained power from the organization [Gray, 1988, p. 29].

In stark contrast to this approach, another urban partnership maintains a policy of open participation, continually trying to involve new participants with its ongoing agenda while maintaining a regular core group of stakeholders.

Stakeholders often disagree about the legitimacy of other

stakeholders, but successful collaboration depends on including a broad enough spectrum of stakeholders to mirror the critical components of the problem. As Rogers and Whetten (1982, p. 62) have pointed out, "if one organization interprets another as a threat, whether it be founded or unfounded, future attempts at coordination will generally fail." Third parties often need to mediate these disputes over who will be at the table before negotiations about the substance of the problem can begin.

Necessary Trade-Offs. In complex disputes involving hundreds of stakeholders, it is virtually impossible to create a seat at the table for everyone. Some attention must be given to the size and manageability of the group at the table. Administratively, it is often impossible to have every stakeholder participating. Hence, issues of representation must be considered. The selection of participants for a negotiated investment strategy in Malden, Massachusetts, provides a useful illustration. The negotiated investment strategy was a collaborative process undertaken by citizens, businesses, and city government to devise the best ways to utilize public and private funds to address pressing city problems. Among those representing the citizens were individuals from the Malden Interfaith Clergy Association, the YWCA, the Boy Scouts, the Malden Human Rights Commission, and TRI-CAP (a community action group for low-income residents). Representatives from the chamber of commerce, private health care practitioners, the Rotary Club, a manufacturing firm, and several small businesses were among those representing business interests. Choosing representatives for the business and citizen teams proved problematic, however, because not all the stakeholders were obvious initially, and some key stakeholders, who were skeptical of the project's ability to succeed, initially refused to participate (Susskind and Madigan, 1984).

In such circumstances, it may be helpful if a mediator convenes the various constituency groups individually and helps them organize the constituency and identify a suitable representative. Flexibility to add representatives of new constituencies can also be designed into the early phases.

The decision of whom to include is often a paradoxical one that forces conveners to choose among competing benefits. For example, the conveners of the National Coal Policy Project limited the number of stakeholders in order to keep the project manageable. They intentionally excluded representatives from government agencies on the belief that it would be impossible to involve agency officials who had sufficient authority to make decisions. They also opted to omit several other classes of stakeholders (such as Indian tribes, farmers, and transportation interests) who also had an interest in the future of coal use in the United States. While these decisions greatly enhanced the conveners' ability to administer the NCPP, they imposed severe constraints on the NCPP's subsequent attempts to implement its recommendations (Gray and Hay, 1986). (See Chapters Five and Six for a detailed discussion of these constraints.)

Differing Levels of Participation. While it may be important to include a large number of stakeholders, they may not all participate to the same extent or at the same time in the process. In some cases, rotation of representatives from interested groups can be used to reduce an unwieldy sized group (Emery, 1976). In other cases, all the stakeholders must be present, or an agreement will be meaningless.

In joint ventures, deciding levels of participation up front is critical. When partners are of different size, often the largest one assumes overall leadership for the venture. While this establishes clear responsibility, it does not guarantee that the resources of all the partners are effectively being utilized. Unless more equitable provisions for decision making are negotiated, smaller partners are often skeptical that their interests will be protected (Moxon and Geringer, 1985). Delicate deliberations about the extent of technology transfer, compatibility of management philosophies, and levels of risk can sour potential partners if these talks are characterized by misunderstandings or mistrust. Effective collaboration initially over distribution of responsibilities and benefits can greatly enhance the ease of managing a joint venture.

Legitimacy Within Stakeholder Groups. Legitimacy may also be an internal issue for some stakeholder groups. If there is considerable division within a group of stakeholders, no legitimate spokesperson may be apparent. This has been a major stumbling block to U.S. efforts to establish negotiations in the Middle East. Among the Palestinians and the Israelis, representation is an issue because factions within each group have divergent views on settlement options (Saunders, 1985). Internal legitimacy issues also damaged regulatory negotiations over farmworker protection standards for agricultural pesticides. The United Farm Workers left the negotiations after four meetings, ostensibly questioning whether the negotiations were the appropriate forum for expressing their views. Speculations are, however, that a more compelling reason for the Farm Workers' departure was their desire to save face with their constituents back home and to avoid going on record as supporting a compromise. The problem of negotiators maintaining credibility with constituents is a very delicate issue that needs to be deliberately managed during collaborations. This problem will be addressed in more detail in discussion of the implementation phase.

When leadership concerns among a particular group of stakeholders interfere with getting to the table, a convener or mediator may need to intervene to assist that group in selecting a representative. Possible interventions include calling a meeting to convene unorganized parties, working with them to clarify their interests, mediating internal disputes among those stakeholders, and constructing a process by which they identify a representative.

Convener Characteristics

The identity and role of the convener are another critical component in the problem-setting phase. The inspiration to collaborate may come from the convener or from one of the stakeholders, but it is up to the convening organization to invite and/or persuade other stakeholders to participate. For some domains, an already existing umbrella organization may be able to serve as convener (Provan, 1983). This is likely to be the case in established networks of social service or medical providers, for example, where the umbrella organization may be a central funding agency on which the others are mutually dependent (Kaplan, 1982; McCann, 1980). The convener may be a government agency (such as the EPA in the case of regulatory negotiations) that has statutory authority for promulgating a new regulation.

The convener may or may not be a stakeholder in the problem. The role of the convener is to identify and bring all the legitimate stakeholders to the table. Thus conveners require convening power, that is, the ability to induce stakeholders to participate. Convening power may derive from holding a formal office, from a long-standing reputation of trust with several stakeholders, or from experience and reputation as an unbiased expert on the problem. The conveners' tasks are distinct from those of a third-party mediator, although in some collaborations one person has assumed both roles.

For domains in which a formal authority exists, the formal authority may need to be pressed into service by appeal from one or more of the stakeholders (Friend and Jessop, 1969). This was the case in the mortgage-lending dispute that is analyzed in the next chapter. In that case citizens appealed to their municipal government to convene a committee to hear and address accusations of discrimination against mortgage lenders in the community.

In the absence of a putative authority, one or more relatively powerful stakeholders may serve as conveners, perhaps assisted by a third party. In cases referred to mediation by the courts, a judge serves as convener, effectively mandating the collaboration and appointing a third party as special master. Whether the convener is a stakeholder or a third party, it is essential that other stakeholders believe the convener has legitimate authority to organize the domain. A classic case concerning a proposed dam and water-treatment facility in Colorado provides an example in which the first mediator, Congressional Representative Pat Schroeder, who offered to convene the negotiations was rejected by one key stakeholder (Susskind and Ozawa, 1983). Subsequently, Representative Tim Wirth offered to mediate and was accepted by all the parties. Wirth himself was a strong advocate for the environmentalists, but in principle he also supported the proposed dam and water-treatment facility, the merits of which were being debated by several state and federal agencies and environmental groups. Wirth's perceived legitimacy was described by Susskind and Ozawa (1983):

> Congressman Wirth's acceptance as a mediator was particularly noteworthy because of his public stand on the issues in dispute. His position allowed him to bring both subtle and direct pressure to bear on the negotiating parties. He had enough political clout that the federal agencies involved felt he might "cause problems for them" if they did not make concessions. The local organizations and actors involved believed he represented their best interests, although, officially, Wirth was accountable only to the voters in his congressional district [p. 258].

As Touval and Zartman (1985) observe for international disputes, mediators also have self-interests that motivate them to mediate the dispute. Thus, some parties will prefer a mediator because of what he or she is expected to favor.

However, if the convener (or third party) is suspected of bias, other stakeholders may refuse to participate or even try to subvert the collaborative attempt. For example, the efforts of two university professors to convene a forum on nuclear power were sabotaged when the university's president contemporaneously agreed to serve on the board of the local power company, which operated two nuclear reactors. Environmental groups used this event to discredit the conveners and thereby dissuade a funding agency from supporting the project. Ultimately, the legitimacy of the convener enhances or limits her or his ability to exert the authority needed to organize collaboration at the domain level (Friend and Jessop, 1969; Stein, 1976).

In addition to legitimacy, conveners need appreciative skills. That is, they need to appreciate the potential value of collaborating. The skill of a convener is to see the wisdom in collective appraisal of the consequences of contemplated future actions (Vickers, 1965; Emery, 1977; Friend, Power, and Yewlett, 1974). Conveners also envision a purpose to organizing the domain (Sarason and Lorentz, 1979), and they need to propose a process by which this purpose can be carried out. Additionally, successful conveners have a sense of timing and the ability to create the appropriate context for the negotiations. Finally, they need to identify other stakeholders. Conveners may enlist the help of a third party to accomplish these tasks. For example, third parties can help stakeholders to analyze their alternatives to negotiations and can help ameliorate power differences among stakeholders by promoting norms for equal participation (Susskind and Cruikshank, 1987). When third parties assist one stakeholder to convene the others, they may have to recontract with the entire group in order to reaffirm their credibility before continuing in the role of mediator or facilitator during the negotiations.

Identification of Resources

In most multiparty negotiations, some resources are needed to launch the deliberations. Unless they are being conducted under agency auspices (such as regulatory negotiations), the parties themselves will incur the costs. This may impose hardship on one or more of the stakeholder groups, in terms of both actual dollar costs and the cost of their representative's time. Therefore, one final aspect of problem setting may be securing enough resources to ensure that stakeholders may participate equally in the proceedings. Resources may also be needed to fund joint information search as the negotiations proceed and to pay for the services of one or more mediators. Sometimes these funds are secured from foundation sources. Sometimes corporate stakeholders contribute to an overall fund for the other stakeholders. Sometimes mediators volunteer their services. For regulatory negotiations within the EPA, the agency creates a resource pool that can be used for participants' transportation or information needs.

To summarize, then, several issues must be dealt with

during problem setting: defining the problem, identifying stakeholders and gaining their commitment to collaborate, ensuring the legitimacy of the stakeholders, identifying a skilled convener and possibly a third party, and securing resources. Unless these tasks are accomplished during problem setting, subsequent efforts to prepare for and engage in negotiations will be hampered. Thus, the above tasks can be thought of as important outcomes of the problem-setting phase and as critical preconditions for the next phase. According to John T. Dunlop, a former secretary of labor who has been instrumental in creating and mediating a number of important multiparty negotiations:

> The most critical steps in alternative dispute resolution, in their legislative or rules-making modes, are the formation of the forum—i.e., who is to be a member, who is to chair or mediate the sessions, and by what process or legitimacy does the chair exercise its role [1987, p. 6].

For a list of the steps in the problem-setting phase, refer to Table 4.

Direction Setting

During the direction-setting phase, positive outcomes are associated with important procedural and substantive issues. During direction setting, stakeholders identify the interests that brought them to the table. They sort out which of their interests are the same, which are opposed, and which are unique or different and can form the basis for eventual trade-offs. This phase has been called direction setting (McCann, 1983) because stakeholders articulate the values that guide their individual pursuits and begin to identify and appreciate a sense of common purpose or direction. The discussion takes life as the stakeholders begin to realize that at least some of their desired ends can, in fact, be achieved. The direction-setting phase can be broken down into several components, each of which will be discussed in detail below. These components include establishing ground rules, agenda setting, organizing subgroups, joint fact finding, exploring options, and reaching agreement and closing the deal. The objective of this phase is to achieve coorientation. McLeod and Chafee (in Harris and Cronen, 1979, p. 19) describe coorientation as a state in which two or more individuals are "focused on the same set of objects where each has some estimate of what the other person thinks about the object." We use it here to convey the idea that during direction setting each side develops a realistic understanding of how the other stakeholders view the issues and what their interests are. The stakeholders can then jointly assess how well the various proposed solutions satisfy these interests (Fisher and Ury, 1981).

Establishing Ground Rules

Reaching agreement about how the stakeholders will interact with each other is vital to direction setting. Establishing ground rules that outline acceptable and unacceptable behavior for parties in their discussions can have a positive effect on the process (Fisher and Ury, 1981). Ground rules can remove some uncertainty for the participants and lessen the likelihood of misunderstandings (Fox, 1982b). They can also set the tone for the meetings and signal to the parties how these proceedings will differ from other conventional processes (for example, public hearings, legal proceedings, and the like). Agreement on the ground rules should involve all the parties, should precede discussion of substantive issues, and can provide the parties an initial sense of confidence in their ability to reach agreements.

One example of ground rules that specify how parties should interact with one another was provided in the following list from the *Rule of Reason:*

1. Data will not be withheld because "negative" or "unhelpful."
2. Concealment will not be practiced for concealment's sake.
3. Delay will not be employed as a tactic to avoid an undesired result.
4. Unfair "tricks" designed to mislead will not be employed to win a struggle.

5. Borderline ethical disingenuity will not be practiced.
6. Motivation of adversaries will not unnecessarily or lightly be impugned.
7. An opponent's personal habits and characteristics will not be questioned unless relevant.
8. Wherever possible, opportunity will be left for an opponent's orderly retreat and "exit with honor."
9. Extremism may be countered forcefully and with emotionalism where justified but will not be fought or matched with extremism.
10. Dogmatism will be avoided.
11. Complex concepts will be simplified as much as possible so as to achieve maximum communication and lay understanding.
12. Effort will be made to identify and isolate subjective considerations involved in reaching a technical conclusion.
13. Relevant data will be disclosed when ready for analysis and peer review—even to an extremist opposition and without legal obligation.
14. Socially desirable professional disclosure will not be postponed for tactical advantage.
15. Hypothesis, uncertainty, and inadequate knowledge will be avoided.
16. Unjustified assumption and off-the-cuff comment will be avoided.
17. Interest in an outcome, relationship to a proponent, and bias, prejudice, and proclivity of any kind will be disclosed voluntarily and as a matter of course.
18. Research and investigation will be conducted appropriate to the problem involved. Although the precise extent of that effort will vary with the nature of the issues, it will be consistent with stated overall responsibility to solution of the problem.
19. Integrity will always be given first priority [Wessel, 1976, pp. 23-24].

These ground rules were devised by Milton Wessel, a seasoned trial attorney. After years of adversarial practice, Wessel became increasingly concerned that complex social issues could not be satisfactorily resolved through litigation. Instead, he proposed alternative proceedings guided by the Rule of Reason. These ground rules became the guiding framework for the National Coal Policy Project, discussed in Chapter Six.

An anecdote from the National Coal Policy Project illustrates how the ground rules can influence the discussion. During a task-force meeting, one participant directly attacked the motives of another. The offender was reminded of one of the tenets of the Rule of Reason: "Motivation of adversaries will not unnecessarily or lightly be impugned." The offender facetiously pointed out that the Rule of Reason prohibited impugning the other side's motives "lightly" but that there was no prohibition against impugning them "seriously." The remark turned an anxious moment into a lighthearted one, and the substantive discussion proceeded without further incident (F. S. Murray, personal communication, September 24, 1982).

> Ground Rules address very basic details of the negotiations. Procedural issues can include deciding whether to allow the use of alternate representatives, selecting meeting sites, scheduling meetings, handling confidential information, using outside experts, deciding how to handle relations with the media, and determining whether agreements will be put in writing and, if so, in what form [Bingham, 1986, p. 106].

In particularly sensitive negotiations, agreements on ground rules may also address the "shape of the table," who will sit next to whom (Saunders, 1985), and whether or not smoking will be permitted during the negotiating sessions. Table 5 illustrates typical issues addressed by ground rules.

Depending on the context in which the negotiations are occurring, some ground rules may be prescribed by statute. For example, the Federal Advisory Committee Act requires that negotiating sessions are regularly open to the public. Also, rule-making negotiations convened by a federal government agency are bound by the provisions of the Administrative Procedure

✓

Table 5.   Typical Issues Covered in Ground Rules.

What is the role of representatives?
  Do they represent the views of a constituency?
  Do they have authority to take binding action on behalf of their con-
    stituency?
  Can alternates serve in a representative's place?
Is there a deadline for the negotiations?
  What is the timetable for meetings?
  What happens if a timely agreement is not reached?
How will confidential information be handled?
How will media publicity be handled?
  Who will speak to members of the press?
  When and in what form will information be released?
  What information will be kept confidential?
Will parties receive compensation and/or reimbursement for expenses for
  their participation?
How will a record of the proceedings be kept?
  What will be recorded? By whom?
  Who will have access to it?
How will consensus be determined?
  Must all parties reach agreement on all issues before decisions are pre-
    sented to sponsors or others?

Act. The major provisions of this act that have implications for
rulemaking proceedings are (1) prohibitions on delegation of
authority by government officials, (2) limits on ex parte communications, (3) prohibition of ultra vires agency action, and
(4) judicial review under the arbitrary and capricious standard
rule. The implications of the first point for regulatory negotiations are that the convening agency must retain the right to promulgate any agreed-on regulation. This responsibility cannot be
delegated to the negotiating parties. Also, the agency must provide an independent justification for the rule it promulgates.
Thus the negotiators and the agency must agree at some point
on who will take credit for which arguments on paper. The second point, on ex parte communications, seeks to prevent some
parties from having private access to the agency during rulemaking. While the legal precedent is not definitive on this point, according to Perritt (1987, p. 909), if the negotiations represent
a balance of interests, and summaries of the negotiations are
entered into the record so participants can comment, the ex

parte prohibitions will likely be satisfied. The third and fourth points provide for judicial review of the proceedings to ensure that the agency does not exceed its authority or render a capricious or unfounded decision. To date there have been no challenges to negotiated rulemaking on any of these grounds.

Ground rules can also work to the detriment of reaching consensus, if their implications are not carefully considered at the beginning of a negotiation. For example, in OSHA's regulatory negotiations over the benzene standard, negotiators agreed up front that they would only pass their deliberations on to OSHA if they reached agreement on all the issues. No partial agreements would be transmitted. When negotiators failed to reach complete agreement on all points, no report was sent to OSHA. Since OSHA had not participated in the negotiations, they did not benefit from learning even the limited areas of agreement that the parties reached.

Agenda Setting

Early in the direction-setting phase attention must be given to what the substantive aspects of the collaboration will be. Agenda setting is a delicate task in that parties who do not believe that the agenda reflects their interests may lose their commitment to the negotiations. "The agenda is often the object of intense debate since some parties will work hard to add or delete issues of special concern" (Susskind and Madigan, 1984, p. 185). Creation of a preliminary agenda requires considerable care and skill, as trade-offs must be considered and a reasonable timetable presented. Generally the agenda will reflect the breadth of the issues being discussed and will parallel the number of stakeholders who are present. Once again, the trade-off between the number of stakeholders and the ease of managing the process must be addressed. Large numbers of stakeholders can make the project difficult to manage and consensus difficult to achieve, but if legitimate stakeholders are left out, the quality of the recommendations can be weakened, and the agreements reached may not be lasting (Fox, 1982).

Collaborative activities can also be criticized if they address issues that some stakeholders perceive have already been settled or are the domain of someone else to solve. The stage of an issue in its public life cycle may affect the responsiveness to it (Buckholtz, 1986; Post, 1978). For example, businesses may be unwilling to join negotiations on issues that are early in their life cycle and have not captured national attention or have not been sufficiently politicized to merit priority attention.

Organizing Subgroups

The way conveners organize the collaborative process will affect their success at promoting consensus. Often it is advantageous to create subgroups or task forces if the number of issues to be discussed is large or the number of stakeholders exceeds the twelve-to-fifteen-member limit for effective group functioning. Organizing into task forces allows the group to address several issues simultaneously. The task forces are typically charged with exploring one or more issues each and preparing a report to a larger plenary group along with recommendations for addressing the issues. Membership on the task forces should be as diverse as possible so that the widest range of input can be brought to bear on the issue.

Another design that may be used concurrently with task forces is the caucus. Caucuses can play a constructive role when the stakeholders are composed of two or three subgroups initially representing distinct positions. For example, in the National Coal Policy Project two caucuses, one representing the environmentalists and the other the industrialists, were formed. The caucuses allowed the leaders of each side to meet separately with their members to review positions, test tentative agreements, and draw support for proposals. Caucuses also can regulate the behavior of their members with respect to the ground rules.

For example, in one environmental negotiation, an industry participant exhibited a very belligerent and dogmatic stance, which disrupted the work of his task force. In the privacy of the industry caucus, his counterparts learned that he felt intimidated by two Ph.D. economists on the other side. Frustrated by his inability to counter their arguments, he had resorted to power tactics. The caucus chastised the member for violating the ground rules and secured their own Ph.D. economist as an adviser.

Joint Information Search

Often stakeholders find that they are working off of very different sources of data or that neither side has sufficient data to answer questions that arise during their deliberations. In these circumstances, it is useful for stakeholders to undertake a joint information search.

Searching for "the Facts." An important ingredient in building a consensus is reaching agreement on the facts supporting the problem definition and the proposed solutions. If the stakeholders base their interpretations on different sets of facts, much time can be spent arguing over whose facts are right. Sometimes it is sufficient to review both sets of data. But when there is bitter disagreement about the facts, or none of the parties have the data, the parties may need to jointly search for the information. Mutually examining relevant data can help the parties develop a common basis for discussion; it can also encourage the disputants to discuss specific elements of discrimination between shared, opposing, and differing interests. In reflecting on the difficulties of creating a joint data base from diverse backgrounds, one of the senior industry participants in the National Coal Policy Project observed:

> We all found that we were discussing broad generalities, and I soon found that we were talking about entirely different things. For example, when the term "strip mine" was mentioned, I visualized a mine with which I was familiar in eastern Ohio with a three-foot seam of coal, 80 feet of very difficult overburden to handle, and a reclamation process that gave me the benefit of 40 inches of rainfall a year. My friend Mr. Curry (Robert R. Curry, a University of Montana geology professor who

was vice co-chairman on the environmental side) visual-
ized, as you would expect, a strip mine in Montana with
a 50 to 60 foot seam of coal, very unconglomerate
overburden, and he was faced with reclaiming the property with 10 inches of rainfall a year. So it was obvious
we were not going to come to any agreement on anything because we were not really talking about the same
things [Committee on Interstate and Foreign Commerce,
1978, pp. 119–120].

Researching "the facts" together often produces seren-
dipitous outcomes. It allows the parties to get to know one another as people instead of as adversaries on opposite sides of the
table.

When environmentalists meet industrialists in a board
room, Congressional hearing or press conference, sparks
fly. But get them out on the road in work clothes and
blue jeans and the mistrust and inhibitions break down
[Kosnet, 1977, p. 2C].

Personal interactions like that one create a basis for increased
trust among the parties and allow subsequent debates over issues
to proceed more smoothly. In addition, joint information search
often leads to shared solutions (Gricar and Brown, 1981), as the
parties have a common basis from which to draw inferences. Focusing on joint research rather than on opinions defuses controversial, emotional issues and fosters more dispassionate analysis.
Joint research helps parties evaluate the relative weight to give
to their own position and in some cases prompts parties to
change their opinion on an issue.

Managing Complex and Controversial Data. For complex
technical problems involving scientific terminology, mathematical projections, perceptions of risk, and large quantities of data,
special methods for reaching agreement on these aspects of the
problem may be needed. Several designs for dealing with the
complexities of and controversies over data have evolved. Often,

for controversial issues, a panel of technical experts is invited to help the stakeholders sort out and reach agreement on relevant technical facts. Choosing the panel of experts is itself often contentious, but, if the parties collectively query each other's experts, they can often gain a more subtle appreciation of the "factual" bases for their own differences. Additionally, they can narrow the range of issues in contention by permitting the experts to stipulate some fundamental areas of agreement among themselves. Sometimes, by probing the technical issues in depth, the parties are able to set or agree on broad parameters that address their most significant areas of interest and to relegate to technical experts the details of these technical issues. Other times the parties realize that pushing for the specific technical outcome is secondary or unnecessary if a satisfactory process for monitoring outcomes is agreed on. A dialogue among ecological modelers, computer scientists, economists, businessmen, and local townspeople from Obergurgl, Austria, was designed to create a mathematical model of economic development for the area. While the intended model was never completed, the dialogue greatly improved communication among the stakeholders and fostered insights into local problems (Raiffa, 1982).

Role of Third Parties in Information Search. Third parties can assist in information search in a number of ways. They may be able to recommend expert witnesses who would be acceptable to all parties. They may even do research at the behest of the negotiators. Third-party involvement of this kind precipitated a collaboration among the Amalgamated Clothing and Textile Workers Union (ACTWU) and the men's shirt manufacturers. In an eleventh-hour effort to settle contract negotiations, they approached two professors at Harvard University to investigate the competitive status of the apparel industry. The unfavorable predictions in this report stimulated the parties to launch an unprecedented partnership (which also includes textile manufacturers). The partnership is called the Textile/Clothing Technology Corporation, or $(TC)^2$ for short (Dunlop, Salter, and Sanabria, 1987).

Third parties may also serve as repositories for information that is proprietary or that by law must be kept confidential (Susskind and Cruikshank, 1987). For example, when sharing information may constitute a violation of antitrust laws, the neutral can provide a summary of the data that introduces the essential ideas but still protects confidentiality through anonymity.

Exploring Options

The importance of exploring multiple options before foreclosing on any of them has been stressed by conflict-management practitioners (Fisher and Ury, 1981). It is especially important in multiparty conflicts since, with multiple interests at stake, it is unlikely that a single option will satisfy all the parties equally. Fisher and Ury propose inventing options of differing strength as a way of increasing the number of potential solutions. This process forces the parties to think in terms of trade-offs among interests and to be creative in recognizing a range of possible solutions. Parties should be encouraged to invent options that satisfy their own interests and those of the other parties (Fisher and Ury, 1981).

Options may be most completely scrutinized in subcommittee meetings. Subcommittees may also be instructed to present multiple options to the plenary group so that they, too, have the benefit of considering trade-offs. Where multiple issues are on the table, trade-offs can also be made across issues. Comprehensive proposals can be drafted in which interests are satisfied to differing extents. Third parties often play critical roles in helping to forge acceptable packages through private conversations with each coalition of interests. If necessary, options can be proposed by outside experts (Moore, 1986), or an intermediary (such as a well-known political figure) can be asked to gather suggestions from the parties and to formulate one or more options for consideration (Kolb, 1983; Touval and Zartman, 1985; Carpenter and Kennedy, 1988). These approaches inject new sources of creativity and objectivity into the options under consideration. Precedents established in similar cases can also serve as useful models for stimulating options. Using an intermediary to offer proposals can protect parties from reprisals from constituents for making public concessions (Moore, 1986).

Another procedure for generating options is the single-text-negotiating procedure (Fisher and Ury, 1981). The procedure involves initiation of a draft proposal (for example, by the mediator), which is circulated among the parties, who sequentially amend it until it is acceptable to everyone. This approach is used when parties cannot meet face to face, but it can also be a useful tool for constructing an agreement among parties who are mistrustful or unwilling to publicly support draft proposals.

Reaching Agreement and Closing the Deal

The final step in the negotiation phase is reaching agreement and closing the deal. Reaching an agreement means gaining commitment of all the parties to a single option or to a package of options. For agreements involving multiple issues, the final agreement can be forged by sequentially negotiating agreement on each issue and then combining these individual agreements. This approach, called the building-block approach (Carpenter and Kennedy, 1988), allows the parties to reduce the problem to manageable pieces and to move forward at different rates on various issues. Thus, progress can be realized as each issue is settled.

Another approach is to strive for agreements in principle that provide a general framework of agreement within which details can be subsequently worked out. An agreement in principle for an environmental dispute might be that a safety clause will be written into any subsequent agreement that is fashioned. In a joint venture, firms might agree in principle on the kind of business information that would remain proprietary to each firm. This approach permits parties to experience a sense of accomplishment and to maintain momentum by striking a preliminary agreement on something early in the process. As the negotiations proceed, increasingly specific proposals that fall within the earlier agreement in principle are considered (Moore, 1986). Agreements in principle can be tested for at any time simply by asking the stakeholders to list possible areas of agreement.

Sometimes it is more useful to structure package agreements by considering multiple proposals that address several options simultaneously and then selecting the best package. This procedure for closing a deal is especially useful when the importance of various options differs considerably among the parties. In such a case trade-offs that allow parties to maximize on their most important interests are possible. By considering the whole package of solutions together, no party has to be the first or the only to offer a concession.

Shuttle diplomacy by a mediator can enhance closure, especially if parties are reluctant to commit to an agreement. If a mediator is conducting private sessions with each side in a dispute, the mediator may be able to sense agreement and make a trial proposal to each side individually to test for consensus. In some cases the agreement needs to be backed up by a statement of rationale, which, while typically prepared by a subgroup, must also often pass muster with the full plenary. Usually, agreements are finalized in written form, but commitment of the agreement to writing can often reopen the deliberations. Participants should be prepared for such a temporary setback. They should proceed by identifying the underlying stakeholder interests that the wording violates and by then reformulating the agreement to satisfy those interests. Or a single-text procedure can be adopted by circulating the draft until an acceptable version is produced.

Implementation

Carefully forged agreements can fall apart after agreement is reached unless deliberate attention is given to several issues during the implementation phase of collaboration. These issues are dealing with constituencies, building external support, structuring, and monitoring the agreement and ensuring compliance.

Dealing with Constituencies

Representatives to any negotiation have to deal with the back-home or "two-table problem" (Colosi, 1985). That is, they are faced with persuading their constituencies that the agreement is the best they could secure. Often the other parties in a collaboration can assist stakeholders in devising a compelling case to present to their constituencies. If parties do not take time to ensure that the various stakeholder constituencies understand the rationale for the trade-offs made and support the final agreement, any or all of them may disavow the agreement at some future date.

Building External Support

Garnering the support of those who will be charged with implementing the agreement is also critical.

> A general problem, particularly for public agencies and corporations, is that often the individuals with decision-making authority who can speak for the organization are not the same as those with specific technical expertise on the issues. Also, in large organizations, it is often not possible for the policy makers to spend their time to be present personally in all negotiations. Establishing clear and effective internal communications between meetings so that representatives can check with policy makers can be very helpful [Bingham, 1986, p. 115].

Some negotiations produce draft legislation for which a sponsor must be found. For example, in 1982, after two years of informal talks, the Virginia Toxics Roundtable, a dialogue among business leaders including E.I. DuPont de Nemours & Company, government, public citizens, and environmentalists devised a draft bill for the Virginia general assembly. A special subcommittee of the roundtable was responsible for working with the legislature until the bill was signed into law in March 1984. Thus implementation required mustering considerable public support for the agreements reached as the first step in getting the agreements implemented.

Structuring

The extent of effort needed for implementation depends on four factors: (1) whether the collaboration was designed for information exchange or decision making, (2) how much organizational change is required (Cummings, 1984), (3) who has the resources to accomplish the change, and (4) whether the agreements reached are self-executing or not (Young, 1972). Collaborations organized solely for information exchange may lead to efforts among the stakeholders to coordinate their actions or to endorse actions by selected parties. However, these outcomes are ad hoc and voluntary in contrast to formalized agreements for which enforcement provisions must be specified. In joint ventures, for example, if a product is being jointly produced, precise agreements are reached about each partner's responsibility for designing, manufacturing, and marketing.

More extensive implementation efforts will be needed for agreements that are non-self-executing. Self-executed agreements are either implemented at the time of agreement or formulated so that adherence will be self-evident, whereas non-self-executing agreements require "continuing performance which may be difficult to measure in the absence of special monitoring arrangements" (Young, 1972, p. 58). Implementation of an agreement devised through negotiated rulemaking officially falls to the sponsoring agency, who, after an appropriate review-and-comment period, promulgates the agreement as a regulation. Indirectly, however, the parties to the agreement also implement it through their future compliance with the regulatory provisions.

If implementation requires new relationships or substantial changes in the way existing stakeholders interact with one another, stakeholders should remain closely involved during implementation.

> Structures intended to standardize existing information exchanges among organizations could likely be implemented by outsiders, such as higher authorities or management consultants, while new methods for joint decision making are likely to require higher member involvement for implementation [Cummings, 1984, p. 407].

Often, the same organizations will participate in implementation, but the representatives from them will change. Making this transition can be particularly problematic because the second wave of participants do not share a joint history together.\

Several steps can be taken to maintain continuity during this transition. First, implementers should be involved as early as possible. Preferably, at least some of the original members should remain throughout implementation. It may be necessary to review some of the steps that led up to an agreement to recapture the appreciative-level change that occurred. Appreciative-level change involves the jointly constructed perceptions and understandings that underlie more concrete agreements about task-level changes (Trist, 1983; McCann, 1983).

/Often it is necessary to create a temporary organization to oversee implementation of the negotiated agreement.\Stakeholders may agree to empower a new or existing organization to carry out or monitor agreements they have reached. Generally, these organizations, which Trist (1983) refers to as referent organizations, continue the association of all the stakeholders within a more clearly delineated framework of roles and responsibilities.

> Through structuring, stakeholders generate a system for sustaining coincident values and establishing order within the domain. Specific goals are set, tasks are elaborated, and ongoing responsibilities are assigned to stakeholders [Gray, 1985, p. 918].

While the establishment of a formal structure is often thought of as occurring at a fixed point in time, in reality the process of structuring refers to the gradual institutionalization of the agreements reached. If an existing organization is assigned responsibility to implement the agreement, often an advisory committee of the other stakeholders is created for consultation (Carpenter and Kennedy, 1988). Thus, as details of the agreement are fleshed out during implementation, the original parties can be advised, and any new disagreements that arise over these details can be renegotiated.

A case in point is the commission established to work out collective bargaining agreements among the Farm Labor Organizing Committee (FLOC) (which represents migrant farm

workers in Ohio and Michigan), the tomato and cucumber growers who hire these workers, and Campbell Soup Company. The
commission (chaired by former Secretary of Labor John Dunlop) grew out of an understanding reached between FLOC and
Campbell after a bitter labor dispute, including a six-year boycott of Campbell's products by the union. The commission
"provided an institutional forum for the evolving relationship
between FLOC, the growers and Campbell Soup Company"
(Kennedy and Goldberg, 1985, p. 2) by acting as a kind of private labor relations board. The first major task of the commission was to determine whether the farm workers wanted FLOC
to represent them. After conducting elections that demonstrated
support for FLOC as the bargaining agent, the commission conducted negotiations among the union, the growers, and Campbell. The talks focused on the economic context of the tomato
industry in Ohio, the inability of the growers to improve their
contracts with the company, and the housing and health care
problems of the migrant workers. The negotiations laid groundwork for subsequent formalized collective bargaining agreements
involving all three groups.

Stakeholders may want to manage their interactions in an
increasingly systematic manner as a result of negotiation. For
example, they may agree to some form of self-regulation of the
domain (Trist, 1983; Emery and Emery, 1977). To the extent
that stakeholders "regard each other as potential coproducers of
desirable changes in their shared environments" (Williams, 1982,
p. 12), they need to create long-term structures to support and
sustain their collective appreciation, a forum for future problem
solving, and a regulative framework for the domain. The Dunlop
commission provided an organizing structure for the vegetable-
growing and -harvesting domain and a mechanism by which the
parties could create institutional arrangements for regulating
their ongoing relationships. Similarly, the Jamestown Area Labor Management Committee (JALMC) serves a self-regulating
function. JALMC has been in existence for fourteen years and
continues to tackle issues related to economic improvement in
the Jamestown area. One of the steps JALMC undertook was to
encourage the development of labor-management committees
within local companies. Sixteen firms introduced these struc-

tures, which were instrumental in reducing Jamestown's unemployment from 10 percent to 4 percent in the first three years of the project (Lundine, 1987).

Referent structures provide a mechanism for the operationalization of negotiated agreements. Depending on the agreement, many specific concrete actions may be necessary to implement it and to initiate change in the domain. Lobbying of legislative bodies may be required to influence the passage of desired legislation. Applications for permits or licenses may need to be made. Contracts may need to be drafted and let to begin construction. In the case of research and development consortia and joint ventures, sites must be selected, provisions for technology transfer must be determined, and organizational and management structures need to be put in place. Implementation should also include preparing for future contingencies, including provisions for handling subsequent disputes. The completion of these steps is usually enhanced by the formation of a temporary referent structure to administer the agreement.

Once implementation is under way, stakeholders may find that it is necessary to renegotiate some of the original provisions of the agreement or to modify implementation plans. For example, after several months of operation, the MN Community Services Council redirected its efforts from information gathering about the unemployment needs of laid-off workers to providing resources for all unemployed in Great River (Taber, Walsh, and Cooke, 1979). A reorganization of the referent organization accompanied this shift in direction (Taber, Walsh, and Cooke, 1979).

Monitoring the Agreement and Ensuring Compliance

Another function of referent organizations can be monitoring the stakeholders' compliance with the agreement. Despite their good-faith efforts during consensus building, organizations do not always follow through on their commitments.

> Organizations change their personnel and their policies.
> One party in a settlement may discover that a program it
> promised to initiate is going to be much more expensive

> than it anticipated and top management says no. Or an
> organization's goals and priorities change. The person
> in the organization responsible for carrying out an
> agreement leaves and no one is left to implement the
> organization's commitment. . . . The parties may have
> an argument after the close of negotiations and a
> representative may become so angry that he or she
> decides to renege on promises made earlier [Carpenter
> and Kennedy, 1988, pp. 153-154].

These or other problems that none of the parties anticipated
may arise, which can lead to a violation of the agreement. Under
these circumstances, the noncompliant party must be approached
and steps taken to ensure compliance. Renegotiations of certain
aspects of the agreement may be required to accommodate
changed circumstances. New representatives may need time to
"get up to speed" and feel ownership. In extreme cases, it may
be necessary to invoke sanctions (if they are available) against
the offending party or to apply public or peer pressure to induce compliance. The responsibilities of those charged with
monitoring should be clearly prescribed in the negotiated agreement before it is implemented. For example, monitors may be
limited to identifying infractions (whistle blowing) or to enforcing sanctions (Moore, 1986).

Collaborative agreements determined under judicial auspices have the force of the court to enforce the agreements.
Failure to comply can lead to several possible remedies: dam-
ages, recision of the contract, or court-ordered compliance
(Strauss, Clark, and Susskind, n.d.). Executive action can also
be used to ensure implementation. In negotiated rulemaking,
the agency has administrative authority to conduct implementation and to ensure compliance. Enforcement of a mediated
agreement reached over flood-control measures on the Snoqual-
mie River in the state of Washington was handled by the governor's office (Moore, 1986).

Collaboration is especially susceptible to collapse during
implementation. If the relationships among stakeholders have
been historically characterized by mistrust, despite success at

reaching substantive agreements, they are likely to be suspicious of each other's commitment to follow through. Implementation may also be impaired by cultural differences and expectations that were taken for granted and not explicitly addressed during the negotiation phase. Japanese and U.S. automakers are finding the subtle details of organizing their joint ventures particularly problematic because of embedded cultural values and expectations about the nature of human interaction (Holusha, 1988). Blending the cultures of public- and private-sector institutions in public-private partnerships has also been an obstacle to successful implementation (Berger, 1986).

If implementation issues are not assiduously anticipated during the negotiation phase, implementation is guaranteed to pose new conflicts.

> Insufficient consideration of implementation may result in settlements that create devastating precedents that may result in reluctance to negotiate in the future; damage interpersonal relationships; and financial, time or resource loss [Moore, 1986, p. 248].

Issues of implementation are considered further in Chapters Five, Six, and Eleven.

The importance of process cannot be overemphasized in planning and conducting successful collaborations. Good-faith efforts to undertake collaboration are often derailed because the parties are not skilled in the process and because insufficient attention is given to designing and managing a constructive process. Good intentions are insufficient to counteract the typical dysfunctional dynamics that interfere with productive group performance in work groups or the political dynamics that characterize interorganizational relationships. Stakeholders' predispositions, stereotyping, institutional mistrust, and historical animosities create powerful disincentives to collaborate unless opportunities are created in which they can be tested and modified. For example, the training phase of the Citizens' Radiation Monitoring Program provided ample opportunity for the monitors to test and challenge assumptions about nuclear power.

Similarly, a boat trip on very turbulent seas, which thrust participants into a common fate, helped to break down barriers among business and environmental leaders in the early stages of a collaboration over offshore oil drilling (Redford, 1987).

Steps to counteract typical group behavior (such as rushing to solutions before adequately investigating interests and insufficient listening) can greatly enhance constructive agreements. Listening, for example, can be improved through use of ground rules and skillful facilitation by a third party. Posturing is another dynamic that, if constructively managed, can have a place in but not dominate group discussion.

Successful outcomes greatly depend on how the dynamics of collaborating unfold. In the next chapter, the Urban Heights case illustrates the three phases of collaboration in detail and expressly points out how the process influenced the outcomes achieved.

4

Turning Conflict
into Collaboration:
A Case Study

*I am not struck so much by the diversity of testimony as
by the many-sidedness of truth.*
                                                    —Stanley Baldwin

This chapter follows a case example of a successful collaboration through the sequential steps of the process, from problem
setting through implementation. The collaboration was initiated
to deal with a conflict among activist citizens and lenders in a
racially integrating community. The city government convened
the consensus-building efforts after the citizens charged the
lenders with using discriminatory tactics called redlining to
avoid making loans in the community. After considerable education of each other, the stakeholders were able to agree on a
problem of joint concern. Over the ensuing two years, they initiated several collective efforts to ensure that sound investments
could continue in the community.

The chapter begins by presenting the details of the case,
followed by an analysis of what occurred during each phase of
the collaboration. In the final section of the chapter, several lessons about collaboration are drawn on the basis of the Urban
Heights experience.

Reinvesting in Urban Heights

Urban Heights is a city of about sixty thousand people built
during the early 1900s as an upper-middle-class residential sub-
urb of an adjacent urban center. In the mid 1960s black resi-

95

dents from the inner city began to migrate into Urban Heights. As in other white suburbs that experienced an influx of blacks, some "white flight" and racial "steering" by real estate agents had begun to occur. White flight refers to a rapid, extensive exodus of white residents, which creates a glut of available properties and a drop in property values. Racial steering is the practice of showing properties selectively on the basis of race. In addition, the community was facing continued deterioration of some local commercial strips and of the housing stock, which was largely frame.

Urban Heights had long had a tradition of active civic involvement among its residents. In 1968 leaders from several local churches, educational institutions, and civic organizations formed a community congress. The mission of the congress was to preserve the character and integrity of the city's neighborhoods while facilitating transition from being an all-white community to one that welcomed and integrated people of multiple races.

Over the next several years the black population of the community increased gradually. While there were proven instances of steering by real estate agents, integration proceeded fairly smoothly. Although discriminatory real estate practices were largely in check, concerns about adverse lending practices had begun to surface. In 1974, a citizens' group affiliated with the community congress became increasingly concerned that, because of the community's age, racial composition, and proximity to other deteriorated neighborhoods, lending institutions might begin subtle disinvestment of the community. Disinvestment was a trend that was contributing to resegregation in other integrated areas across the United States. The citizens' group suspected that local financial institutions were already disinvesting in Urban Heights by restricting home mortgage loans (a practice called redlining). To test those suspicions, the group gathered and analyzed data from the county recorder's office on all mortgages granted in the community over the previous seven years.

The citizens' research suggested that some lending institutions had in fact begun to disinvest the community. The citizens' group confronted several major lenders with their analysis, first privately and later publicly. The lenders categorically denied the accusation of redlining privately and in every available public forum. In fact, the Regional Association of Lenders issued statements insisting that the practice did not exist. Additionally, the lenders argued that the primary responsibility for preventing neighborhood decay belonged to homeowners and to the local government, and that it was the responsibility of the lending institutions to ensure that sound investments were made in the community.

Unable to influence the lenders to take their analysis seriously, the citizens then presented their data and interpretations to the city government and requested that the city exert pressure on the lenders. The tempers of both citizens and lenders were frayed by this time, and there was reason to believe that the conflict might escalate. In other U.S. communities, citizens protested discriminatory lending practices by staging boycotts and sit-ins and by threatening withdrawal of institutional deposits. The redlining issue was concurrently gaining national attention, congressional hearings on the subject were under way, and the Urban Heights community congress was among those planning to testify. About this time, a local newspaper carried the story about the citizens' data and the accusations against several of the well-known lending institutions.

Against this background of simmering conflict and in response to pressure from the citizens' groups, the city manager convened a new municipal advisory group called the Committee on Residential Lending (CORL). Membership included representatives of two major banks, two savings and loan associations, one mortgage banker, two appraisers, three realtors, four citizens, and one member each from the city council and the school board. The city manager chaired the committee, and several of the city administration's staff and a staff member on loan from the community congress assisted with the administrative work of the committee. At the first meeting, the mayor explained the city's intervention:

> While there had been no clear evidence of policies which show disinvestment, there have been specific complaints,

which when coupled with extensive research by the citizens' group, indicate possible first stages of disinvestment [Gricar and Brown, 1981, p. 881].

The mayor then charged CORL with the task of reviewing the data and coming up with a plan to ensure continued investment in the community.

During the first several meetings, various stakeholders were given an opportunity to present their views on the factors contributing to lending patterns in the community. First the citizens presented their findings. Then several lenders and the mortgage bankers offered interpretations from their point of view. For example, the lenders argued that "sound banking practices" compelled them to avoid "marginal loans." Presentations were also made by the appraisers and realtors, each of whom introduced specific details that were considered in mortgage-lending decisions from their perspectives. The citizens charged that the lenders had responsibility to make sure that overall mortgage money continued to be available to residents of Urban Heights.

After everyone had an opportunity to make an initial statement, members were invited to propose topics for discussion at subsequent meetings. Table 6 shows the distribution of interest in topics proposed by various stakeholder groups. The citizens and city administration were particularly anxious to design a system to monitor the mortgage-lending patterns of the lending institutions. Not surprisingly, the lending institutions showed less enthusiasm for that topic but joined the realtor and city government representatives in calling for discussion of federal loan programs. Several groups proposed a community education program to acquaint residents with a number of issues related to community preservation. There was no clear focus overall among the stakeholders about the agenda for CORL at this stage. In fact, the proposed agenda items represented preferred solutions to problems rather than definitions of the problems themselves. Table 6 reveals this lack of stakeholder consensus about the problem domain.

Over the next four months, committee meetings were

Table 6.   Agenda Suggestions by Stakeholder Type.

Stakeholder Group	Mean Number of Suggestions	Agenda Item			
		Education	Revitalize Community	Federal Loan Programs	Monitor Lenders
Lenders (n = 3)	2.3	0	30%	56%	14%
Realtors (n = 1)	3.0	33%	0	67	0
Citizens (n = 4)	7.0	10	25	21	44
City administration (n = 1)	3.0	67	0	0	33
City government (n = 1)	2.0	25	0	75	0

Source: Gricar and Brown, 1981, p. 883.

characterized by frequent disagreement, misunderstandings, and discussion at cross purposes as representatives of each group defended their initial positions. One proposal by the citizens drew strong objections from the lenders. The proposal called for the city to publish a preferred lenders' list and to prohibit depositing city funds in institutions not on the list. The following conversation illustrates the debate that ensued:

Lender: On first blush I have real problems with a preferred financial institution list. It sounds like some are unpreferred. If they don't treat the city equally, then educate them. You will not find any institution not putting money back into the community. I get my hackles up talking about restricting city deposits to a select few. I prefer not using muscle.

Citizen: It (the preferred lenders' list) bothers me, too. A preferred list still doesn't guarantee good lending (Gricar and Brown, 1981, p. 883).

Despite these differences, as a result of the discussions, the stakeholders' collective understanding of the alleged causes and consequences of disinvestment eventually became more differentiated and complex.

At this point, the city manager, who had been setting the agenda, inviting presentations, and chairing the meetings, presented this overall list of the issues the city hoped the committee would attempt:

- work with financial institutions to develop, promote, and implement a strategy of investment and reinvestment of funds in this city
- examine pertinent policies and practices of financial institutions and determine how they affect Urban Heights
- recommend constructive changes in policies and practices that affect Urban Heights negatively or that could have positive effects
- recommend depository policies for public and other institutional funds
- involve financial institutions in an aggressive, affirmative incentive program that will enhance the realization of goals
- advise council on matters that relate to mortgage lending and financial health of Urban Heights

He also established three subcommittees. One investigated disinvestment and reinvestment (including monitoring of lenders); a second focused on specific practices used in granting mortgages; a third addressed education of lenders and the community about the proactive efforts of the community to sustain integration.

Work in the subcommittees brought CORL members into closer contact with others of differing views. The six to eight members of each subcommittee were responsible for gathering data and generating specific recommendations to the committee as a whole. As research in the subcommittees progressed, a consensus began to emerge in CORL as a whole that home buyers, mortgage bankers, lenders, and the federal bureaucracy were all partly responsible for aspects of disinvestment. The lenders admitted that subtle redlining practices were employed by some lenders; citizens conceded that not all lenders were redlining; the city administration acknowledged that the local government should take a more active stance in ensuring that the housing stock was adequately maintained. In the subcommittee charged with monitoring lending institutions, for example, two lenders at first vehemently opposed monitoring, claiming, "It's like holding a brick over our heads!" At the first three subcommittee meetings, the discussion was repeatedly tabled. But after several months of joint investigations, citizen representatives and lenders had developed enough rapport by cooperating around other issues that the sensitive issues related to monitoring could be reintroduced and discussed openly:

Citizen: Our facts raise questions. How can we get answers? We are willing to try meetings, but what about subtle redlining? We need monitoring.

Realtor: I'm opposed to monitoring. It drives lenders away. But there are middle managers who discriminate by discouraging people from the city.

Lender: There are some subtle ways—middle managers fixing of loan rates, etc. You should go to those [lending institutions] who are at fault directly and ask them, but not through questionnaires; you don't learn anything that way (Gricar and Brown, 1981, p. 884).

As the subcommittees began to reach agreement on some aspects of the disinvestment problem, the focus of discussion shifted from responsibility for disinvestment to a concern for preservation. As one lender put it:

We'd all like to see something happen in the city that's never happened anywhere—to keep the city integrated in areas below $75,000. I'd like to see a place that has stayed integrated [Gricar and Brown, 1981, p. 885].

It was finally under this overarching problem definition that CORL was able to proceed toward drafting solutions.

Identification of this common purpose paved the way for discussion of preventive actions. After eight months CORL had developed some generally accepted objectives that included interviewing local lenders, revitalizing the community's commercial areas, promoting interior home inspection, and eliminating abuses in government-insured mortgage programs that were contributing to foreclosures and vacant properties. To accomplish these objectives, CORL needed to influence other organizations including local lenders, the Federal Housing Administration (FHA), the Veterans Administration (VA), and the Urban Heights city council. Soon after the education subcommittee was formed, it began to conduct visits with the management of individual lending institutions whose lending activity had decreased over the years studied. At these visits, city staff presented mortgage data on the specific institution and asked the lenders to explain the patterns observed. Efforts were made to discern any overall negative impressions of the community conveyed by lenders during these visits and to counteract these by publicizing the city's active housing programs as well as the work of CORL. Additionally, CORL appealed to the FHA and VA to tighten up their mortgage-loan procedures to reduce the number of foreclosures in Urban Heights. Subsequently, the number of foreclosures in the community dropped substantially; however, it is impossible to assess how much of this was due to CORL's efforts and how much to a general downturn in the housing market that occurred at that time.

Another major effort was launched to persuade the city council to institute an interior inspection program. Despite previous long-standing opposition to such action, the council did pass such legislation at CORL's urging. With respect to monitoring, the following agreement was reached: The community congress was given a contract by the city to develop a monitoring program and to report annually to the CORL. The capability to monitor lending practices had been greatly enhanced by the passage of a federal statute (the Home Mortgage Disclosure Act of 1976) requiring lenders to furnish annual data on loans granted by census track.

By the end of two years, two programs conceived by

CORL had been initiated: a local development corporation to promote commercial revitalization and a foreclosure rehabilitation program for which the lenders raised funds. The committee continued to operate for an additional two years, addressing new housing issues such as tax abatement and insurance redlining as concerns about such issues arose in the community. Meanwhile, two years after CORL's inception, the regional planning agency began systematic monitoring of lending practices for the metropolitan area that included Urban Heights.

Case Analysis

This case illustrates virtually all of the steps in the collaborative process outlined in Chapter Three. Considerable time was required to move this collaboration through each of the three phases. For example, the problem-setting phase lasted for over one year, the direction-setting phase another eight months, and the implementation phase continued for several years. During this time, as new issues arose, CORL recycled through the second and third phases of collaboration. The most significant aspects of each phase are explored below.

Problem Setting

Little, if any, consensus about the problems in Urban Heights existed in 1974 when the citizens began to collect data. Because there was no consensus, the problem-setting phase for this collaboration was conflictual and protracted.

Common Definition of the Problem.   Prior to the citizens' analysis of mortgage trends in the community, the "problem" of mortgage redlining had not attracted much, if any, public attention in the metropolitan area in which Urban Heights was located. National attention to the problem began to pick up during 1975, when a community group called National People's Action began to publicize redlining by lenders in neighborhoods in and around Chicago. However, not until the congressional hearings had the issue received any local publicity. Precisely because a shared definition of the problem did not exist on the public agenda, the citizens' group in Urban Heights had neither a constituted forum within which to present its concerns nor the bargaining power to convene other stakeholders or to get the issue onto the agenda for public review. Getting a common agreement on the problem would only come after the lenders were persuaded that they had something to gain from participating in a dialogue with the citizens.

Commitment to Collaborate. Getting to the table was clearly a difficult aspect of this collaboration. By garnering data on lending practices, the citizens built bargaining power. Then, using this bargaining power, they sought to persuade the lenders to address their concerns. Because the lenders, however, did not share the citizens' definition of the problem, they refused to participate in a dialogue with the citizens to address a problem the existence of which they disputed.

The citizens then enlisted the support of the municipal government to generate a commitment to collaborate among the lenders. By collecting data about individual institutions, by organizing those data to address sensitive issues, by threatening to reveal the information, and by gaining media attention to the problem, the citizens were able to get the ear of the municipal government. The data also afforded them bargaining power vis-à-vis the lenders, since the lenders did not have and could not easily retrieve the data about their own institutions that the citizens had acquired. This, coupled with the power of the city government as convener, brought the lenders to the table.

Clearly the lenders' assessment of the outcomes to be gained from collaborating changed when the city stepped in as convener. This change may be attributed to several possible inducements. First, the prospect of withdrawal of municipal deposits may have increased the lenders' incentives to collaborate. The city government's role as convener may have created a more neutral, less emotionally charged setting for discussion. It is also possible that the lenders agreed to participate to prevent the development of an alliance between the city and the citizens.

The convening of CORL represented a preliminary commitment to collaborate by all the parties. A temporary or working agreement about the problem was provided by the mayor at the first meeting. The problem definition did not conclude that redlining was occurring but left open the possibility for investigation by the committee. Specifically, the committee's task was to investigate the allegations of redlining and to devise a strategy to ensure or promote reinvestment in the community.

Identification and Legitimacy of Stakeholders. Identification and solicitation of stakeholders for CORL were done by the city manager in consultation with the community congress. The appointment of members of the citizens' group to CORL acknowledged their legitimacy as stakeholders. The mayor's opening remarks at the first meeting supported the research conducted by the citizens without laying blame on the lenders. Inclusion of realtors and appraisers in CORL illustrates the advantages of broadening the scope of interests beyond just the disputing parties. Clearly, both of these groups influenced and were influenced by lending decisions in the community, and they could provide firsthand anecdotal evidence about how lending decisions were made. They would also be negatively impacted if lenders withdrew their investments in the community.

Convener Characteristics and Resources. The convener in this case was appropriately the government of the municipality in which the problem was allegedly occurring. The city government was clearly an interested stakeholder, one with sufficient clout to movitate others to participate. Aside from the fact that the city's intervention made sense, the convener's role was enhanced by the individual characteristics of the city manager himself. His evenhanded management of the process contributed a great deal to its success. He carefully designed an opportunity for each stakeholder group to present its initial views on the question of redlining and sound lending practices, and he ensured that other stakeholders listened and did not disrupt these presentations. He also exhibited considerable patience while at the same time challenging the group to take its mission seriously. Resources for the operation of the committee were provided by the city government, with additional staff support from the community congress.

Direction Setting

With a working agreement about their charge, CORL began the direction-setting phase of collaboration. Stakeholders devoted considerable time to investigating current mortgage-lending practices in the community and gradually constructed a shared appreciation of problems associated with the current system. After eight months, consensus about the problems began to emerge along with preliminary proposals for preventing disinvestment.

Establishing Ground Rules and Agenda Setting. The city manager played a significant role in helping CORL to establish ground rules and in setting the agenda for early meetings of the committee. At the first meeting he made it clear that each group represented would have sufficient time to present its initial points of view and to raise issues and questions relevant to CORL's mission. The city manager closely controlled CORL agendas to guarantee equal time for different points of view. In addition, he actively managed discussion of sensitive topics to prevent escalation and to ensure that critical issues were not overlooked.

After the initial series of opening presentations, the city manager solicited suggestions for the future agenda from the participants. The diversity of proposals, reflecting those in Table 6, demonstrated that group members were still focusing on their initial positions. The agenda suggestions were cast as solutions to very different definitions of the problem. Rather than accept any one of the solutions or the problem definitions on which they were predicated, three subcommittees were formed to gather additional information on whether or not disinvestment was a problem for Urban Heights.

Between CORL's second and eighth months of operation, conflict between the groups continued to dominate much of the exchange, but gradually a structure and informal norms governing the members' interactions evolved. Work in the subcommittees permitted more informal though nonetheless lively exchanges. As members aired their different viewpoints in these informal settings, they developed a more sophisticated and differentiated understanding of the others' perspectives on the issues. They also identified gaps in their collective understanding and posed questions for the staff to research. Gradually the discussion was reoriented from blame and defensiveness to recognition of mutual responsibility and capability to prevent disinvestment.

Subgroups and Joint Information Search. It was not until after several months of subcommittee work that the stakeholders began to discuss their real interests and to candidly acknowledge that their initial positions masked their shared interest in a more fundamental concern, that of preserving the racially integrated character of the community while maintaining housing values. Reaching this understanding was key to drafting proposals for action. With this shared concern identified, it was easier for lenders to acknowledge how subtle discrimination could adversely affect the community. The appraisers and real estate agents played pivotal roles at this time, because they could point to specific aspects of home buying and selling where the potential for discriminatory practices existed without incriminating any specific lenders. The citizens also came to realize that not all negative lending decisions were deliberate attempts to discriminate. Gradually, CORL members began to appreciate that the collective effect of several practices in use in the housing delivery system was detrimental to integrating communities. These joint appreciations formed the basis for several proposals for action.

Generating Options, Reaching Agreement, and Closing the Deal. After eight months of work, each subcommittee had devised several preliminary plans, which were presented to the whole committee for approval or modification. Because the staff had been coordinating closely across committees, gaining agreement from the whole group on subcommittee proposals presented few problems. Some of the plans involved actions that CORL members themselves could take. The visits to local lending institutions, for example, became the ongoing responsibility of the education subcommittee members and city staff. The subcommittee investigating specific lending practices recommended that the full committee investigate government-sponsored lending programs, and this was done during several subsequent meetings of CORL. Still other agreements took the form of drafts of new legislation for consideration by the Urban Heights city council.

Implementation

Between the eighth and twenty-fourth months, CORL developed several policy proposals and undertook steps to promote them with groups such as the city council, whose approval of legislation was needed for implementation. In some cases extensive lobbying of these external groups was necessary.

Dealing with Constituents and Building External Support. Here the support of the constituents was needed. Because the citizens' group was closely aligned with the community congress, widespread support from local neighborhood associations was easy to muster. Additionally, a realtor on the committee was also a member of city council. His eventual support for the proposal helped pave the way for the passage of the proposed legislation.

Presenting a unified front in these other arenas enhanced the resolution of conflicts within CORL as well. For example, CORL recommended that the city adopt an interior home inspection program. CORL proposed a point-of-sale inspection process that was designed to ensure that properties satisfied housing code standards before properties were transferred to new owners. In the past, proposals for interior inspection had traditionally met with resistance from city council and the real estate community. The lenders, however, were able to persuade other members of CORL of the importance of interior inspection to maintaining home values and ensuring commitment from lenders. With the backing of CORL, the council passed legislation authorizing the city's housing office to establish an interior inspection program. Within a year and a half the program was under way. Interestingly, the community congress had been lobbying council for interior inspection for some time, but to no avail. Because of the broad base of institutional support that CORL represented and the compelling arguments in support of reinvestment they could muster, they persuaded council to adopt the measure. Further, because of their active participation in the work of the subcommittees, members of the city's housing staff were well prepared to implement the code enforcement legislation once the city council enacted it. Still, this aspect of implementation took over a year before code enforcement actually began, and the citizens' group maintained pressure on the city until the program was in place.

Structuring. Once CORL's initial efforts were concluded, the city saw fit to extend the committee's tenure in order to address other issues relevant to investment in the community. Essentially, CORL served as a temporary referent organization. That is, CORL provided an institutional forum within which a dialogue could be maintained among the stakeholders concerned about housing and investment in the community. Through CORL the stakeholders were able to regulate mortgage lending and related housing issues in the community for several years.

Monitoring the Agreements. Although no formal agreements were reached about monitoring, it was handled by the community congress, which set itself up as an unofficial watchdog to ensure that follow-through occurred. Since implementation of many of CORL's agreements eventually fell to the city's staff, monitoring primarily consisted of prodding them to act. On one occasion, when it appeared that the city was dragging its feet, neighborhood groups began to pressure the city for action.

Lessons from Urban Heights

In addition to illustrating the gradual stepwise process by which collaboration unfolds, the Urban Heights case highlights several other important lessons about how the process of collaborating

impacted the outcome. First, collaboration prevented this conflict from escalating to other arenas, such as public protest
(which was occurring in other cities where redlining was a problem), or to the courts through the filing of lawsuits (a practice
that the community congress had used in the past to challenge
discriminatory real estate practices). By addressing the conflict
within the community, a comprehensive approach to the problem that went well beyond the initial dispute was achieved.

Second, the case demonstrates how a local government
official knowledgeable about group process and design skills can
effectively convene and facilitate collaborative problem solving.
The services of a mediator were never used in the Urban Heights
dispute. The city manager, with the ceremonial help of the
mayor, served as convener and as quasi mediator. That is, he
took pains to ensure that agendas were set, that all parties had
time to present their views, and he generally set a conciliatory
tone for the proceedings by encouraging debate and exploration. The staff of the community congress and the city's housing office greatly facilitated CORL's work by providing necessary research, organizing subcommittee meetings, and preparing
draft and final agreements. Without this jointly sponsored back-
up and the strong leadership of the city manager, it is unlikely
that agreements would have emerged or that any programs
would have been implemented. In this regard, CORL offers a
model for the role local officials can play in making effective
use of multiparty collaboration.

Third, although CORL represents a successful collaboration, there was still room for some improvement in CORL's process. For example, continued participation by certain lenders
was always uncertain, especially when the "intentions" of the
lenders were at issue. At these times, an impartial mediator
could have helped the parties by working both inside and outside the committee meetings to ensure that the lenders' interests
were being served by the process and to help all the parties invent constructive options. A mediator could also have helped
CORL establish more productive relationships with external
agencies such as the FHA and VA, who could have been asked
to join the group when their role as stakeholders became evident.

Fourth, collaboration in Urban Heights was not possible without the exercise of power. The case raises awareness that collaboration does not take place in a context devoid of power. Indeed, collaboration in Urban Heights would not have been possible if the citizens' group had not initially employed power tactics to enlist the city government and the lenders in a dialogue. Those contemplating the pros and cons of collaboration should not underestimate the power relationships present in any collaboration. How power is developed and shared during collaboration is the subject of the next chapter, on the political dynamics of collaborating.

A final lesson from the Urban Heights case deals with domain transformation. The problem domain in this case involved preservation of a potentially deteriorating community. Once the stakeholders came to appreciate their joint concerns about Urban Heights, they were able to initiate actions to address the problem. CORL's efforts resulted in major community improvements, which enabled the community to realize its desire to remain a well-preserved, economically sound, integrated community.

5

Understanding the
Political Dynamics
of Collaboration

Heaven's eternal wisdom has decreed that man should ever
stand in need of man.

—Theocritus

Differing Concepts of Power

Central to the notion of collaboration is the concept of shared
power. Stakeholders in a collaboration essentially share the
power to define a problem and initiate action to solve it. This
chapter explicitly addresses the notion of collaboration as power
sharing. It examines how power dynamics influence efforts to
initiate collaboration during prenegotiations, how power is
shared during negotiations, and how power shapes the course of
implementation.

As noted in the previous chapter, collaboration does not
occur in a political vacuum. Nor are stakeholders altruists pursuing some greater good. Quite the contrary: Even when collaboration is initiated in order to advance a shared vision, stakeholders are anxious to advance their own interests (Benson,
1975; Dahl, 1982) associated with that vision. However, if any
of the stakeholders are capable of exerting unilateral control,
collaboration does not make sense. It is precisely because stakeholders hold countervailing sources of power and their fates are
interwoven that collaboration is made possible.

To clarify the political dynamics of collaborating, the first
section of this chapter will draw some general distinctions among
several mechanisms of political behavior. Following Gaventa

(1980), three models of political behavior are presented: pluralism, elitism, and control of consciousness. While collaboration is similar to pluralism, several critical distinctions are introduced in the second section of the chapter. This is followed by an examination of the specific political dynamics associated with each phase of collaboration.

Contrasting Models of Political Behavior

Pluralism. Pluralism refers to a political process in which diverse groups representing a variety of different interests clash with one another (Stepan, 1978). Conflicts among these groups are resolved through intense bargaining in prescribed arenas among groups of relatively equal power, none of which has full sovereignty (Dahl, 1982). The net effect of this clash of interest groups is taming power, securing the consent of all, and settling conflicts peacefully (Dahl, 1967). Power is wielded openly by contending interest groups, which try to influence policymakers on the basis of bargaining strength. The medium of exchange is resources; that is, power is equated with personal efficacy, organizational strength, money, and votes. Participation in the process is available to any group that organizes. Pluralistic models have been used repeatedly to distinguish the public policymaking processes in the United States from interest group representation in other countries (Dahl, 1982; Schmitter, 1974; Wilson, 1982; Ziegler, 1988).

Groups in a pluralistic process are all trying to exert influence over decision outcomes. These claimants may extract a range of responses from political authorities (Schumaker, 1975). At a minimum, a claimant may achieve "access responsiveness." That is, the group gains the ear of a political authority so that their concerns may be aired. A second level of response is "agenda responsiveness." In this case, the group's concerns become the subject of more deliberate review by the authority. A third level, "policy responsiveness," is achieved if some legislative or administrative action is taken in response to the concerns. Two additional levels of response, "output" and "impact responsiveness," refer to implementation of the policy and elimination of the original grievance, respectively. In order to collaborate, the citizens' group in Urban Heights expended considerable effort before achieving agenda responsiveness (that is, the convening of the advisory committee).

Proponents of pluralism argue that it provides the widest access to decision-making arenas of any political process (Truman, 1951; Dahl, 1967, 1982). Groups who want to influence political agendas have the freedom to organize and to express their viewpoints through public hearings, use of the media, lobbying, and so forth.

> Where citizens or other actors can more or less freely express and advocate their interests (as they perceive them), and where organizations can be more or less freely formed, activists form joint organizations in order to advance their interests. Organizations in turn create, advance, protect, strengthen, and preserve some of the interests of some of their members [Dahl, 1982, p. 43].

In the pluralistic process, interest groups are expected to organize themselves and strive to build bargaining power to influence public policy in their favor. Thus the power to mobilize a group is a critical component of pluralist politics. The power to mobilize is also a critical assumption of collaboration that will be discussed further in the third section of this chapter.

Elitism. The second model takes as its starting premise that access is not equally available to all groups. One party or a select group controls access to the decision-making forum. Control over access and agendas is restricted to a powerful elite. Depending on your point of view, these elite either legitimately represent the interests of non–decision makers, or they define social problems in a manner optimal to themselves (Downs, 1976; Perucci and Pilisuk, 1970). Decisions in this model are, at best, consultative. That is, those with authority to make policy decisions may or may not consult the nonelite before rendering a decision. In effect, they exercise and maintain power over the decision criteria and over the decision itself, often without a mechanism for counteracting their own limitations and biases (Bozeman and Cole, 1982; Rittel and Webber, 1973). /Some argue that elitism involves the intentional suppression of conflict because the concerns of the less powerful are systematically dismissed. According to Bachrach and Baratz (1963), power is wielded not only among participants within the decision-making process but also to deliberately exclude certain interests from being considered. Requests that run counter to the interests of the more powerful decision makers (or pose challenges to the existing allocation of benefits) are precluded through non–decision making. Thus, through the application of systematic bias, prohibitions, or stalled implementation, the interests of certain groups are advanced at the expense of others. A select few have greater power and control access to decision making.

Control of Consciousness. The third mechanism involves control of beliefs that support the powerful. In this use of power, less powerful groups acquiesce to decisions that are contrary to their interests because they subscribe to overarching myths that make those decisions appear legitimate (Brown, 1986). The powerful maintain their domination by controlling the awareness of the less powerful through socialization processes, information control, the use of symbols, and so forth (Edelman, 1960, 1967; Deutsch and Rieselbach, 1965). A consequence of this exercise of power is not only that grievances are "excluded from entering the political process, but they might be precluded from consideration altogether" (Gaventa, 1980, p. 20). For any number of reasons (for example, fear of retribution, inappropriately targeted grievances, ineffective strategies, or perceptions of immutability), the interests of the less-powerful are not advanced.

Collaborative Model of Power

How, then, is collaboration different from these three traditional models of how power operates? To answer this question, it is necessary to consider some recent critiques of pluralism and to show how collaboration addresses them.

Contrasts with Pluralism

Three criticisms of pluralism have been raised. The first is that despite the open invitation for groups to enter the fray, pluralism in fact fosters inequality because some groups cannot muster the resources to organize. Thus, pluralism produces the unintended consequence of favoring organizations that are already well off (Aldrich, 1977; Warren, 1974; Lowi, 1969; Dahl, 1986). Lowi (1969), in a criticism of "interest group liberalism," argued that pluralism was biased toward those with more resources and greater voice. When power battles are the currency by which decisions are made, some groups always end up losing.

A second possible consequence of pluralist decision making is the inability to get any decisions made because of countervailing or blocking power among the parties. Political theorists struggle with how to redress the inaction that results from such stalemates. The typical answer is to recommend a centralization of authority—for example, giving more power to the President (versus Congress) or moving to a more-elitist power structure at the expense of the less-powerful stakeholders in order to generate enough unity for action. Thus "governments sometimes resort to the use of independent public authorities because these authorities can do the job faster, free of the hindrances of the political arena" (Aharoni, 1981, p. 183).

Dahl summarizes the limits of pluralism in this way:

> A stable system can develop in which the most disadvantaged are unorganized or poorly organized and therefore comparatively powerless to remedy their condition; . . . in which, major public problems go unsolved because every solution that does not have substantial agreement among all the organized forces, is in effect, vetoed; in which public politics in every sector are pretty clearly not determined by considerations of what might serve the best interests of the greater number but result instead from the play of organized groups, each concerned exclusively with its own interests. . . . A particular constellation of organizational pluralism, then, can produce

a stable system in which mutual vetoes prevent the
reduction of inequalities and, more generally, structural
changes in the status quo [1982, pp. 254-255].

The sheer volume of initiatives on the November ballot in California shows how pluralism can contribute to inaction. In some areas, such as San Francisco, over seventy different initiatives, each sponsored by a different interest group, were before the voters in 1988. The consequence is a splintering effect. There is a proliferation of partial, myopic solutions, none of which leads to a constructive resolution or advances the public interest (Aldrich, 1977, p. 25).

At some point groups become so splintered that each
lack the power to exercise responsible leadership. . . .
Divided responsibility and compromise become ends in
themselves, while genuine political needs go unheeded
for lack of leadership [Davis and Frederick, 1984, p. 138].

A third criticism of pluralism, then, hinges on the question of whether or how the public interest is advanced in the face of such stalemates. Elitist models assume that the public interest can be discerned by decision makers who act in the interest of those who do not participate. This view is, of course, challenged by those who attribute more insidious motives to those in control. Turning over the authority to more central organizations to determine what is in the "public good" is unsatisfactory, since individual organizations will consciously or unconsciously seek to advance their self-interests.

According to the pluralists, the concept of the public good is fallacious (Stepan, 1978) because it is difficult to ascertain how the public good can emerge from the clash of particularistic interests. According to Dahl, what is in the public good would always be subject to intense debate (1986, p. 256).

How, then, can stalemates be overcome simultaneously with consideration of the public good? Here, collaboration offers a possible answer. Collaboration offers four improvements on pluralism. (1) It is possible for interest groups to reach consensus on the public good because the alternative of taking no action is clearly worse for all concerned. Collaboration assumes that the particularistic interest of each of the parties includes the resolution of stalemate. (2) The parties in addition to elected officials assume responsibility for searching for the collective good. Unlike with pluralism, no one party attempts a priori to discern or promote the nature of the collective good. (3) A wide array of interests is explicitly included in, rather than excluded from, the deliberations to enhance the possibility of reaching a consensus on the public good. (4) By changing the process by which the parties exert influence over one another, the chances of discovering a mutually beneficial accommodation are increased. The process involves multilateral stakeholder interactions rather than a series of bilateral interactions between stakeholders or between stakeholders and policymakers. In this and other ways, collaboration differs from strict interest group mediation (Reich, 1985) characteristic of pluralism (Fiorino, 1988).

In these four respects, then, collaboration offers a nonelitist alternative to pluralism. It creates a process by which the stakeholders themselves must wrestle with the question: How can I satisfy my interests in the context of what is in the collective good? Thus, collaboration urges a distribution of power among those whose interests are most keen. With this distribution, however, comes the responsibility to grapple with risks and make hard choices about the allocation of limited resources. With a collaborative approach, the final agreement defining the common good is not the proclamation of a ruling elite or the result of political logrolling and majority rule, but rather a consensus agreement among those chiefly involved. Even when a collaborative agreement serves as input to a traditional legislative or administrative body (and thus becomes subject to pluralistic bargaining in that arena), opposition to the collaborative consensus should be minimal if a wide enough set of stakeholders participated in its development.

The preceding analysis asserts that collaboration is not devoid of political dynamics but that a different model of political behavior is involved.

Collaboration as Power Sharing

Collaboration operates on a model of shared power. In collaboration, problem-solving decisions are eventually taken by a group of stakeholders who have mutually authorized each other to reach a decision. Thus, power to define the problem and to propose a solution is effectively shared among the decision makers. This does not mean that parties to a collaboration are equal in power, that those in positions of power must relinquish it in order to collaborate, or that all the resources that are brought to the table are distributed equally. It does mean, however, that major inequities in power are a major deterrent to collaboration (Nemeth, 1970; Smith, 1982). It means also that to achieve collaboration all parties must have some form of countervailing power. "Power parity is reached when each interest group is unable to impose its proposed solution on the other affected parties" (McCarthy, 1984, p. 13). Thus, the parties must in some ways be dependent on each other.

As in a strictly pluralistic model, when some stakeholders can exercise substantial power over the others, the weaker parties must first develop their capacity as stakeholders. They need to establish some form of countervailing power. The extent of this power building will depend on the degree of asymmetry in the relationship. In highly unequal power differences, a "process of issue and action formulation" (Gaventa, 1980) or "conscientization" (Freire, 1971) will be necessary in which parties who have acquiesced to control by others come to recognize their right to express a grievance. This level of intervention is required if parties are to move from the low-power dynamics of latent conflict to become legitimate stakeholders. Efforts of this type have been undertaken by community development, community education, and grass-roots organizing programs throughout the world. (See especially Gaventa [1980], Friere [1971], Alinsky [1969, 1971], and Parenti [1970] for in-depth discussions of these approaches.) We note these organizing efforts not because they are a component of collaboration but because they often generate domain-level concerns for which collaborative initiatives can provide viable answers, and they may be deliberately undertaken prior to proposing collaboration.

The power dynamics associated with collaboration generally involve a shift from the kind of unequal distribution of power associated with elitist decision making to more participative, equally shared access to the decision-making arena. Collaboration opens up control over access and agendas to wider participation. This empowers some stakeholders to participate who previously may not have had access directly or indirectly. Typically, the power that is shared through collaboration is agenda-setting power for the domain. Stakeholders collectively participate in defining the problems before them. The mechanisms by which power is shared through collaboration are not unproblematic, however, and must themselves often be "negotiated." As we saw in the Urban Heights case, for example, mobilization and considerable jockeying for access power by the citizens were necessary before any dialogue between the citizens and lenders could begin. As convener, the city government served as a kind of power broker in that case, helping all parties come to the table.

Some have noted that collaboration, like pluralism, is susceptible to the same criticism about biased representation (Abel, 1982; Fiorino, 1988). This criticism is tempered by the fact that collaboration deliberately attempts to incorporate a wide array of stakeholders in the deliberations. Conveners are urged to consider potential as well as vocally active stakeholders, essentially any party that has relevant information about the problem and/or the potential to block an agreement, should they decide to muster their resources. Thus, stakeholders who are organized enough to have capacity will be included. In this way collaboration can disperse power to a wider group than would normally be guaranteed agenda or policy responsiveness in the traditional pluralist process. In Urban Heights, the realtors and appraisers were not likely to participate in strictly pluralistic bargaining over restrictions on lenders, but they had key knowledge necessary for constructing a viable collaborative agreement.

Through collaboration, stakeholders may also share influence over policy responsiveness for the domain (Schumaker,

1975); that is, they may participate in proposing and selecting action steps. Collaborations differ, of course, with respect to the extent that stakeholders can enact policy or implement action steps. These issues will be addressed in more detail as we consider the power dynamics at each phase of collaboration.

Power Dynamics in Each Phase of Collaboration

Power sharing is a necessary ingredient for collaborating, but it cannot be taken for granted. Power can be manifest in a number of different ways during each phase of collaboration. Stakeholders and third parties need to be aware of power dynamics throughout the process and to make conscious choices about how it is exercised.

Power Dynamics During Problem Setting

In the early phases of collaborative endeavors, the boundaries of the problem domain are sufficiently unstable, ambiguous, or contested that the relative distribution of power among potential stakeholders is often largely unknown and untested. In a development dispute, for example, the precise nature or extent of local opposition to a proposed plan is difficult to discern before the plan is made public. This is especially true where new groups are organized in response to the specific problem domain. In such cases, who defines the nature of the problem, how it will be addressed, and what actions will be taken with respect to solving it are all political matters. That is, power to make these determinations will be distributed among the stakeholders. Defining the forum in which the deliberations will occur is also a political matter.

Stakeholder Legitimacy. A significant step in initiating a collaboration is identifying who has a legitimate stake in the issues to be addressed (Gray, 1985; McCann, 1980; Walton, 1972). In Chapter Three the notion of legitimacy was introduced. A stakeholder is viewed to have legitimacy when this individual or group is perceived by others to have the right and the capacity to participate. Legitimacy involves perceptions of entitlement. People believe they are entitled to participate when they will be impacted by the decisions taken. Collaboration presumes that their voice is also critical to arriving at comprehensive and fair resolution of a problem. Questions of legitimacy, however, often create conflict during problem setting. In establishing the forum at Three Mile Island (discussed in Chapter One), pro-nuclear technocrats from government and industry were reluctant to admit that antinuclear groups in the community had a legitimate stake in decisions about community safety. Meanwhile, community groups vehemently asserted their stake in the problem. The collaborative forum created recognized this stake, along with the others on which the problem was dependent for resolution.

Stakeholder Capacity. Capacity refers to the possession of some degree of power over the domain. Capacity for some stakeholders derives from their acknowledged expertise with respect to the issues under consideration. Others may be powerful because they control an established part of the public policy process (for example, they may be regulators, lobbyists, or nongovernmental policy agencies who have the administrative authority to support or oppose the decisions). Capacity also derives from the ability to represent constituencies. Such groups may have the capacity to block implementation of whatever agreements policymakers reach. They may organize resistance, invoke legal injunctions, or file expensive future claims against other stakeholders. Their participation may be sought by those who are more powerful in order to preserve the status quo.

The power distribution in an underorganized domain is usually uncertain at the outset. The stakeholders' power in other settings related to the problems will likely have some bearing on their capacity for influence within the new domain. For example, some stakeholders will hold greater control over critical resources for solving problems than will others (Aldrich, 1977; Benson, 1975; Provan, Beyer, and Kruytbosch, 1980). Elites who are already active in other civic and philanthropic activities of a community (Galaskiewicz, 1985) may have greater capacity in the form of travel resources, time, or access to information. Organizations represented in such elite inner circles are often important stakeholders who can marshal large commitments of private resources needed for collaborative initiatives, such as public-private partnerships, or who can muster political support for a project. In these cases, participation by major corporations, key civic and religious groups (for example, the League of Women Voters, Rotary Club, and the like), and local government officials are often critical to a project's success.

Power to Mobilize. Involvement of stakeholders less connected to the established power structure is also critical, however. Frequently it is these less powerful stakeholders who first call attention to issues for which domain-level solutions are needed. This was the case in Urban Heights. Interestingly, in that situation certain institutional members of the power structure were targets of the less powerful citizens' attacks. It is important to recognize that during the problem-setting phase, power challenges may be launched by groups who are trying to elevate the level of attention given to a problem or who are trying to gain access and agenda power (Schumaker, 1975) to an arena in which a problem can be addressed. This is called the *power to mobilize.* Sometimes stakeholders with no voice (Hirschman, 1970) must engage in power-building tactics in order to gain access to domain-level discussions.

Tactics of this type, including group protests, pickets, and use of the media to publicize an issue, have been reported by Alinsky (1969, 1971) and Gamson (1975). The aim of such power-building tactics is to force the more powerful to acknowledge the capacity of the less powerful to influence the domain. In doing so, those with more power are forced to acknowledge their dependence on the less powerful and grant access power to them. As a result, the power relations within the domain shift from elitist to pluralistic initially.

Power to Organize. In some collaborations there is no existing forum for addressing the problem, or the existing forum is not amenable to multiple stakeholders. Thus, no interorganizational forum is legitimately constituted. Domains with these characteristics have been referred to as underorganized (Brown, 1980; Gricar and Brown, 1981) and underbounded (Alderferer, 1979). There is no accepted institutional mechanism for addressing the problem. Thus, if the problem is to be addressed collaboratively, someone must create or arrange for a forum. An intervention is needed to convene the stakeholders. Intervention in these interorganizational settings thus becomes a process of creating boundaries where none—or only loosely defined ones—have previously existed (Gricar and Brown, 1981). Creating these boundaries is in and of itself a highly political activity. Identifying and selecting stakeholders to collaborate, in effect, circumscribes the boundaries of the domain and empowers a specific group to address the problem. The power of conveners, then, is the *power to organize.*

To select appropriate participants for a collaboration, the conveners must be able to identify the legitimate stakeholders and be able to elicit their participation. In site-specific disputes, the prospect of including the relevant stakeholders is high, unless local groups themselves are not sufficiently organized to select a representative. In that case, the convener or mediator may have to facilitate the selection process. For disputes with large numbers of stakeholders, the politics of choosing a group of manageable size are not insignificant.

> The determination of legitimate interests in public-policy debate is a risky process for several important reasons. Administratively, if the issue is broad enough, it will incur expenses and delays. Politically, if all parties are not represented, a lasting agreement is not likely to be achieved. Parties that are left out may disrupt the proceedings or ultimately challenge the outcome reached, while parties that stay out are implicitly challenging the effort as it begins. In either case, these groups may want to reenter later, often at the cost of whatever progress has been made to date. It is thus usually better to include too many interests rather than too few [Fox, 1982b, p. 402].

One model recently tried in regulatory negotiations is the use of multiple tiers of participants. In this arrangement, the key stakeholders (those in the first tier) are designated to conduct the negotiations, while those in second tier observe the proceedings and confer with the negotiators periodically throughout the process. Third-tier participants are invited to review the agreement before it is ratified. Again, this provides an opportunity for a wider set of interested parties to gain access, agenda, and policy responsiveness than would a strictly pluralist process.

For public-private partnerships, frequently members of the power elite can play effective roles as conveners because of their ability to induce others also to participate. Typically, a well-respected, influential figure has a better chance of persuading parties to participate (Carpenter and Kennedy, 1988). In the New York City Partnership, for example, the founding inspiration came from David Rockefeller. Because of his prominence and network of contacts, Rockefeller was able to enlist participation of several other key civic leaders to launch the partnership. This advantage can also be offset if an elitist convener tries to restrict the participation of legitimate interests.

The extent of the convener role can vary considerably. In a dialogue among the Farm Labor Organizing Committee, Campbell's Soup Company, and the vegetable growers, John Dunlop's credentials as a labor economist and mediator allowed him to convene the negotiations, for which he then served as mediator. In the case of the NCPP, the conveners were also stakeholders, one from the environmentalists and one from the industrialists. As Carpenter and Kennedy (1988) note, the initiator and the convener may not be identical, since the convener must have the power to organize.

The power held by the conveners also affects the character of the collaborative effort. To secure the participation of other stakeholders, the conveners themselves must be seen as legitimate and powerful and must be accepted by other stakeholders as having sufficient authority to convene the others and to control the selection of participants. Like other stakeholders, conveners derive power from their ability to influence outcomes in the domain (for example, through their expertise, resources, links to legitimate authorities, and so forth). Their power also depends on their credibility with other stakeholders. Conveners' credibility derives from their expertise and experience in the domain, from their breadth of connections and representativeness, and from perceptions of objectivity or bias attributed to them by other stakeholders.\

The power of conveners to select participants significantly shapes the collaboration. In selecting others to participate, conveners make political decisions about who can use the collaborative process to influence the domain. As Fox (1982b) noted above, other stakeholders too can exhibit certain power by their willingness or refusal to participate. These decisions themselves may be made on the basis of power. Unless stakeholders perceive that they have sufficient capability to influence the outcomes of the project, they will be unlikely to participate (Gricar and Brown, 1981; O'Toole and O'Toole, 1981; Walton, 1969). As Fox (1982b, p. 402) notes, "The weaker party may view collaboration as an attractive alternative to the current situation, but the stronger one will see no value in negotiating away any of his or her strength." Thus, powerful stakeholders who perceive little or no interdependence with other stakeholders will resist collaborative efforts that seek to balance the power differences among the stakeholders, unless they can be persuaded that their own interests will be jeopardized by not participating. This may be the case if all the other stakeholders have agreed to participate, and the one holding out fears missing an opportunity to influence a decision.

Thus, interactions during problem setting have the potential to shake up entrenched power dynamics and to restructure existing power relationships with respect to the domain in question. They do this through the power to mobilize and the power to organize the stakeholders of the domain.

Power Dynamics During Direction Setting

Power associated with direction setting derives largely from control over how issues are appreciated. Processes for sharing power in this phase include joint influence over the group's agenda and exchange of critical information about the domain. Although some groups may have more access to information than others, unless provisions for sharing the information and agreeing on its value are established, shared agreements are unlikely to emerge.

Power to Strategize. One type of power that is shared during the direction-setting phase is essentially the *power to strategize* about the agenda for the domain and about appropriate solutions to undertake. The extent to which parties in a collaboration have the ability to make recommendations or to actually establish policy and the extent to which they can ensure implementation will vary depending on the design of the collaboration. In search conferences, for example, parties simply share the power of idea generation and influence through information exchange or persuasion. There is no expectation that policy recommendations will emerge from a search conference, although joint agreements are not precluded. Similarly, in policy dialogues, stakeholders exert influence on each other to craft agreements but are not directly empowered to enact their agreements. Instead, their influence on policy is more diffuse—by creating a compelling and widely shared appreciation or vision about how the problem should be addressed and by agreeing to exert pressure on legislative bodies to enact their recommendations. In regulatory negotiations, in contrast, the regulatory agency in effect shares the power to create policy with the other stakeholders (unless they cannot reach agreement, in which case power reverts to the agency). In mini-trials the power to craft and to implement decisions rests fully with the parties, who basically agree to a contractual agreement out of court.

Information Control. Once stakeholders have agreed to participate, power dynamics during the direction-setting phase are largely played out through efforts to control the process of the negotiations and the flow of information. Here the role of a third party can be critical in structuring a process of information exchange that ensures that (1) all parties' concerns are heard and addressed and (2) the stakeholders themselves make process as well as substantive decisions. Disputes often arise during direction setting over the qualifications of technical experts called by one side or the other. Here, again, the third party can structure a process that elicits agreement from the parties on the credentials of expert witnesses or ensures that multiple experts are consulted.

> The inequality of information is particularly relevant to disputes involving complex or scientific facts. Environmental disputes are often characterized by one side controlling the technical data . . . data can only be obtained at great expense and scientifically analyzed at even greater expense. The party with control of data has the power to unilaterally influence the dispute. This party is often reluctant to share such data with an adversary because it would create the equalization of power and would decrease the ability to unilaterally affect the dispute [Riesel, 1985, pp. 109–110].

In cases like this, the mediator needs to even out this disparity of power. This can be done in several ways, depending on the circumstances. (1) The mediator can call the more powerful party's attention to the value of educating the other stakeholders so that they can understand the more powerful party's perspective and consider its merits. (2) Access to data can be exchanged for knowledge of the others' specific objections to it (Riesel, 1985). This enables the more powerful party to learn the weak links in its own case. (3) Assurances can be built into the ground rules so that data revealed during consensus building cannot be used by opponents in subsequent court proceedings if negotiations break down. (4) The party with the data can make general stipulations with respect to their content, and/or the mediator can serve as a repository for data that are proprietary but the general content or validity of which needs to be certified.

Power Dynamics During Implementation

The implementation of agreements introduces yet another set of power dynamics with which the stakeholders must contend.

Power to Exercise Influence or Authorize Action. As noted in Chapter One, collaborative initiatives serve different purposes, and, as a result, they differ in the extent to which the parties assume responsibility for implementing the agreements they draft. The power available to parties in this phase can be described as *power to exercise influence* or *power to authorize action.* Even in exploratory collaborations, such as search conferences, parties can exercise some influence over the domain by acting in concert with the joint visions they establish. In the case of policy dialogues, while the parties themselves cannot authorize policy actions, they can individually and collectively exercise influence over the passage of legislation that advances their collaborative visions. As in mini-trials, public-private partnerships, and other interorganizational consortia, implementation is typically prescribed by a contract and monitored through some form of institutionalized arrangements. In these cases, parties jointly authorize each other or a subset of the stakeholders to implement the agreements. That is, parties exercise self-regulation over their actions that affect the domain.

In some cases, the convener's choices about who to seat at the table will directly affect subsequent implementation efforts. Parties who are not at the table may be inclined to block legislation or may refuse to comply with voluntary agreements. For example, after the U.S. Department of Energy and a local citizens' organization (the Oak Ridge–Roan County Citizen Task Force) negotiated a plan (including mitigation, compensation, and economic as well as noneconomic incentives) for the siting of a nuclear waste storage facility in Oakridge, Tennessee, the plan was challenged by several state-level environmental groups and the state legislature and eventually was rejected by the governor (Peelle, 1987). Several key stakeholders were not included in this negotiation, and, as a result, the plan was received with skepticism and generated widespread opposition.

Designers of collaborative efforts cannot ignore the larger context within which their efforts are embedded. "Stakeholders must understand the role the dynamic larger environment plays in defining their problem since events within the larger environment ultimately determine what they can and cannot do" (McCann, 1983, p. 183). A shifting political climate may severely hamper implementation efforts by limiting the power of the parties to take the actions they desire. Successful implementation requires skill in politics, both within the domain and with respect to the wider environment, to ensure that sufficient political support for the agreements can be sustained (Horwitch and Prahalad, 1981; Pfeffer, 1981; Sapolsky, 1972). Proponents of the supersonic transport (SST) project were unsuccessful implementing it because they failed to heed a major shift in public opinion and consequently could not sustain a public constituency in favor of the project. In another example, a successfully sited hazardous waste landfill in Maryland closed after one year of operation because of insufficient market demand.

This chapter has put forth a view of collaboration based on shared power. While this perspective seeks to overcome the limitations of unequal access and inaction inherent in pluralistic politics, the model is not based on idealistic notions of equality for equality's sake. The underlying premise to collaboration is that shared power is becoming increasingly necessary to advancing both private and public interests. In order to move ahead as a society, we must devise ways to share power.

6

Coping with
Power and Politics:
A Case Study

*Leave a half dozen of the group, three environmentalists
and three industrialists, stranded in a West Virginia holler
while the rest of the field trip participants—and the buses—
are nowhere to be seen, and they'll find a lot in common.*
                                                    —*Coal Outlook*

This chapter takes an in-depth look at how political dynamics
shaped the course of a large-scale collaborative effort. The National Coal Policy Project (NCPP) is one of the classical efforts
to establish a collaborative problem-solving process among a
wide array of stakeholders. It has been touted as an example of
how bitter adversaries can put aside their differences in a spirit
of searching for common ground. Critics, on the other hand,
cite the NCPP as an example of a poorly conceived attempt at
collaboration that suffered from flaws in design and was plagued
by concerns about good-faith bargaining by stakeholders on
both sides. Issues of stakeholder exclusion, constituency representation, convener credibility, and implementation failure were
primary issues in the NCPP's history.

The National Coal Policy Project case provides a comprehensive, albeit not entirely successful, example of collaboration
at work. Some of the most compelling lessons provided by the
NCPP case are those concerning power and collaboration. Despite the NCPP's unprecedented ability to bring together and
forge agreements among some long-standing political adversaries,
political dynamics also played a role in limiting the NCPP's success. Three dynamics in particular curtailed the NCPP's overall
effectiveness in achieving a widespread consensus and gaining
acceptance of their agreements in their wider policy arena:

(1) the politics of selecting participants, (2) the role of power in stakeholders' decisions to participate, and (3) the power of the project as a whole to influence the public policy arena.

The story of the NCPP is included here because of the rich opportunities it provides for learning about political dynamics. In particular, the case underscores the complexities of organizing and managing a multiparty collaboration and demonstrates how political dynamics significantly influenced the outcome. This analysis draws heavily on Gray and Hay (1986) and Hay (1983).

The case spans several years, from early 1976 through 1980. A chronology of events is provided in Table 7.

Table 7.   Chronology of Events in the NCPP.

January 1976	Early exploratory meeting between Decker, Moss, and representatives from ten environmental groups.
July 1976	"Test meeting" at Arlie House Conference Center. Industry and environmental caucuses were formed following this meeting.
January 1977	First official meeting of NCPP. Beginning of Phase I.
February 1978	Close of Phase I work. First set of recommendations released.
December 1978	Phase II launched.
March 1980	Phase II recommendations completed.

Historical Relationship

After the oil embargo of 1973, there was a resurgence of interest in the use of coal as a major energy source in the United States. Business was prepared to pursue the use of coal, since it represented a cheap and relatively abundant fuel, but had been hampered from aggressively doing so by environmental legislation. By 1974, however, there was general agreement that coal development was an essential response to the energy future of the United States. While an agreement in support of coal use was emerging among business, government, and environmental interests, major disagreements surfaced concerning the standards governing its extraction and use. Moreover, since no clear government policy existed with regard to current or future coal use, industry was saddled with uncertainties about the future of coal as an energy source. Disagreements over standards for coal use existed against a backdrop of hostilities between business and environmental groups, who had spent years battling each other over environmental policies dealing with air and water quality, land use, resource extraction, and energy issues.

By 1976, when the National Coal Policy Project was proposed, the relationship between environmental groups and business was characterized by polarized viewpoints, bitterness, and mistrust. Many environmentalists had come to view their industrial counterparts as motivated only by profit and insensitive to ecological concerns; many industry members, in contrast, saw environmentalists as radicals who wanted only to stop business growth. Indeed, proposals to arrest energy growth were viewed by business as proposals to "arrest economic growth" (Fox, 1982, p. 462). Typically, the conflicts between these two groups were played out in Congress, in the regulatory arena, or in the courts, forums in which the format as well as the substance of the disputes were highly structured and largely out of the control of the disputing parties. The process encouraged parties to present and defend extreme positions on the issues, thus contributing to the polarization of issues and a win-lose climate. The NCPP was proposed as an alternative forum in which parties could explore their differences and search for agreements outside the traditional legislative or adjudicative arenas.

When it was proposed, frustrations were running high on both the business and the environmental side over the lack of clear federal policies with respect to coal. In addition, concern over the perceived ineptitude inherent in the traditional policy-making processes was mounting. For different reasons, the situation had become so unsatisfactory for many parties on both sides of the dispute that the climate was ripe for an alternative. For example, many of those who later participated in the National Coal Policy Project characterized their feelings as "a nearly unanimous dissatisfaction, often rising to the level of frustration, with the decisions rendered by the traditional system" (Murray and Curran, 1982, p. 27).

One of the two individuals who appreciated the depths of the stalemate and initiated a search for a better way of resolving the protracted conflicts was Gerry Decker, Dow Chemical Company's corporate energy manager. In reference to the coal industry disputes, Decker observed, "We were getting nowhere; we were killing each other off" (Hay, 1983, p. 12). Over the years Decker had had some unpleasant experiences with environmentalists, particularly in the courts, and he wondered whether the two sides could resolve their differences in another way: through face-to-face negotiations. Decker was well aware of the limitations of the legal system to resolve the complex conflicts between business and environmentalists over energy use. As Dow's corporate energy manager, Decker had tangled with environmentalists in the courts over the site of a nuclear power plant in Midland, Michigan. The litigation had delayed completion of the plant by at least ten years and had at least tripled the original cost estimates because of legal fees and delayed construction. As a member of the Federal Energy Administration's (FEA's) Environmental Advisory Committee, Decker had also experienced the "serious intent of the environmentalists to develop pragmatic solutions to the new energy crisis" (Fox, 1982a, p. 459). Believing that alternatives could be created to escape the less-than-satisfactory results of litigation, Decker, at the urging of several of his industrial colleagues, began to explore negotiation. He believed that numerous issues such as emission control standards and power plant sitings were potential topics for negotiation.

Dissatisfaction with the existing methods for resolving conflict was experienced by some environmentalists as well. Protracted court battles strained the financial resources of many environmental organizations, and in some cases the environmentalists' persistent protests against industry had created ill feelings toward them on the part of the public. Additionally, being forced to depend on the courts, the legislature, or some other third party to arbitrate disputes did not always produce satisfactory results. For example, Michael McCloskey, the executive director of the Sierra Club, cited the example of some negotiations between environmentalists and the timber industry over wilderness boundaries in Idaho. Initial discussions were unsuccessful because of the destructive role played by the Forest Service (Carter, 1977, p. 278). However, private negotiations, from which the government agencies were excluded, eventually led to accommodation between industry and environmental representatives.

Despite the prospects for success, many environmentalists were wary of negotiations because these demanded large amounts of time, time needed to lobby for or against legislation being considered by Congress. Additionally, some environmentalists believed they had been winning the war with the coal industry in the traditional arenas like Congress and the courts. Thus, their motivation to search for alternatives was considerably less than that of their industrial counterparts.

> Clearly, much of the motivation for industrialists to participate comes from an awareness that industry has been kept on the defensive in the federal and state legislatures and in the courts. "We've lost almost every battle on Capitol Hill," Decker says, overstating the case but indicating accurately enough the general drift of things [Carter, 1977, p. 278].

Launching the NCPP

It is no wonder, then, that Larry Moss was skeptical about Gerry Decker's proposal to establish negotiations about coal policy. In January 1976 Decker and some of his industry colleagues met with Moss (a former member of the Sierra Club) and representatives from ten environmental groups to explore the possibility of negotiations. Decker knew Moss because they had worked together on the FEA's Environmental Advisory Committee, which Moss chaired. Among the environmental organizations who attended these preliminary discussions were the Environmental Defense Fund, the Environmental Law Institute, the Natural Resources Defense Council, the National Wildlife Federation, the John Muir Institute for Environmental Studies, the Environmental Policy Center, and the Sierra Club. Industry participants included Dow Chemical, U.S. Steel, PPG Industries, and Detroit Edison (an electric power company).

Decker described the January meeting as "the roughest meeting I had ever sat through" (Alexander, 1978, p. 96), since hostilities normally expressed at a distance were aired openly. At the conclusion, the environmentalists requested time to discuss the proposed negotiations among themselves. The environmentalists privately expressed several reservations. (1) Some believed participation in the negotiations detracted from lobbying efforts to influence the Clean Air Act amendments and the surface mine legislation being contested in Congress; (2) some questioned the appropriateness of resolving disputes outside of legitimate forums, especially when they believed that environmentalists were "winning" in these arenas; (3) others considered legislation recently passed by Congress to represent a hard-fought consensus that should be recognized as such. Other legislation pertaining to coal policy (such as a strip-mining law) was also being debated in Congress at the time. Despite his initial skepticism, Moss agreed to support the proposal. In the months that followed, Decker and Moss were able to persuade several environmental groups to participate in a "test meeting" to learn whether the two sides could engage in productive dialogue with one another.

Administrative and financial support was also crucial to successful launching of the negotiations. The Georgetown Center for Strategic and International Studies (CSIS) at Georgetown University in Washington, D.C., offered to serve as a neutral sponsor for the project and provided administrative and staff support and office space. Four foundations agreed to fund the project, whose cost was initially estimated at $650,000. Foundation support was crucial, since the environmentalists could not accept expense money from the industry side in order to participate. The original industry participants also contributed financial support for the project, but they agreed that it would be inappropriate to finance the environmentalists' travel and living expenses and instead provided $150 per diem for time spent on the project.

The "test meeting" was held in July 1976 at Arlie House Conference Center in northern Virginia. Each side was permitted to select one item for the agenda. The industrialists proposed deterioration of air quality; the environmentalists chose energy pricing. The latter was a highly contested topic and proved to be a difficult subject throughout the life of the project. Despite the controversy, discussion was facilitated by the use of a set of behavioral ground rules called the Rule of Reason (see Chapter Three). These rules were compiled by Milton Wessel (1976), who argued that litigation was an ineffective method for resolving complex public issues. The NCPP adopted the Rule of Reason to help guide the negotiations. Former Secretary of Labor John T. Dunlop served as facilitator of this meeting, and his skill as a mediator contributed to the successful outcome.

Dunlop was determined to establish a realistic atmosphere for the negotiations. He immediately challenged the conveners' plans to conclude the negotiations by 9:00 P.M., insisting that negotiations are not serious if they do not extend into the night. He also advised the parties that the disputes they would encounter within their own constituencies were likely to be more difficult to resolve than those between the industrialists and the environmentalists.

One small skirmish (which foreshadowed much of the dialogue to follow) occurred in preparing for the meeting. A disagreement arose over whether or not ashtrays would be available for smokers during the negotiation sessions. Some environmentalists objected to distributing ashtrays. A hasty agreement was reached that enabled the parties to begin dialogue on coal issues.

Some surprises occurred for both sides at the Arlie House meeting. Industry participants were amazed to discover that their environmental counterparts favored using higher energy prices rather than government regulation to promote conservation. Environmentalists observed that the industry side was far from monolithic in its view on energy pricing. Moss had approached the test meeting with some skepticism. By the close of the meeting, however, Moss was convinced of the NCPP's potential. He commented, "The discussion surprised me. It was honest and intellectual. We made good progress" ("A Promising Stab . . . ," 1977, p. 25). After the test meeting each side met separately to consider whether or not to formally proceed with the NCPP.

Organization of the NCPP

One outcome of the test meeting was the creation of two caucuses representing industry and environmental participants. Decker and Moss were selected to serve as the respective chairs of these caucuses. Additionally, five task forces were established with equal participation by environmentalists and industrialists. Each task force would address a different topical issue related to coal development: mining, transportation, air pollution, energy pricing, and fuel utilization and conservation. Each task force had a roughly equal number of industrial and environmental members and cochairs from each side. The cochairs took turns conducting the meetings. Each caucus was responsible for selecting its own members.

The task forces were assisted by a plenary group, which also was composed of an equal number of industrialists and environmentalists. The plenary group consisted of the task force cochairs, caucus chairs Decker and Moss, and plenary chair Frances X. Quinn, a Jesuit priest and experienced mediator in coal industry labor disputes. The plenary group was responsible for discussing and giving final approval to all task force recommendations, thus ultimately deciding the NCPP position on each issue. The task forces forwarded policy recommendations to the plenary group, which either accepted them or remanded them for further study by the task force. The two caucuses usually met separately before each plenary group meeting. This provided an opportunity for each side to review progress, test agreements, and muster support. (See Figure 1 for a diagram of the NCPP's organization.)

Quinn and the project director, Frank Murray (a professor at CSIS), deliberately took a neutral, relatively passive role

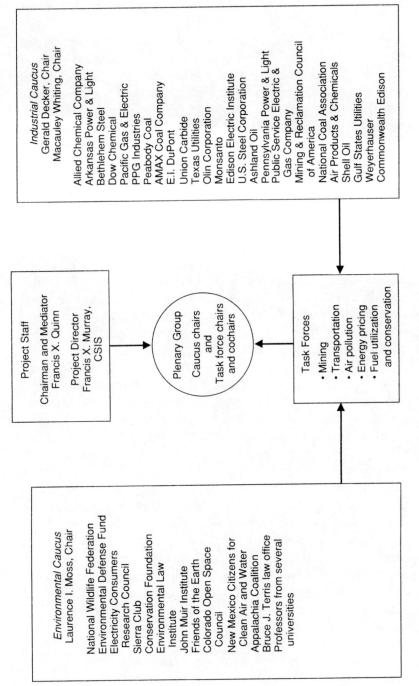

Figure 1. Organization of the NCPP.

in NCPP discussions. In instances in which intervention was necessary to resolve a dispute, it was Decker and Moss—the two convening stakeholders—who intervened. The caucuses also played a major role in assuring that the ground rules were followed. In the "privacy" of the caucuses, for example, caucus members who violated the Rule of Reason could be disciplined. Indeed, a prominent member of one caucus told an offending member quite bluntly to either change his behavior or resign from the project.

Selection of Participants

The first official meeting of the NCPP was held in January 1977. Several critical decisions were made by the project's conveners in selecting the members of the NCPP. The conveners decided to address a relatively large domain of issues relating to coal development in the United States: mining, transportation, coal use, pricing, and pollution were among the issues that they included. This decision meant that a large number of interest groups—for example, coal companies, miners, farmers, unions, environmentalists, consumers, and transportation interests—would have a stake in the project and would be affected by the eventual recommendations. However, NCPP organizers decided to limit the number of project participants to two broad classes of interest groups: environmentalists and representatives of coal-producing and coal-consuming industries. The primary reason for limiting the number of participants was to keep the project at an administratively manageable size. Too many participants, it was believed, would result in an unwieldy, expensive process and would make it more difficult to reach agreements. The organizers recognized that by choosing a smaller forum, they might experience difficulties later in implementing the project's recommendations. But, they reasoned, because the project was an experiment to see if any agreement could be reached on very controversial topics, they opted to limit the number of participants in hopes of facilitating agreement.

   Some stakeholders were invited but chose not to participate. Prospective participants from the aluminum and paper industries as well as several environmental organizations declined invitations to join the project. Also, a well-known leader of a powerful coal industry lobby, while privately supportive of the NCPP, expressed concern that it would be politically disadvantageous for him to publicly participate in the project. Instead, a board member from his organization took his place.

After the work of the NCPP had been under way for several months, the conveners again brought up the issue of stakeholder selection, giving consideration to the possibility of adding more participants. The task force discussion had gone surprisingly well, and project leaders thought it might be feasible to expand the project membership to include representatives of other interests beyond the industrial and environmental viewpoints. Conveners approached a few groups informally at this point, but the response was lukewarm; some groups perceived themselves as being considered for the NCPP only as an afterthought, and both the groups involved and the NCPP conveners feared that members who were added at this juncture would be inferior in status to the existing members. A further complication was the issue of equal numerical status. The NCPP had thus far included roughly equal numbers of industrial and environmental interests. Would it now need to include an equal number of members representing consumers, labor transportation, and so on?

The NCPP organizers concluded that the difficulties and expense involved in expanding the project's membership after several months of operation outweighed the potential benefits and decided to continue with just the two initial groups. Again, the conveners recognized that their decision might mean that the project's eventual recommendations would carry less weight; however, they decided to accept this trade-off as one of the project's limitations.

Among the stakeholders considered for possible inclusion in the project at this stage was the United Mine Workers (UMW) union. The union, however, declined to participate because its leadership was embroiled in a bitter fight for the union presidency. Consequently, the NCPP conveners decided to avoid considering issues such as mine safety and health in which the

miners' input would be essential. However, one environmentalist who chose not to participate in NCPP, Louise Dunlap, maintained that the union's absence adversely affected the NCPP's
work since the project did debate other coal-related issues in
which the union had a stake (for example, strip mining). Dunlap
thus claimed the NCPP negotiations were not legitimate.

The NCPP's leaders also considered including representatives of government agencies in the project, believing that the
project would be more readily accepted and its recommendations would stand a better chance of being implemented if government officials were involved from the outset. However, after
considerable debate, the decision was made to not include government representatives. Two reasons were given:

> Only high-level officials have any real degree of flexibility
> at the policy level and even that may be limited. Realis-
> tically, these individuals would be unlikely to attend
> meetings on a regular basis due to the demands and re-
> sponsibilities of their positions. This raised the second
> concern that these individuals would be forced to dele-
> gate this responsibility to their subordinates. Such
> individuals would have limited flexibility in considering
> policy and perhaps little influence at the decision levels.
> In effect, a layer of bureaucracy would be added, and the
> main purpose of the NCPP, bringing leaders together with
> each other, would be defeated [Murray and Curran,
> 1982, p. 22].

The NCPP conveners settled on a compromise. They invited government officials to participate as observers rather than
as voting members. There were occasionally other instances in
which stakeholders not officially included in the NCPP's membership had input into the project's work. For example, input
from local stakeholders was sought during a project field trip,
one such as those taken by the mining task force.

Several criteria were important in the selection of participants. According to Robert Curry, the environmental cochair of
the Mining Task Force:

It is worth noting that the participants were very carefully selected to represent wide ranges of points of view and interests. Each person selected was highly qualified in technical matters of coal mining, regulation, and impact assessment or had access to staff that was so qualified. In addition, many of those selected represented organizations with significant national interests in coal energy policy. Many were nationally respected persons with frequent opportunities for input to energy policy decisions. On both (industry and environment) sides we sought a mixture of representation of groups concerned with coal as well as those with regional expertise on problems of coal development in specified different regions of the United States [Committee on Interstate and Foreign Commerce, 1978, pp. 124–134].

The NCPP conveners also recognized that a prospective participant's willingness to try an alternative conflict-resolution approach was important to the success of the project. Decker and Moss sought persons who would be objective and would abide by the Rule of Reason. Some persons who, in the assessment of Decker and Moss, did not meet these criteria were not invited to participate, and a few invitees whose behavior at the July 1976 test meeting was deemed inconsistent with the Rule of Reason were asked to leave the project.

The degree of influence that participants would be able to exert in their respective constituencies was a selection criterion that proved to be a serious issue for the NCPP. This issue was of particular importance because none of the NCPP members were participating as official representatives of their organizations. It was agreed that participants would take part in the project as individuals (without constituencies). In this way any agreements reached in the NCPP would reflect the views of the participants only and would not be binding on their organizations. Since the NCPP was an experiment to see if people could reach agreement, the conveners wanted the members to participate as freely as possible. They believed it would be far more difficult to explore differences if participants felt obliged to

present the official position of their organizations. The choice
of some participants, however, was contentious precisely because they did not speak for a constituency. Louise Dunlap, of
the Environmental Policy Center, a Washington-based lobbying
group that served as an umbrella organization for a number of
grass-roots environmental groups, contended that the project
failed to include enough people who could "turn off the tele-
grams," that is those who spoke with a powerful voice in the
coal debate. For example, Dunlap claims that John Corcoran
(the former chairman of Consolidation Coal who cochaired the
Mining Task Force) had been a central figure in the 1969 debate over the Deep Mine Health and Safety Act, but that, since
he was no longer active in the industry in 1976, he was no longer
a "big player" in coal debates. On the other hand, Corcoran was
a well-known public figure, someone who was respected by both
sides in the debate.

The selection of participants for the Transportation Task
Force illustrates other trade-offs in stakeholder selection. On
the environmental side, only one member of the task force, a
transportation economist from the University of Pennsylvania,
had had any direct involvement with transportation issues. Two
other members had expertise in water resources; a third had no
distinct experience with transportation. The industry side purposely chose to include members from coal-consuming rather
than coal-transporting industries. Robert J. Ferguson, Jr., the
task force's industry cochair, explained the decision this way:

> I must say that our initial concepts were that direct
> representation of the transportation industry would not
> lead to a very successful kind of operation, because I can
> assure you that were members of the railroad industry,
> the pipeline industry, the barge industry and the trucking
> industry part of this task force there would have been no
> consensus [Committee on Interstate and Foreign Com-
> merce, 1978, p. 255].

The NCPP's decisions about which stakeholders to seat

were among the major reasons why some environmentalists chose not to participate in the project. According to Louise Dunlap, one major reason her organization chose not to participate was that key interest groups who had been working on coal issues for several years were not included in the NCPP's negotiations. She also questioned the credentials of convener Moss, who, although active in the SST debate some years earlier, was not seen as a mainstream environmentalist on coal issues. Initial discussions with Moss about the NCPP caused Dunlap to believe Moss was insensitive to other environmentalists' investments in consensus-building activities vis-à-vis surface-mining legislation. Richard Ayres of the Natural Resources Defense Council also expressed concerns about the NCPP's selection of participants and about their authority to make decisions affecting coal policy at all. He charged that the NCPP's recommendations did not represent a "legitimate consensus" among those stakeholders interested in coal issues. In a February 1978 letter to Moss, he explained his reasons for not participating.

> I disagreed with the proposition that private discussions among a small group of privately selected people from among business and environmental organizations would be a more appropriate or productive means of resolving major issues of public policy than the constituted processes of our government. . . . In my view, the Constitution provides the only processes for legitimately resolving disputed issues of public policy through the Congress, the Executive, and the Courts [letter from Ayres to Moss, February 7, 1978].

Thus, not all environmentalists shared Decker's and Moss's dissatisfaction with the traditional process of settling disputes or their enthusiasm for trying an alternative process. Indeed, some, like Louise Dunlap, believed they were "winning more amendments than (the industry side) on the Hill and had nothing to gain" from the proposed negotiations (personal communication with Louise Dunlap, November 18, 1982).

Work of the NCPP

Despite these setbacks, the NCPP held its first official meeting in January 1977. Several topics for negotiation were identified by the task forces. Some of these topics were the development and use of new emissions control technology, fair competition among all transportation sectors on coal haulage, siting of new coal-fired power units, efficient and expeditious reclamation of abandoned mine lands, the impacts of proposed coal slurry pipelines on water resources in the West, provisions in state regulatory programs for modifications to federal regulations for coal surface mining, increasing citizen participation and reducing procedural delays in energy facility siting, and price information for electricity users (a similar but longer list appears in Fox [1982a]).

In order to study these questions, each task force was charged with establishing its own agenda and securing the data it needed to investigate the questions before it. This meant acquiring a joint data base that both sides believed was accurate and complete. On several occasions, the participants took field trips together to collect data and to collectively witness illustrations of controversial issues. The Mining Task Force visited coal fields in Wyoming, Montana, Illinois, Pennsylvania, and other states as well as in Europe to get a firsthand view of existing and potential mining sites, reclamation areas, and strip-mine operations. The reasons for the trips were explained by the industry cochair of the task force:

> We all found that we were discussing broad generalities, and I soon found that we were talking about entirely different things. For example, when the term "strip mine" was mentioned, I visualized a mine with which I was familiar in eastern Ohio with a three-foot seam of coal, 80 feet of very difficult overburden to handle and a reclamation process that gave me the benefit of 40 inches of rainfall a year. My friend Mr. Curry (Robert Curry, the University of Montana geology professor representing the environmental side) visualized, as you

would expect, a strip mine in Montana with a 50 to 60 foot seam of coal, very unconglomerated overburden, and he was faced with reclaiming the property with 10 inches of rainfall a year. So it was obvious we were not really talking about the same things [Committee on Interstate and Foreign Commerce, 1978, pp. 119–120].

One of the key agreements in the NCPP emerged from the field trips to the strip mines, as the opportunity for both sides to view the same mines resulted in some participants (in this case, the environmentalists) changing their stand on an issue.

One such issue concerned high walls around strip mines. The industrialists had generally favored allowing high walls to remain after strip mining, while environmentalists wanted the land to be restored to its original contour. Upon viewing some reclaimed areas during field trips to strip-mining sites, the environmentalists discovered that attempts to avoid high walls sometimes produced erosion problems, and that allowing high walls to remain in some cases actually was the better alternative for reclaiming the land. As a result, the NCPP generally recommended that disturbed land be returned to its previous condition but noted that, in some cases, high walls should be allowed to remain. Thus, through careful, joint research, both sides were able to arrive at a satisfactory compromise on high walls.

This decision proved extremely controversial, however, because of its timing. Just one year earlier the environmentalists had successfully persuaded Congress to adopt an absolute ban on high walls in the Surface Mine Control and Reclamation Act (SMCRA). The NCPP recommendation, therefore, was considered a victory for the industrialists (by environmentalists not participating in the NCPP) because it gave up ground "won" in SMCRA the previous year.

The NCPP's deliberations took place in relative privacy, for the most part. Although task force meetings were open to the public, few observers ever attended; a few members of the news media occasionally accompanied the task forces on their information-gathering field trips. No doubt being able to conduct their discussions away from the public eye helped NCPP participants in their attempt to seek areas of agreement. Privacy afforded the participants the opportunity to express doubt, uncertainty, or even ignorance without losing face, to change their minds, and to retreat from previously stated positions.

Work in the task forces also promoted personal interaction among the participants. Many of the NCPP's discussions were lively and heated, but rarely did disputants resort to acrimony, personal attacks, or bitterness. The Rule of Reason had been read aloud at the first meeting, and occasionally the participants invoked it to deal with controversy when it arose.

Outcomes

On February 8, 1978, the NCPP concluded Phase I of its work and released its first set of recommendations from each of the six task forces. In the nine months that followed, the project focused on communication of these recommendations to a wide audience including Congress, regulatory agencies, industry and environmental leaders, academicians, and others interested in energy policy. During this time the project received wide media coverage as well. The NCPP did not engage in any lobbying efforts, however, because as an arm of Georgetown University it was prevented from doing so by university policy.

It is important to emphasize that the NCPP's founders never envisioned the project to be a wholesale substitution for traditional methods of policy development. The original objectives of the NCPP were experimental and modest in scope: to see if an alternative method of interest mediation was viable and if a constructive dialogue among opposing parties was possible. Finding that it was, after one year of study, the NCPP was faced with the problem of how to disseminate its agreements and to influence the traditional policymaking apparatus. Since the NCPP was not convened under the auspices of any recognized authority, no organization was bound to accept its results. On the issue of dissemination, the project wrote in its final report:

> It was hoped that broad dissemination of NCPP's findings and recommendations would stimulate expanded dia-

logue and increase the quality of the coal policy debate
. . . and to determine whether those recommendations
were, in fact, reasonable, workable, and in the national
interest. Finally, the project sought to create support
among various constituent groups and the broader public
for adoption of the recommendations ["National Coal
Policy . . . ," 1981, p. 14].

Whether or not the NCPP was successful in influencing
public policy is debatable. The impact of the NCPP on subsequent decisions rendered by Congress and the regulatory agencies cannot be definitively traced. Since the NCPP members only
represented themselves in the project, their respective organizations were not bound to support the NCPP's recommendations
in the legislative or regulatory arenas. Indeed, some NCPP critics
charged that the agreements reached in the project were relatively meaningless because they represented the consensus of a
group of individuals rather than the consensus of the affected
interest groups.

Still, the project director points to a number of initiatives
and decisions taken by federal agencies that are consistent with
NCPP recommendations. Each of these is discussed below under
the specific task force that generated the recommendation.

In December 1978 the NCPP decided to embark on Phase
II in order to address unresolved issues from Phase I. Work during Phase II was conducted by three task forces: mining, air pollution, and a cogeneration task force that grew out of proposals
from Phase I. The specific work of each task force during Phases
I and II is summarized below.

Mining Task Force

As a result of its visits to coal fields across the United States,
the Mining Task Force emphasized the need to tailor mining
control and reclamation policies to specific regional conditions.
Since SMCRA was passed by Congress during the NCPP's deliberations, the Mining Task Force opted to focus on implementing and enforcing SMCRA. One of the task force's recommendations was subsequently promulgated by the Office of Surface
Mining (OSM):

[The] Mining Task Force recommended that abandoned
mine reclamation programs be implemented on a water-
shed basis. Recognizing the problems related to state
boundaries, the NCPP further recommended that OSM
should coordinate reclamation efforts. The example used
by the Mining Task Force was the Tug Fork River Basin,
which includes parts of Virginia, West Virginia, and
Kentucky. Nearly one year later, OSM approved its first
coordinated reclamation program—for the Tug Fork
River and surrounding area ["National Coal Policy . . . ,"
1981, p. 25].

NCPP participants also believe several other OSM actions
were influenced by the Mining Task Force's recommendations.
For example, the NCPP recommended that OSM compile an in-
ventory of abandoned mine problems; in 1980, OSM awarded
moneys to several states to develop such inventories; the task
force also recommended in 1979 that OSM provide assistance to
operators of small coal mines, and a year later OSM awarded
grants to small-mine operators in several states (Murray and Curran, 1981). In June 1979 the NCPP recommended relaxation in
OSM bonding requirements. A year later OSM relaxed its bonding requirements. However, OSM did not mention the NCPP in
connection with any of these actions. NCPP members believe
OSM did not acknowledge their contribution because some
OSM personnel viewed the project as "infringing on their terri-
torial prerogatives" (Murray and Curran, 1981, p. 7). In another
case, OSM approved several experimental programs to allow discretion to individual coal companies. The Mining Task Force
had called for such flexibility, but Section 711 of SMCRA
(passed the same year that NCPP was deliberating) also allows
for such experimental programs. Here, the NCPP may have over-
stated its influence.

    In addition to continuing to work on surface-mining regu-
lations, during Phase II the Mining Task Force addressed the
issue of federal coal leasing. Some new members were added to
make up for a lack of expertise in this area. This new group
struggled to reach consensus and in September 1979 sought to
abandon their efforts. They cited four reasons for their failure:

the difficult nature of the issue, the timing of the discussions, philosophical differences, and difficulties working together ("National Coal Policy . . . ," 1981, p. 17). Urged by the plenary group to try again, in March 1980 they produced a draft agreement proposing improvements to the federal land management program recently promulgated by the Department of the Interior. The draft was given a cool reception, however, since it was released before the new regulations had been tested.

Air Pollution Task Force

Concurrent with the NCPP's efforts to reach consensus, Congress was deliberating amendments to the Clean Air Act. The NCPP, therefore, initially directed its attention to topics outside this purview. For example, the Air Pollution Task Force made two recommendations on power plant siting. The Federal Coal-Fired Powerplant Siting Act was a direct result of these recommendations. It reflected a compromise beneficial to both sides, for which power plant siting had become a costly and time-consuming activity. The bill required a quicker decision by federal agencies on siting decisions and provided "intervener funding" to assist interest groups that could not afford the costs of participating in the hearing process.

A second bill, based directly on recommendations from the Air Pollution Task Force, was an amendment to the Clean Air Act that sought to encourage innovation in air-pollution-control technology by allowing the EPA to grant variances for the use of experimental emissions-control technology. It also proposed an emissions charge plan to improve air quality in areas that did not currently meet EPA's standards.

The task force's influence on other regulatory decisions is less easily verifiable. For example, several proposals endorsed by the task force were conceptually consistent with subsequent positions taken by EPA and the National Commission on Air Quality.

During Phase II, the Air Pollution Task Force tackled several issues previously tabled because during Phase I Congress was considering them as part of the Clean Air Act amendments. No recommendations emerged from Phase II, however, since the proposal favored by task force members generated substantial political and technological opposition among their constituencies.

Fuel Utilization and Conservation Task Force

The initial work of this task force was directed to general themes that characterized the NCPP's general views on coal use, namely, conservation, limited expansion of coal use in the United States as an intermediate step toward use of sustainable resources, and selective government intervention. The task force also supported the role of the federal government in basic and applied research into new coal technologies.

During Phase II members from the Fuel Utilization Committee and the Energy Pricing Committee merged to form the Cogeneration Task Force. (Cogeneration is a process for producing usable heat energy along with mechanical or electrical energy.) The impact of this task force can be directly observed in the regulations for cogeneration promulgated by the Federal Energy Regulatory Commission (FERC). FERC invited members of the Cogeneration Task Force to provide input into standards it eventually promulgated to regulate cogeneration.

Transportation Task Force

Several recommendations stressing the theme of competitiveness among transportation modes were developed by this task force. Among them were that waterway user charges should be imposed based on the full costs of operation, maintenance, repair, and construction of the waterways, that federal subsidies to inefficient railroads should be ended, and that truckers should be charged for environmental damage in addition to highway wear and tear. These recommendations generated major opposition from those transportation interests that were not part of the NCPP; understandably, the recommendations were not implemented in any subsequent legislation or rulemaking.

Participants' Reactions

The NCPP's ability to promote change in the participants' attitudes and behaviors was highly touted by the project director.

"Our success at reaching agreements exceeded our most optimistic expectations" (Personal Communication with Frank Murray, May 31, 1984). Many participants reported changing their
perceptions of their adversaries as a result of participating in the
project. John Corcoran of Consolidation Coal recalled that before the NCPP, "I knew few environmentalists and I came to the
judgment that they were all misguided" ("Industry, Activists
...," 1978). Environmentalists and industry representatives
both publicly agreed that their original perceptions of the
other side were founded on inaccurate stereotypes and that this
realization made it easier for them to work together toward
consensus.

Longer-Term Impact

The NCPP also inspired two proposals in Congress in 1980 for
creating regulatory negotiation commissions. These regulatory
commissions, charged with advising governmental agencies on
the development of federal regulations, would be composed of
representatives of interest groups with a stake in the issues under consideration. The advice would represent a consensus developed by relevant interest groups using a collaborative process
like that of the NCPP. Hearings on the bills were held by the
Ninety-sixth Congress. Subsequently, the Regulatory Mediation
Act of 1981 was introduced with similar intent to the earlier
bills. While none of this legislation was enacted, it did contribute to a dialogue about negotiated rulemaking that culminated
in an endorsement of the practice by the Administrative Law
Conference in 1985. Several U.S. regulatory agencies (including
EPA, OSHA, FAA, and the Federal Trade Commission) have
subsequently made use of negotiated rulemaking. (See Chapter
Nine for a review of these efforts at collaboration.)

Analysis: Political Dynamics of the NCPP

In this section three political dynamics of the NCPP are examined in detail. These dynamics represent generic issues that are
likely to characterize any collaborative effort, and especially
those in which public policy issues are being considered.

Politics of Selecting Participants

The NCPP's conveners defined the domain of their collaboration quite broadly. It included many aspects of U.S. coal policy, including recovery (mining and land reclamation), transportation (including coal slurries), and usage (including effects on
air quality and electricity costs). For each of these specific areas
there were specialists among environmental and industry organizations as well as other organizations that had a stake in one or
more of the issues under consideration. Rather than including
the wider set of stakeholders, however, the NCPP conveners
elected to restrict their group to environmental and industry
participants. These decisions were made largely to enhance the
possibility of demonstrating that these two groups could reach
accommodation. Recognizing that such decisions might limit the
impact of any forthcoming recommendations, the conveners decided to accept this trade-off in order to demonstrate solidarity.

The experience of the NCPP's Transportation Task Force
illustrates many of the issues involved in drawing the boundaries
of a project and choosing from a wide set of stakeholders. As
noted earlier in the section on selection of participants, limitations were consciously placed on the diversity of the industry
representatives seated on this committee. The reason given for
this, according to the industry cochair of the task force, was
that too much diversity would prevent any possibility of a consensus. As it turned out, however, although agreements were
reached among task force members, their likelihood of garnering widespread support among those affected by them was slim.
For example, the task force agreed that waterway user charges
be imposed based on the full costs of operation, maintenance,
repair, and construction of the waterways; that federal subsidies
to inefficient railroads be ended; and that trucks be charged for
both environmental damage and road wear. No doubt these
agreements reached by the Transportation Task Force would
have been hotly contested by transportation industry stakeholders had they been invited. It is also plausible that consideration
of their viewpoints might have resulted in other constructive
solutions with better chances for implementation had the transportation interests been granted a place at the table initially.

The politics of stakeholder selection also become apparent in the decision to exclude representatives of the UMW from the NCPP. When the conveners reconsidered the selection of stakeholders several months after the project's inception, they decided not to include the UMW, whose leaders at that time were absorbed in internal problems and had little time to participate. Because the UMW, a powerful stakeholder, was absent, NCPP conveners chose to avoid considering such issues as mine safety and health for which the miners' contribution to discussions would be essential. Louise Dunlap, of the Environmental Policy Center, argued, however, that the union had a stake in other coal-related issues the NCPP did address. As a result, the EPC challenged the legitimacy of the negotiations in the absence of the mine workers and refused to support the NCPP's recommendations.

NCPP conveners also traded off political and administrative considerations when deciding whether to include representatives of the federal government as participants. Although the conveners recognized that Congress and the regulatory agencies would be more likely to implement the NCPP's recommendations if government officials were involved from the outset, the NCPP ultimately elected to proceed without them.

The conveners believed that high-ranking government officials would not attend and that their designees would not have sufficient power as stakeholders to warrant their full participation. A compromise was struck in which government representatives were invited as observers rather than as decision makers in an effort to keep lines of communication with the agencies open.

Overall, the act of limiting the boundaries of the NCPP was fraught with politics. The final decisions effectively restricted some legitimate stakeholders from participating and raised questions about the validity and strength of the consensus recommendations.

Questions about political legitimacy also surfaced with respect to one of the NCPP's conveners. While industrialist Decker and environmentalist Moss were able to persuade many stakeholders to come to the table, skepticism about Moss was voiced by some who elected not to participate. Louise Dunlap cited

both Moss's lack of familiarity with coal issues and his inability
to be unbiased during the negotiations as reasons for the EPC's
boycott of the project.

Role of Power in Stakeholders' Decisions to Participate

There were indications at the time of the NCPP's inception that
power differences among the key stakeholders influenced their
willingness to come to the table.

> Clearly much of the motivation for the industrialists to
> participate comes from an awareness that industry has
> been kept on the defensive in the federal and state legis-
> latures and in the courts. "We've lost almost every battle
> on Capitol Hill," (Jerry) Decker says, overstating the case
> but indicating accurately enough the general drift of
> things [Carter, 1977, p. 278].

Some environmentalists, on the other hand, preferred the traditional congressional hearing process over the alternative forum
provided by the NCPP, because environmentalists believed they
had the upper hand in the former arena. The Natural Resources
Defense Council, for example, chose to boycott the NCPP, preferring to apply their limited resources to battles in traditional
arenas where they felt confident of success. Louise Dunlap justified the EPC's boycott on several grounds, including the need to
speak for a wide constituency that was not adequately represented in the NCPP. This constituency included farmers, ranch-
ers, Indians, and other groups for whom the EPC provided a
voice in Congress. As a lobbying arm for many grass-roots environmental groups, the EPC was unwilling to relinquish the access
and agenda power they had gained in the legislative arena and
that they believed was working to their advantage. They viewed
the NCPP as an attempt by the industrialists to regain power
lost in the traditional legislative arena.

Timing also played a role in some environmentalists' decisions not to participate. Several of the issues on the NCPP's
agenda had recently been addressed in the legislative arena (for

example, amendments to the Clean Air Act), and these groups, arguing the legitimacy of the legislative process, were unwilling to submit certain issues for reconsideration. According to Louise Dunlap, "It was presumptuous for the Coal Policy Project to go off to one side to develop a so-called consensus at a time when Congress had already been working for six years on one" (Alexander, 1978, p. 102). Thus EPC resisted collaborative interventions that it perceived were designed to balance power among the stakeholders in order to preserve its individual control over the domain.

Power of Project to Influence Domain

For the NCPP to implement its consensus, the participants had to persuade Congress and several regulatory agencies administering policies governing coal use (particularly the Office of Surface Mining within the Department of the Interior) to adopt the NCPP's approximately two hundred recommendations. To accomplish this the NCPP needed to mobilize a strong coalition of stakeholders to lobby for its recommendations. For several reasons, however, it was unable to do so.

The NCPP did not adequately consider the environment in which its consensus building was taking place. This is probably because the NCPP was conceived as an experiment and was never intended to be a wholesale substitution for traditional policymaking. However, once the NCPP's designers decided to implement the agreements that were reached, they overestimated their own role in the interconnected web of agencies dealing with coal policy and underestimated the inertia of the Congress, the Department of the Interior, and the courts, which were already embroiled in coal issues. They did not anticipate how dependent their own efforts were on the established policymaking apparatus and were not prepared to implement their consensus in this political environment.

The exclusion of key stakeholders was another reason for the NCPP's implementation problems. Clearly the recommendations of the Transportation Task Force would have been more favorably received had the affected interest groups participated in drafting the recommendations. In hindsight the project sponsors acknowledged the costs of the trade-off they made: "[The Transportation Task Force experience] proved to be an interesting lesson. Although the approach made the search for agreement much easier, it severely complicated the implementation efforts" (Murray and Curran, 1982, p. 16).

The NCPP's decision to limit government participation to observation also hampered implementation of certain agreements, particularly those directed to the Office of Surface Mining. Clearly the NCPP did not establish productive linkages with OSM. Agency officials were not invited to participate and perceived the NCPP as an intrusion on OSM's rule-making authority. A new article at the time reported: "At the Department of Interior there has already been some grumbling about the mining task force's recommendations, which are regarded as an intrusion by an unaccountable elite into already settled issues" (Alexander, 1978, p. 102). The shift from a Democratic to a Republican administration in 1980 further weakened any ties to OSM. While some subsequent actions by the agency were consistent with the NCPP's recommendations, OSM never credited the NCPP's influence on any of these decisions.

Questions of representativeness also plagued the NCPP's influence attempts. Although ostensibly the NCPP's members were selected because of their institutional affiliations, it was informally understood that they did not speak for those organizations. Member acceptance of the NCPP's recommendations did not constitute organizational commitment to them. As a result, some participants were unable to enlist their organizations' backing for the recommendations. Other organizations privately endorsed the recommendations but were reluctant to do so publicly. They were willing to experiment with consensus building but shied away from a more visible public posture.

As the legitimacy of the "representatives" was questioned, the strength of the consensus was undermined. This occurred for two reasons. First, efforts to get constituents on board sometimes led to considerable delays and objections to the agreements forged in the task forces. In Phase II, the Air Pollution Task Force was unable to overcome objections to its proposals from within the members' own organizations. As a result, no agreement was publicized. A second reason for the NCPP's consensus to be undermined was that observers questioned just how robust the agreements were when public support for them was not forthcoming from the constituent organizations. The NCPP was vulnerable to accusations of not having its own house in order.

Finally, efforts to implement the NCPP's recommendations were also severely constrained by the failure of many outside the project to accept it as a legitimate forum for resolving the disputed issues. Early decisions as to the inclusion and exclusion of stakeholders facilitated the achievement of a consensus but restricted the perceived legitimacy of the project at the policy implementation phase. Not surprisingly, environmental groups that had declined to participate publicly opposed the recommendations, charging that the participating environmentalists had "sold out" on issues such as the high walls around strip mines.

Coping with Political Dynamics

In many ways the NCPP provides a worst-case scenario about the political dynamics associated with collaboration, and many have learned from its failures. Nonetheless, by its very nature (the fact that parties are interdependent) collaboration evokes political dynamics. These dynamics must be recognized and managed if effective consensus building is to ensue. Preliminary analysis of conflicts needs to consider the relative distribution of power. Third parties can play pivotal roles in helping the parties to appreciate each other's power and to direct this power toward constructive solutions. For example, developers may underestimate the ingenuity and perseverance of local residents in blocking a proposed project and in initiating a lawsuit if necessary. "Decision makers often leap to conclusions about their ability to force a decision on their adversaries only to be confronted by unexpected difficulties that confound orderly plans and progressively increase costs" (Carpenter and Kennedy, 1988, p. 217). In cases like this, third parties can anticipate the potential leverage the other side can exert and ensure both parties of the opportunity for influence at the table. Alternately, power may be unilaterally controlled by one side (for example, when a developer has satisfied all zoning requirements, permits are approved, and time is not an issue) (Susskind and Cruikshank, 1987). Under these circumstances a third party can assist other stakeholders to make a realistic appraisal of the futility of initiating a collaboration.

7

Fostering
Collaborative Outcomes:
A Mediator's Role

Blessed are the peacemakers for they shall be called the
children of God.
—New Testament
Matthew 5:5

Mediation as a Distinct Third-Party Role

Not every multiparty collaboration requires the services of a
third party in order to reach a successful agreement among the
stakeholders. In fact, most multiparty collaborations are managed without the assistance of a third party. However, third parties can assist the parties in a number of critical ways during all
three stages of a collaboration, and many times mediators have
made the difference between success and failure in achieving a
settlement. In this chapter specific tasks that third parties play
to assist a collaboration are described and some general observa-
tions about third-party intervention are offered.

Types of Third Parties

Before elaborating the specific roles of third parties for collaborative initiatives, it is important to draw distinctions among several general types of third parties. The term *third party* generally
connotes a variety of roles including judge, arbitrator, fact finder, mediator, and facilitator. Generally, third parties play important roles in shaping conflicts and their outcomes (Boje and
Wolfe, 1988; Kolb, 1983; Gross and Greenfield, 1986; Mather
and Yngvesson, 1980–81). However, there are important dis-

tinctions in the roles and procedures third parties use to intervene in disputes. Judges and arbitrators ultimately render a decision on the merits of the case presented by the disputants. They follow formal procedures (for example, rules for the introduction of evidence) and rely on a body of legal precedent to guide their decisions. Their job is to decide the substantive issues in a dispute, and their decisions are binding on the parties. In fact finding the procedures for presentation of evidence and deciding the merits of the case are usually more informal, and the fact finder's decision is often only advisory and not binding on the parties. In all three roles, however, the procedures vest the third parties with the obligation to impose or offer (in the case of fact finders) a solution. The third party makes a decision for the disputants.

Mediation operates on a very different premise. The mediator has no power to render a decision or to impose a solution. Instead, the mediator helps the parties themselves to work out their differences and to construct a mutually acceptable solution. In fact, if the mediator attempts to impose a solution, that puts his or her power to settle the dispute in jeopardy because one source of their power to extract an agreement is to threaten the possibility of a less desirable solution should the mediation fail (Touval and Zartman, 1985). Parties voluntarily elect mediation because they believe they can advance their interests in some way through the process (Touval and Zartman, 1985; Gulliver, 1979), but they are not bound by any decision reached.

The process by which the mediation is conducted is in the hands of the mediators.

> Mediators have procedural flexibility not available to judges or to decision makers who function in a quasi-judicial capacity. They need not to be concerned with prohibitions against ex parte communications, with supervising the formation of a record or with other formalities which would prohibit or impair confidential relationships with the parties and would inhibit settlement efforts. A mediator may adopt procedures or

methods of operation which meet the needs of each situation, and may alter those procedures if the need arises [McCrory, 1981, p. 56].

Processes differ considerably from case to case, particularly when there are multiple parties involved. Studies of mediation have found that mediators, too, vary in their style of operation. In a study of federal compared to state mediators (Kolb, 1983), the former assumed a hands-off role, allowing the parties to formulate their own decisions. They were characterized as "orchestrators." The state mediators, in contrast, who adopt a more proactive role in proposing agreements, were described as "dealmakers."

Facilitators represent still another type of third party. The primary role of a facilitator is to assist parties to have a constructive dialogue. Facilitators usually help groups set an agenda and manage the process of the discussion. Facilitators have been usefully engaged as "traffic cops" for public meetings on controversial subjects. For example, facilitators help the parties to recognize how their own styles of interacting or the institutional prejudices that they embody may interfere with constructive problem solving. Here the objective is to promote understanding among the parties. Additionally, facilitators may propose a series of process steps to keep the discussion on target. Facilitators may also explicitly help parties find a mutually agreeable solution to a dispute.

In multiparty collaborations, a third party can be anyone acceptable to the disputing parties who is brought in to help them communicate more constructively and to resolve their differences. Generally speaking, the third party's role is to assist the stakeholders in getting to the table, in exploring their differences constructively, and in reaching an acceptable agreement. To accomplish this the third party may serve either as a mediator or as a facilitator. Third parties in multiparty collaborations are concerned with establishing a context within which the parties can constructively confront their problems and take responsibility for solving them. This last point is especially important, since an agreement to collaborate involves the "explicit recogni-

tion that the parties are willing to work toward an agreement"
(McCarthy, 1984, p. 4), and that they themselves will construct
the details of that agreement. Third-party efforts are directed
toward influencing the process of the collaborating rather than
toward exerting influence over the substantive outcome of the
negotiations. "One of the significant problems frequently faced
by mediators . . . is that adversaries mistake their procedural
problems for substantive ones" (Patton, 1981, p. 8). Adversaries
are often locked into firm positions because bargaining is structured to encourage such outcomes, thereby narrowing the range
of options. Mediation offers a change in the process. By focusing on interests, different ways of constructing the problem and
choices for dealing with it become available to the parties. A
wider field of choices increases the likelihood of agreement
(Fisher, 1978).

For ease of presentation throughout this chapter, the
term *mediator* will be used to describe the third-party role in
collaborations.

Leverage of the Mediator

Ostensibly, a mediator enters a collaboration to help the parties
arrive at an agreement they cannot conceive of, construct, or
execute on their own. In addition to believing that collaboration will advance their interests, parties must see value to themselves in third-party intervention. At a minimum, parties must
conclude that the mediator will enhance their ability to reach
agreement and that their opponents will not gain an advantage
from mediation. Often, stakeholders have much loftier beliefs
about the mediator's impact. Disputant motives for agreeing to
a mediator in international disputes, for example, are quite explicit. They include:

1. the desire to save face (by making concessions through the
    third party)
2. the potential of averting an internal crisis (for example, by
    choosing military escalation or retreat)
3. the belief that the mediator will promote their interests

4. the desire for normative approval
5. the prospect of winning the mediator's favor (for exam-
    ple, in subsequent interactions) (Touval and Zartman,
    1985)

Mediators, too, are typically not totally disinterested
parties. To a lesser or greater degree, depending on the issues
under consideration and the scope of the conflict, mediators
also have something to gain from participating (Gulliver, 1979;
Touval and Zartman, 1985; Smith, 1985). Mediator motivations
are perhaps clearest in international disputes, when the number
of possible candidates who can serve in a mediative role is severely limited and the mediator is representing powerful national
or organizational interests. Mediators in these disputes are either
major powers, medium states, or coalitional organizations (such
as the Commonwealth of Nations, the Organization of African
Unity, or the United Nations) or humanitarian organizations
(such as the International Committee of the Red Cross). While
the motives of these mediators vary, Touval and Zartman (1985)
argue convincingly that mediators' interests (whether to avoid
external influence in a region, to prevent expansionist moves by
another superpower, or to strengthen their relationship with
one of the parties) are primary to their motivation to mediate
and to their ability to exercise leverage in the situation. For example, Algeria's success at freeing the U.S. hostages held by Iran
in 1979 is attributed to Algeria's close relationship with the
Ayatollah Khomeni regime in Iran and to Algeria's desire to
curry favor with the United States, who had an interest in another dispute involving Algeria and Morocco (Touval and Zartman, 1985).

The stakes for the mediator in other disputes may not be
nearly so critical when they do not involve national interests.
Still, they are worth examining. A mediator may be interested
in establishing precedents for how certain disputes get settled or
in advancing her or his professional reputation. The key point to
emphasize for collaboration is that selection of a mediator is
also a political activity. The power to mediate is derived, at least
in part, from the mediator's affiliations and particular interests.

The success of the mediator, then, hinges on the ability to influence each of the parties in the collaboration and on the parties'
willingness to be influenced by the mediator's actions.

Tasks of the Mediator

There are certain tasks and skills that enhance a mediator's ability to move parties toward agreement. Mediators vary in their
personal styles, particularly in the extent to which they actively
participate during negotiating sessions (Gulliver, 1979; Kolb,
1983). The following are several tasks that mediators can be expected to perform.

- assessing overall readiness to collaborate
    determining interest of parties
    assessing self-interest
- getting the parties to the table
    exerting leverage
    heightening awareness of costs of stalemate
    creating standards of fairness
- minimizing resistance
    creating a safe climate
    displaying empathy
- ensuring effective representation
    ensuring appropriate stakeholders participate
    assisting less organized stakeholders to select a representa-
        tive
- establishing a climate of trust
    dampening or removing violent interactions
    establishing and enforcing ground rules
- modeling openness, optimism, and perseverance
- designing and managing the negotiation process
- managing data
- getting consensus
    transmitting information
    reproposing concessions
    formulating solutions
    highlighting consequences of nonagreement

Mediators' roles will depend on the phase at which they enter the collaboration and the degree of overt hostility exhibited.

Assessing Overall Readiness to Collaborate

Before a mediator agrees to work with the parties, he or she must carefully assess the state of the dispute. This assessment, conducted during the problem-setting phase, includes identification of the stakeholders in the dispute, their incentives for pursuing a negotiated settlement, external pressures bearing on the dispute, including the need for a timely resolution, the political context of the dispute, and the parties' expectations about winning and losing and alternatives to a negotiated settlement. The mediator conducts this analysis through individual conversations with all of the stakeholders as well as other nonparties who are familiar with the dispute and can offer a disinterested view (Carpenter and Kennedy, 1988). Secondary source materials (such as newspaper articles, radio and television stories, and published reports) also provide background for the controversy.

An important characteristic of the mediator is the ability to absorb a great deal of information, often of a very technical nature, that is relevant to the dispute. The mediator must be able to develop a basic understanding of this information and be sufficiently conversant in it to recognize and call attention to subtle differences between the parties that may offer windows for agreement. This familiarity is also key to a mediator's ability to envision possible new options and potential trade-offs that the parties, because of their vested interests, cannot see or are unwilling to put forward for fear of losing face with constituents or a wider audience.

The purpose of this inquiry is to assess whether or not the conflict is negotiable and whether the parties are amenable to mediation. Frequently, after talking with several parties, the mediator will conclude that mediation is not appropriate or feasible under the circumstances. If one party is certain of victory in court, for example, that party will reject mediation. Mediation would also be inappropriate if one party wanted to use it as a delay tactic. After listening closely to the parties, the mediator must make a judgment about the ripeness of the dispute for mediation. Frequently, the parties themselves reject mediation. In a study of eighty-one environmental mediation cases, only 30 percent of the parties agreed to proceed with mediation after the initial inquiry (Buckle and Thomas-Buckle, 1986, p. 61). Interestingly, better than half of the nonmediated cases were resolved among the parties themselves without resort to litigation.

Getting Parties to the Table

The mediator often plays a pivotal role in getting the parties to sit down and explore the issues. The mediator may do this in conjunction with the convener or, in some cases, instead of a convener. The success of the mediator in getting people to the table turns in large measure on issues of leverage discussed earlier. It also depends on the mediator's ability to establish a climate of trust and the perception among the parties that the process will be fair. Success also depends on a realistic appraisal by the parties of the costs of not resolving the conflict. The mediator actively encourages this kind of appraisal by asking the parties about their goals and their likelihood of realization and by providing a reality check that helps the parties appreciate the constraints imposed by the other stakeholders. In cases of stalemate, communication has often so substantially deteriorated, or hostility is running so high, that the mediator may have to conduct several rounds of shuttle diplomacy before the parties will agree to meet face to face. Here the challenge to the mediator is to persuade the parties that they will be worse off by not participating. This may require continued bilateral interaction with each stakeholder or proactive attempts by the mediator to stimulate a perception of need for mediation among the parties by obviating the advantages of unilateral actions (Smith, 1985) and/or enhancing the perceptions of all parties that stalemate offers the least promising outcome (Touval and Zartman, 1985).

Minimizing Resistance

Parties in conflict often are influenced by strong unconscious factors that inhibit their ability to effectively participate in a collaboration. These are behaviors that may be psychological or cultural in origin. In either case, they interfere with effective communication between the stakeholders, increase emotional and seemingly irrational reactions, and generally thwart constructive problem solving. Because they are so deeply engrained in behavior and are typically unconscious, psychological and cultural factors often become sources of considerable resistance that parties are virtually helpless to change by themselves. Under the added stress that overt conflict induces, these factors can become so intractable that parties see no hope of resolution. When this occurs, parties are usually wrestling with internal conflicts provoked by the external situation (Harding, 1965; Folberg and Taylor, 1984).

Mediators can play a powerful role in recognizing and taking steps to ameliorate these blocks to communication that arise during collaboration. The primary role of the mediator in these situations is to legitimize the concerns by providing an empathic ear. "By calming accepting and reflecting the unacceptable perception or the real goal . . . , the mediator can normalize and relax the defense system of participants and elicit their help and cooperation" (Folberg and Taylor, 1984, p. 91).

Mediation, however, is not therapy, so the mediator must also help the parties move beyond the resistance. There are several ways that this can be done, including (1) asking the parties to state the conditions under which they could comfortably participate, (2) asking the parties to offer improvements to a proposed agreement, (3) coupling several issues together in a way that allows the resister to achieve one of his or her most desired outcomes (Moore, 1986), (4) arriving at agreements in principle to govern subsequent negotiations (Moore, 1986), and (5) reviewing the negative consequences of not reaching an agreement. Some of these tactics reveal additional interests that had not previously surfaced but are central to reaching agreement. Others allow the resister to gain a keener appreciation of what is to be gained through collaboration. (For a more detailed discussion of specific psychological forms of resistance and how to cope with them, see Folberg and Taylor [1984] and Schein [1979]. Overcoming institutional and cultural barriers is addressed further in Chapter Eleven.)

Ensuring Effective Representation

When there is no formal mechanism for convening the stake-holders, the mediator can assist the convener to structure a fo-rum and catalyze commitments to participate. In complex nego-tiations involving many parties or in situations in which some stakeholders are not well organized, the mediator may need to work with individual groups of stakeholders to help them estab-lish effective representation in such a forum. Since participation by legitimate stakeholders is a critical aspect of collaboration, special care must be taken to ensure that representation is com-prehensive and fair. Deciding how many representatives of each stakeholder type is often a bit tricky. In federal regulatory nego-tiations to establish maximum exposure levels for a toxic chemi-cal, for example, hundreds of business firms may be affected. In such cases, mediators can help to sort out those with differing interests and make sure that each group is seated. In one case, for example, 95 percent of firms in an industry felt adequately represented in a negotiation by the industry's trade association, while several small firms (about 5 percent) had significantly dif-ferent concerns. The issue of representation was resolved by seating one representative of the large companies and one from the smaller firms. The trade association did not participate di-rectly in the negotiations. It is important to note that the num-ber of representatives from each interest is not critical, since consensus decision making ensures that "a group with one rep-resentative can block agreements as easily as a group with three" (Carpenter and Kennedy, 1988, p. 104).

Some interest groups mobilize almost overnight in re-sponse to a proposed new development or discovery of a local environmental hazard. These groups may need assistance from the mediator to "get organized." This means clarifying their in-terests and choosing an effective representative. For statewide issues, the problem may be coordinating the many local groups into a common voice. Here again the mediator may convene these groups, help them identify and work through internal con-flicts, and prioritize their major interests. Helping the parties to draft clear opening statements for the first meeting can be a constructive intervention (McCarthy, 1984). Mediators can also assist groups in identifying a spokesperson and designing a process for information exchange with the nonparticipating groups. In one case, the mediator helped the parties secure foundation support to hire an information coordinator (Carpenter, 1988).

Establishing a Climate of Trust

A key role of mediation is establishing a climate of trust in which the parties can feel safe enough to explore their differences candidly and civilly. Mediator characteristics such as empathy, patience, self-assurance, ingenuity, and stamina (Zartman and Berman, 1982) go a long way toward fostering the necessary environment of psychological safety.

Openness to ideas and to the parties themselves is also a key trait of mediators.

> The mediator should express willingness to discuss any aspect of the dispute at virtually any time. This sense of availability is a signal to the negotiators that the mediator is genuinely concerned with the issues and encourages the free flow of information necessary for productive negotiations [McCarthy, 1984, p. 41].

Mediators serve as role models for the participants in this regard and in managing the negotiation process generally. Modeling openness and building in safeguards to ensure openness are important to ensure good-faith negotiations.

Designing and Managing a Process

It is difficult for parties who are embroiled in a dispute to be objective enough to analyze how they are conducting their negotiations. Yet their hard-fought efforts to protect their substantive interests may be counterproductive. Mediators can help parties structure a process that protects their interests but still advances the negotiations. This involves carefully designing and managing meeting dynamics.

Within Meetings. One way mediators can help to design a constructive process is to establish an agenda for each meeting and insist that it is followed unless the entire group agrees to modify it.

> Agreement on the topical order of discussion not only symbolizes the willingness of all parties to be reasonable and to work conscientiously toward settlement, it also assures the participants that issues of particular significance will be included in the negotiations [McCarthy, 1984, p. 41].

Mediators also insist on ground rules, because these provide a self-regulating framework for the negotiations and allow the parties to accept ownership for the process. Mediators often propose sample ground rules, but ultimately the parties must adopt rules for themselves. Enforcing the ground rules is a task shared by the mediator and the parties, although often when an infraction occurs, the mediator is in a better position to reprimand the offender than are any of the other parties, who may fear alienating another stakeholder. In enacting this "enunciator" role, mediators remind parties of the moral community to which they belong and call attention to unspoken or unclear shared assumptions (Gulliver, 1979, p. 223).

The design of a mediated negotiation includes time for everyone to express interests clearly. Throughout this discussion the mediator is working to support the legitimate interests of all the parties by ensuring that air time is fairly distributed and by deferring discussion of solutions until all the parties have had a chance to present their interests. The mediator also encourages the parties to question any of her or his actions that do not appear to be neutral. Carpenter and Kennedy (1988, p. 124) describe this step as "educating the parties," because each party has the responsibility to orient the others to his or her concerns.

Another step in managing the process is encouraging the exploration of options. Here the mediator's role is not to propose options but to ensure that multiple options are on the table (Fisher and Ury, 1981). The mediator can propose several techniques for generating options such as adding issues, packaging issues, logrolling, alternation, trading on the time value of money, and use of contingency agreements (Fisher and Ury, 1981; Pruitt and Lewis, 1977; Moore, 1986; Susskind and Cruikshank, 1987). Using small groups for brainstorming and for drafting preliminary proposals is also an effective technique. Mediators can also promote agreements by finessing a party's move from an entrenched position. Because they are not as deeply invested in a particular outcome, mediators can often get away with suggestions that would not be trusted had they been put forth by other parties to the dispute (Rubin and Brown, 1975).

Another key task of third parties is to ensure that different perceptions of risk are considered legitimate and to steer the discussion toward identification of common values by which to judge the options proposed. Mediators also play an effective role in keeping the parties on track and may even interject additional options for consideration. In the case where the mediator is granted status as a special master by the court, the mediator has authority to ensure that negotiations take place and that the necessary information is provided by the various parties. Technically skilled mediators can ensure that the decision reached satisfies technical standards as well as the interests of all the parties.

Whether or not mediators should influence the substantive aspects of collaboration is a disputable issue among scholars and practitioners. Clearly, the practice of mediation runs the gamut from passive to very active roles (Gulliver, 1979). "Dealmakers," for example, are closely involved in making substantive proposals, whereas orchestrators are more passive (Kolb, 1983). Some practitioners argue that mediators must resist temptations to influence the substantive outcome of the dispute. "For many professional mediators this is a difficult role to play. Many of them have extensive knowledge about the substance of the dispute; this means they are likely to have personal feelings about what will work and what will not. Their previous mediation experience, furthermore, may tempt them to 'steer' the negotiations toward solutions that have proven successful in the past" (Susskind and Cruikshank, 1987, p. 163). Ultimately, however, whether the mediator can or should actively shape the outcome will be a function of the mediator's power and how willing the stakeholders are to be influenced by it. Undue influence by any stakeholder (including a mediator) is likely to produce an unsatisfactory and fragile agreement.

Between Meetings. Much of a mediator's job is conducted behind the scenes and in between formal meetings. After each session the mediator contacts each of the parties to review progress and to invite comment on the process and on proposals currently on the table. These contacts allow the parties to express reservations or concerns they do not feel comfortable raising in the negotiating sessions. Often the mediator serves as a conduit for transmitting private messages among the parties between meetings (Susskind and Cruikshank, 1987). Often parties will reveal to a mediator much more candid information than they are willing to present to the other parties. While the mediator must be careful not to breach trust, he or she can sometimes present trial ideas or offer hypothetical circumstances to stimulate a new proposal from one party that the mediator knows the others will likely accept. Carpenter and Kennedy (1988, pp. 165–168) note the following additional activities for mediators between meetings: clarifying perceptions of the parties' moves and proposals, testing ideas, communicating new information, and preparing for subsequent meetings.

Managing Data

For disputes that turn on very technical information and involve the use of proprietary data, the mediator can perform several other useful tasks for the parties. For example, a mediator may provide a critical function as a repository for confidential or proprietary information. In this role, the mediator stipulates to the other parties that the necessary data have been provided and certifies whether they satisfy whatever predetermined criteria have been established.

Where data are not proprietary but parties disagree about

the validity of scientific findings, the mediator can help to structure a constructive process for exploring the technical basis of the dispute. "The mediators must take particular care to ensure that the negotiators do not become captive audiences to competing experts" (Riesel, 1985, p. 110). These concerns can be addressed by identifying experts acceptable to all parties or arranging a questions-and-answer session with a panel of experts chosen by the parties. The intent of these queries is not to pit one expert against the other but to permit the parties to establish a base of scientific data on which they can confidently construct solutions. Where expert projections on the extent of contamination differ, for example, the parties may agree to a minimum acceptable range rather than to a specific level.

Getting Consensus

A critical function of a mediator in getting consensus is listening for, identifying, and reintroducing agreements in principle. Frequently negotiators miss subtle shifts in position by other parties or do not appreciate the full import of an option on the table. Because the mediator is keenly aware of each of the parties' interests, he or she can sometimes spot opportunities for agreement that elude the parties' attention. These can be reproposed in tentative fashion by the mediator and adopted by the parties as agreements in principle. These agreements provide general guidelines within which a more detailed final agreement is constructed (Moore, 1986). For example, in the Franklin Township dispute in Chapter One, the developer and the horse people reached an agreement in principle that the developer would provide access for the riders to the state game lands. The specific path of the access was worked out later.

In the final stages of the negotiations, acceptance of the agreements may require the representatives to be able to "sell the agreement back home." Gaining agreement from constituents is frequently slow and frustrating, and last-minute requests for changes can disrupt a carefully crafted agreement. Anticipating these pitfalls, a mediator can urge parties to communicate with their constituents throughout the negotiations and enlist the other parties' help to anticipate and respond to constituents' objections. Mediators may also be called in to help manage meetings between representatives and their constituents if ratification by those groups does not go smoothly.

On some occasions, the mediator may have concerns about the wisdom or the fairness of the final agreement. Whether or not to introduce these concerns raises an ethical dilemma for the mediator. Ultimately, the mediator's decision will depend on the mediator's own values and contact with the parties. Some mediators feel strongly that they are obligated to question the validity of an agreement that appears exploitative or unworkable (Susskind and Cruikshank, 1987; Susskind, 1981). Others claim that the responsibility for judging the quality of the agreement rests wholly with the parties.

Mediators as Midwives and Myth Makers

Two images, those of midwife and myth maker, offer useful conceptualizations of a mediator's role in the collaborative process. The mediator as midwife conveys the idea that a birthing process is under way. The "baby" in this case is an agreement among the parties. The mediator assists in the delivery process by providing guidance in the appropriate techniques and by offering comfort and support to the parties.

The notion of mediator as myth maker acknowledges that the mediator plays an active role in shaping the parties' interpretation of the dispute and in introducing new ways of understanding the problem domain (Boje and Wolfe, 1988). Exploring idealized futures and reframing the problem to incorporate multiple interests cause alternative images of a problem to emerge. These images, or myths, serve as guideposts for reorganizing the domain. Mediators can create a climate and a process that legitimize the search for new myths.

8

Collaborative Designs
for Solving Shared Problems

*There is one person that is wiser than anybody, and that is
everybody.*

$\qquad$ —*Talleyrand*

Designs for collaborating vary with the circumstances they are
intended to address. While collaborative efforts generally proceed through the three generic phases described earlier (problem
setting, direction setting, and implementation), specific applications differ according to the nature of the problems under consideration and the intended outcome. Some are primarily motivated by competitive pressures, others out of the need to improve
on administrative procedures for regulatory rulemaking, others
because of delays and costs associated with traditional adjudication, and still others as responses to growing urban problems. In
this chapter a framework is presented for classifying different
designs for collaboration. Illustrations and process issues unique
to each design are examined in detail in this chapter and in
Chapter Nine.

Four General Designs for Collaboration

Problems for which collaboration offers a constructive alternative can be conceptualized along two dimensions: the factors
motivating the parties to collaborate and the type of outcome
expected. The motivating factors were described briefly in
Chapter One. Stakeholders are motivated by the desire to advance a shared vision or by the desire to resolve a conflict. Out-

177

comes include the exchange of information or the construction of joint agreements. The agreements may stand alone or may be in the form of recommendations to an authorizing body (such as a legislature or administrative agency). Figure 2 presents a framework for classifying collaborative designs using the two dimensions of motivating factors and expected outcomes. Four general designs for collaboration are identified: (1) appreciative planning, (2) collective strategies, (3) dialogues, and (4) negotiated settlements.

Appreciative planning and collective strategies are designs for advancing a shared vision. They are initiated when someone recognizes that taking action on a problem or taking advantage of an opportunity hinges on pooling complementary resources from several stakeholders. In these designs stakeholders are assembled to diagnose the problem and develop a shared understanding of how to deal with it.

Appreciative planning fosters joint inquiry about the problem without an expectation that explicit agreements will be reached or that actions will ensue. The work of appreciative planning is exploratory and analytical. It encourages joint inquiry by the stakeholders into the problem's context and the interdependent forces that give rise to it. By raising for investigation the value bases of plans (Vickers, 1968), it enables a collective realigning of those values in a mutually reinforcing way. It accomplishes what Ozbekhan (1971) calls the normative phase of planning by fostering an articulation of common ideals. Examples of appreciative planning include search conferences and a variety of community gatherings, which lead to increased awareness about a problem domain and forge a common value basis for future planning. Appreciative planning may also stimulate new initiatives to transform the domain in the desired direction and lead to proposals for collective strategies.

Collective strategies are also motivated by a shared vision, but they go farther than appreciative planning by creating specific agreements to address the problem or to carry out the vision. Collective strategies often emerge from appreciative planning processes, and because they are emergent, the line between them is not definitive. Collective strategies usually result in for-

		Expected Outcome	
		Exchange of information	Joint agreements
Motivating Factors	Advancing a shared vision	*Appreciative planning* Search conferences Community gatherings	*Collective strategies* Public-private partnerships Joint ventures R&D consortia Labor-management cooperatives
	Resolving conflict	*Dialogues* Policy dialogues Public meetings	*Negotiated settlements* Regulatory negotiations Site-specific disputes Mini-trials

Figure 2.   Designs for Collaboration.

mation of ongoing referent organizations to implement agreements reached. Four designs for collective strategies are considered in this chapter: public-private partnerships, joint ventures, R&D consortia, and labor-management cooperatives.

Dialogues convene conflicting parties to explore differences, clarify areas of disagreement, and search for common ground without the expectation that binding agreements will emerge. Facilitated public meetings and policy dialogues fall into this category. These dialogues address generic issues that pertain to many possible sites. They focus on the exchange of information and possible generation of policy proposals for consideration by legislative or administrative bodies.

Negotiated settlements are intended to produce agreements that produce binding agreements or recommendations to an agency that has agreed to ratify them as such. Negotiated settlements are possible for generic issues (for example, regulatory negotiations) or for site-specific disputes. Mini-trials are designs for reaching negotiated settlements in business-to-business disputes (such as disputes over liability for a product failure).

Appreciative Planning

The primary function of appreciative planning is to compare the current state of affairs with a set of ideals. This comparison makes explicit the values underlying potential actions and allows stakeholders to choose those values they wish to pursue together. Two approaches which have been used successfully for appreciative planning are described below.

Search Conferences

The search conference convenes stakeholders with the express purpose of exploring possible scenarios for the future of the domain. The focus of the search conference is on appreciative work, enhancing the stakeholders' shared understanding of the dynamics that operate on the domain. Search conferences in Australia, Canada, and the United States have explored problem domains ranging from traffic congestion to industry development to recreational planning (Emery and Emery, 1978; Williams, 1982). In the United States, a search conference on the "jail of the future" brought together prison wardens, judges, halfway-house directors, and probation officers to contemplate the role of the jail in the criminal justice delivery system (Gilmore, Weiss, and Williams, 1979). The conferees (working in small groups) began by identifying the current internal and external trends that influenced the domain and the expected impact of these trends on jails. Sixty different trends were identified, including population decline and increases in leisure time. In this way participants mapped the domain dynamics and built a collective appreciation of the interdependencies among the stakeholders. Participants then developed idealized conceptions of the jail of the future and reality-tested these against the trends affecting the domain. Noticeably absent from this particular collaboration, however, was one group of stakeholders, the inmates.

The jail of the future conference illustrates a typical search conference process. Stakeholders come together for two to three days in a workshoplike setting. The first session examines trends in society as a whole that will impact the future of the domain. The focus of this session is on brainstorming and wide-ranging exploration intended to legitimize all points of view and to stress the possibilities of various future directions. Idealized futures are introduced by encouraging stakeholders to dream about the way they would like to see the domain transformed. According to Williams (1982, p. 184), by the close of the first session, three outcomes are evident:

First, participants should have developed a shared understanding of what they think is happening in the contextual environment and how it affects them. Second, the session should have demonstrated the possibility of participative and collaborative planning among them. Third, the basic values and ideals to be served by their planned, collaborative actions should have emerged.

In the second session a historical analysis of the problem domain is reconstructed by the stakeholders. This enables them to consider "what of the past should be retained, what should be done away with, and what is missing and must be created" (Williams, 1982, p. 184).

Against the backdrops from sessions one and two, in session three the participants examine the gap between the current state of the domain and their idealized future. They invent general strategies to transform the domain in desired ways. These strategies are subject to reality testing during session four, when relevant constraints and opportunities are considered. From this discussion a few preferred strategies that hold the most promise for change are identified. These preferred strategies are expanded and refined in small-group sessions.

> Using the work done in the previous sessions as context, the task is to examine how wider trends are affecting particular issues, to evaluate current responses to those trends, and to produce new strategies that are more adaptive for pursuing desired directions [Williams, 1982, p. 186].

Reports from the small groups are presented and discussed in a final plenary session. In some cases additional steps are added to permit dissemination of the results to constituents and to elicit their reactions. In Fort McMurray, Canada, a search conference was held to consider development of this rapidly expanding center for new resource industries. The final plenary session was opened to the public in order to facilitate understanding of and build commitment to the proposed strategies (Williams, 1982).

Unlike some of the other designs in this book, the search conference is not designed to produce concrete plans for action or agreements that are binding on all the stakeholders. Three important outcomes are evident, however. First, through search conferences communication between stakeholders is opened up. Second, group articulation of and identification with a set of ideals occurs. Third, a basis for self-regulation of the domain emerges from the acknowledgment of shared values (Emery and Emery, 1978; Williams, 1982). Search conferences serve primarily as problem-setting and direction-setting mechanisms for the domain (McCann, 1983) by facilitating the identification of areas for change and by redirecting stakeholders' efforts toward common objectives. As stakeholders develop a common appreciation about the domain, they can begin to correlate their behaviors toward similar ends. Search is predicated on the assumption that planning should not forecast what will happen in the next twenty years but should identify what people can do now to influence the future (Gilmore, Weiss, and Williams, 1979).

Search is not intended as a decision-making tool but instead as a planning tool. It is an appreciative intervention. That is, the search process is intended to transform the domain by changing stakeholders' assumptions about it and what they think about future prospects. Search creates a common frame of reference that allows stakeholders to move toward a shared concept of what is possible and a joint conviction that what is possible is attainable (Gricar, 1981).

Community Gatherings

In addition to search conferences that create stepwise processes for collaborating, appreciative planning can take place through other community gatherings as well. While the specifics of these designs are less prescribed, Trist (1985), for example, has described several examples of this kind of appreciative planning. These "gatherings" are often inspired by the efforts of a local group (or individual) for a limited purpose but eventually assume a larger community agenda. In a suburban area of Cleveland Heights, Ohio, for example, leaders of several local churches convened a group of citizens and public officials to ask what could be done to quell incidents of racial violence toward blacks who were moving into the community. After several meetings to which additional stakeholders were invited, the decision was made to launch a community congress whose mission would be to facilitate the racial integration of the community while preserving an aging housing stock. The formation of this referent organization launched a series of collaborative initiatives among the residents, city government, churches, schools, and civic organizations, which enabled the city to achieve its objectives.

The city received national recognition as an "All-American City" because of its success in cultivating these collaborative alliances.

A second example is the Craigmillar Festival Society in Edinburgh, Scotland. Begun as a local talent show, the festival grew to become an internationally celebrated event involving dramatical productions and street events. Success with the festival has transformed what had been a poverty-stricken, economically depressed ghetto on the outskirts of Edinburgh into a socially viable community (Trist, 1985). Local leadership from the festival shifted its focus to community affairs. Nine local workshops began meeting to address housing, environmental improvements, employment, and recreational needs of the residents. Eventually external resources from the regional government and the European Economic Community were secured to expand the scope of services the Craigmillar Festival Society was able to provide. One of the outcomes of the society's work is a visionary plan for keeping the community viable in the future. This plan now serves as a model of partnership between voluntary and statutory bodies in Europe (Trist, 1985).

Collective Strategies

Collective strategies go beyond appreciative planning by creating joint agreements for how to transform the domain. Three general examples of collective strategies are presented below. Some involve solely private sector interests; others comprise cross-sectoral interests.

Public-Private Partnerships

Public-private partnerships are designed to merge public- and private-sector resources to counteract a community problem. They have arisen from a combination of factors, including fiscal crises in major U.S. cities during the middle and late 1970s, major cutbacks in federally funded social programs since 1978, and self-interest on the part of the private sector in tackling social problems (especially those associated with urban areas), that bear directly on the local business climate (Lyall, 1986; Davis,

1986). Trist (1985, pp. 27–28) has identified several circumstances that give rise to collaborative partnerships of this type:

1. A critical situation exists that is not being addressed by traditional means.
2. The problem is often a microcosm of a major social problem.
3. The particular version of the problem is local to the community.
4. The problem creates a negative image and negative consequences for the community.
5. Several interest groups are affected by the problem.

Since 1978, partnerships have become an increasingly important vehicle for addressing urban problems at the local level (Committee for Economic Development, 1982). For example, in Massachusetts alone, over 100 public-private partnerships were operating in 1982 (Governor's Task Force on Private Initiatives, 1982).

In some major cities, partnerships were first proposed in response to fiscal crises in the mid 1970s (Lyall, 1986). When major reductions in federal revenues for social programs began in 1978, the problems of urban areas were compounded. President Carter's national urban policy ("A New Partnership . . . ," 1978) clearly identified mutually reinforcing roles for the public and the private sectors in revitalizing urban centers. As federal funds for social programs continued to shrink during the 1980s, the agenda for public-private partnerships expanded to include a growing number of functional areas of urban life, including housing, primary and secondary education, public-policy formation, high-technology business growth (Davis, 1986), and, more recently, illiteracy, youth unemployment (Gray, 1988), homelessness, and substance abuse (Otterbourg and Timpane, 1986).

During the Reagan administration, the President's Task Force on Private Sector Initiatives maintained an emphasis on public-private partnerships largely through publicity and moral persuasion among business leaders (Berger, 1986). An equally

persuasive voice, however, was the growing list of social problems, which began to impinge directly on business's future economic viability. Within both the public and the private sectors
leaders are becoming increasingly aware that "a crumbling social
infrastructure—just like a deteriorating physical infrastructure—
makes a poor environment in which business and business markets can thrive" (Davis, 1986, p. 2). This awareness, coupled
with federal encouragement, has catalyzed business involvement
in partnerships.

   Organization of Partnerships.   The intent and extent of
partnerships can vary considerably. Brown and Wilson (1984),
for example, classify partnerships according to their focus: pro-
grammatic partnerships involve specific contractual agreements
of short duration among limited partners. Developmental partnerships are industry- or regional-level efforts that provide group
benefits. Systemic partnerships are typically long range and societal in scope.

   Public-private partnerships often begin as partnerships
among business leaders and then expand to include nonprofit
and public-sector stakeholders. In New York City, for example,
David Rockefeller (then chairman of Chase Manhattan Bank)
assembled business leaders from major New York corporations
to form the New York City Partnership (NYCP) in 1979. The
stated mission of the NYCP is "to make New York City a better
place in which to live, to work and to conduct business" (New
York City Partnership, 1984, p. 4). The partnership combined
the New York Chamber of Commerce and Industry and the
Economic Development Council under a single 120-member
board. Since its inception the New York City Partnership has
become involved in a host of housing, education, and youth employment initiatives in the greater New York City area. For
each of its substantive areas of interest, a committee for CEOs is
established to spearhead activity in that area. Then working
committees of other stakeholders are convened by the partnership.

   One particularly successful example of a public-private
partnership is the Boston Compact, a partnership that grew out

of a private industry council originally established in 1978 under CETA Title VII funds to provide educational programs for the disadvantaged. A successful summer work program for teenagers eventually led to a major agreement between the Boston school system and area businesses. This agreement, called the Boston Compact, gave priority hiring to graduates of Boston high schools in exchange for specific and measurable improvements in attendance and performance in the schools (Waddock, 1986). The motivation to launch this partnership was derived partly from businesses crying for a skilled work force to sustain growth in high-technology firms in the greater Boston area.

Obstacles to Successful Partnerships. Establishing a common agenda among all the partners is not always easy. While partners are interested in aspects of the same problems, their motivations for joining are not necessarily coincident. For example, one area of concern to partnerships in many cities is education. School-business alliances graphically illustrate the diverse and yet overlapping motivations driving the public and private sectors to work together. For the private sector

> these alliances will enable the school to furnish job-ready workers at a lower cost to the firm than post–high school retraining by business. . . . The rationale for entering into partnerships with schools is further strengthened when these alliances improve community relations and public images of businesses [Otterbourg and Timpane, 1986, pp. 62–63].

From the schools' point of view, partnerships offer a tool for mobilizing supplemental resources from sources the schools cannot tap alone. For example, Adopt-a-School programs, like those in Boston, Los Angeles, and New York, match business firms to individual schools and augment the curriculum by providing tutors, career guidance, and staff development opportunities. Similar initiatives are designed to counteract high dropout rates by guaranteeing job access to those students who remain in school. For programs like these, the predominant motivation for business is to ensure the availability of a qualified work force and to reduce the negative costs to society of large numbers of unemployed. In addition to concerns for the welfare of their children, the schools are also anxious to dissuade dropouts and to improve high school completion rates. Other public and nonprofit agencies support programs (such as apprenticeships and training) to help the most severely disadvantaged. But, as one corporate observer noted, programs to support the underclass fall outside the private sector's agenda and are not going to be driven by business.

Historical alignments pose another obstacle to successful partnerships. Long histories of political maneuvering and suspicion of each other's motives among the public, private, and nonprofit sectors do not engender the kind of trust and open exchange required for collaborative relationships to flourish. For example, in describing difficulties in implementing a program, one corporate executive expressed exasperation over the interminable slowness of the school system's bureaucracy. Her counterpart in the partnership, who represented a city agency, admitted feeling considerable cynicism and skepticism during the early days of the partnership over what business was capable of accomplishing. To be successful, partners must transcend these historical biases and learn to work within the characteristic differences in the institutional styles of their private-sector, nonprofit, and public-sector counterparts.

There is little argument that partnerships are essential to maintaining viable urban centers. Partnership programs clearly support and augment limited public-sector resources. However, as the press of social problems continues, more fundamental questions about the extent of partnership efforts are being raised. For example, can business join the schools in lobbying for more federal assistance without compromising its own economic interest in limiting taxation? Since business-sector involvement in partnerships depends on extensive leadership commitment from civic-minded CEOs, how can these efforts be sustained when corporate priorities change and these leaders move on? Is there a limit to the discretion the private sector should have over the social agenda? Do the disadvantaged have sufficient voice in partnership plans? These as well as more practical questions of how to structure and carry out collaborative agreements across diverse institutions will continue to be salient issues for the management of public-private partnerships in the future.

The Newark Collaboration. In 1984 the city of Newark, New Jersey, initiated a renaissance partnership. The initiative was spearheaded by one of Newark's major businesses, Prudential Insurance Company. At the urging of Newark's mayor, Prudential's senior vice-president for public affairs, Alex Plinio, recruited some 200 of Newark's top leaders to form a partnership aimed at revitalizing the city. The partnership, drawn from Newark's city council, the CEOs of major corporations and nonprofit organizations, has spawned $500 million in redevelopment efforts in the last three years. The remarkable success of this collaborative endeavor has been attributed to the careful attention to process throughout the group's history. Built into the process from day one is a parallel mechanism for designing the processes of all substantive discussions and for ensuring that planning is occurring within stakeholders' constituent organizations simultaneously with cross-stakeholder discussions. With the expert guidance of facilitators from Interaction Associates, the principles of participation, ownership, and equality were continually incorporated into the design and conduct of meetings at all levels of involvement in the partnership.

Not all partners were instant believers in the effort, but as David Strauss of Interaction Associates (facilitator for the initial meetings of the partnership) explained: "Eventually the alligators became advocates" (Strauss, 1988). In a project of this magnitude, identifying all the relevant stakeholders was a multiplicative process. The first ten meetings were devoted to identifying additional parties who should be involved. Eventually, given the scope of the project and the time horizons necessary to carry it out, this partnership, like many others, created a more permanent referent structure. In fact, Strauss believes part of Newark's success is attributable to the permeability of the process, which allowed for continual infusion of new ideas and energy. One result of this permeability was a second collaborative venture, The Newark Education Council, which spun off from the first one.

Joint Ventures

Joint ventures are collaborative alliances among several businesses that hope to gain a strategic advantage in world markets by pooling the distinctive competencies of each form. Many new alliances have been initiated in the automobile, computer, telecommunications, biotechnology, and aerospace industries. These differ from earlier manufacturing joint ventures, which were designed to permit access to protected national markets. These new collaborations are vital to doing business in world markets (Moxon and Geringer, 1985; Perlmutter and Heenan, 1986).

For example, the Dutch firm Philips is teaming up with American Telephone and Telegraph (AT&T) to gain access to AT&T's state-of-the art technologies. In exchange, AT&T gets exposure to Philips's international marketing expertise (Perlmutter and Heenan, 1986). As noted earlier, collaborative alliances within the auto industry involve all the major U.S. and Japanese automakers. "Alliances ranging from investment in rival companies to the importance of Japanese vehicles for sale under American labels, are helping transform the way the domestic industry operates, changing the nature of competition worldwide and blurring the distinction between American and imported cars" (Holusha, 1988, p. 1). These alliances were fostered to give Japan increased access in U.S. markets while improving U.S. automakers' skills in the manufacture of small cars.

R&D Consortia

Another collective strategy that has emerged in recent years is the R&D consortium. According to Dimancescu and Botkin (1986, p. 58), there are five reasons for the formation of these partnerships: (1) strengthening universities, (2) stimulating economic growth, (3) engaging in basic research, (4) creating generic technologies, and (5) developing and delivering specific products. Underlying all these motives, however, is the hope of sustaining and building competitive advantage for industries in need of new technologies. Of special importance in these partnerships is the implementation step, the transfer of technology from the research lab to the production line.

One promising collaboration of this type that has been under way in the apparel and textile industries since 1980 is the Textile/Clothing Technology Corporation [(TC)²]. The original stakeholders in this collaborative venture included four clothing and textile manufacturers and one union, the Amalgamated Clothing and Textile Workers Union. A few years before the inception of (TC)², the union had commissioned a study of the future of the men's apparel industry. That study and a subsequent one done in 1979 urged that a major research and development initiative be launched to create automated manufacturing technology for the industry. Technological changes were seen as the only viable route to retaining market share in an industry in which the United States was at an extreme disadvantage compared to foreign manufacturers with respect to labor costs. Fred Abernathy, who coauthored the study with John T. Dunlop (both of Harvard University), observed:

> It's difficult to say what motivated each of the members to join. It may be that the impetus came from a combination of factors: the flood of imports; the fear that major domestic end-use markets would be lost; the belief that the industry would disappear if nothing were done and that it should not be abandoned without a fight [Hallisey, Sanabria, and Salter, 1987, p. 9].

Regardless of motives, initiating this collaboration was not easy. Initially, participation cost $50,000 per member. This level of investment in research was unprecedented for firms in these industries, and many balked at the cost. Others hoped to profit as free riders, counting on the technology being made available industrywide.

By 1986 (TC)² had achieved a prototype manufacturing line and enlisted the Singer Company to commercialize the technology. That same year the American Apparel Manufacturers Association joined the consortium, followed in 1987 by the International Ladies Garment Workers' Union (ILGWU). Interestingly, so did North Carolina Power and Light, which hoped to stimulate development of the industries to which it supplied energy resources. In order to attract new members, including smaller manufacturers that could not afford the initial $50,000 assessment, a sliding membership fee was instituted. Despite these developments, the real test of $(TC)^2$ hinges on the manufacturers' willingness to adopt the new technology. In an industry long resistant to technological innovation, adoption implies not only substantial capital investment but major organizational and institutional changes on the shop floor as well. Without the collective initiative of $(TC)^2$, however, it is not clear that the industry would remain viable in the 1990s.

Forming community partnerships like the one in Newark or research partnerships like $(TC)^2$ involves many of the same issues that confront conveners of a multiparty mediation. "To form a community partnership, in short, organizers must formulate problems that compel cooperation among diverse participants, identify relevant participants, and arrange credible invitations and sponsorship" (Brown, 1984, p. 8). Clearly, different sources of motivation characterize corporate and community participation in a community partnership than mediated dialogue over a firm's plans to undertake new development. However, in both cases the parties must see some advantage to participation. In the case of $(TC)^2$ this vision was long in coming. Also, in both circumstances, the need to understand different perspectives and to reconcile differing interests and priorities is paramount to success. Parties like those in the Urban Heights case may have different underlying beliefs about the root causes of the problems and about appropriate methods for correcting them. Hence, agenda setting, joint information search, use of subgroups, and skillful facilitation can all enhance partnership efforts. In an R&D consortium, potentially conflicting perspectives are built in from the start simply because these projects are multidisciplinary in scope and must transcend the inherent tensions between basic and applied research in order to get innovative products to market. Accordingly, among their greatest challenges is creating an appropriate way to organize these ventures.

> The relationship between new technologies and new
> management philosophies will have to become a center-
> piece of current or future consortia. It is not enough,
> otherwise, to superimpose new technologies on outdated
> management structures. If America is involved in tough-
> ened global competition that pits management skills
> against one another, a quantum leap must be made in
> inventing better concepts of organization. That leap has
> yet to be made. Knowledge is going to have to be treated
> as a strategic ingredient with information as its raw
> material; financial experts are going to have to learn the
> particularities of laboratory scientists; engineers are
> going to have to talk to nonengineers; technologists are
> going to have to mediate relationships between makers
> and users of knowledge-intensive tools; and business
> schools are going to have to stop producing MBA's only
> superficially prepared to cope with new technologies
> and their strategic implications [Dimancescu and Botkin,
> 1986, pp. 134–135].

Clearly the ability of these partnerships to produce marketable products hinges on their ability to build collaborative organizations across business-academic boundaries and among multiple disciplines. Among the organizational issues these R&D partnerships must confront are the differing expectations and reward structures that characterize for-profit as opposed to academic institutions as well as larger ethical questions about whether universities are being commercialized by such ventures and whether universities can remain on the frontiers of research if they do not become commercialized.

Labor-Management Collaboration

Collective strategies are also proving effective in promoting economic development through improved labor-management relations. Competitive challenges from overseas have all but forced labor and management in many areas of the country to reexamine their relationships in the interest of revitalizing mature industries and attracting new business. Companies looking to open new facilities may be dissuaded by a climate of poor labor relations in an area. Union-management relationships strained by forced plant closings may make introduction of new technologies for modernizing remaining plants more difficult. Moreover, the economic and social needs of laid-off workers and the erosion of the tax base in communities where substantial layoffs or closings have occurred present opportunities for collaboration. In a speech delivered at several universities in the spring of 1988, Elmer W. Johnson, executive vice-president of General Motors Corporation, emphasized the need for "a fundamentally new strategy of cooperation and joint problem solving" between unions and management in the auto industry (Johnson, 1988, p. 1). Part of this strategy was establishment of a partnership with government "to soften the severity of plant closings by providing displaced employees with money, training and other assistance to make the tough transition" (p. 9).

In Pennsylvania, a tripartite commission of labor, business, and government has sponsored the development of regional (as well as in-plant) labor-management committees to address problems of this type. The regional committees tackle issues that cut across management and labor boundaries and have a general affect on economic development in the region. "Areawide labor/management committees provide a forum for improving communication and understanding between labor and management at the area or community level" ("Pennsylvania MILRITE Council . . . ," 1983, p. 15). The Pennsylvania general assembly appropriated funds to support the development of areawide committees, which now operate in thirteen regions of the state. One outcome of these efforts is a proposal for redistributing the financial burden of layoffs through work sharing. During downturns, all workers would work reduced hours and receive proportional unemployment compensation for the time off. In this way continuity of employment could be maintained for younger as well as more senior employees.

The most long-standing and successful labor-management

collaboration is the Jamestown Area Labor Management Committee (JALMC), composed of the general managers and chief union representatives of all the manufacturing firms in the Jamestown, New York, area. In all, twenty-seven companies and locals of ten international unions participate. JALMC was formed in 1972 at the urging of then Jamestown mayor Stanley Lundine, who remained an active player in the committee. Since its inception JALMC has taken initiatives to offset economic decline, raise the quality of working life in the factories, and encourage industrial development in the community (Trist, 1983). After ten years of collaboration, JALMC boasts of several accomplishments: (1) improvement of what was once a very bitter industrial relations climate, (2) rescue of five businesses and retention of 824 jobs and attraction of 1,413 new ones between 1972 and 1981 (Hanlon and Williams, 1982), (3) self-perpetuation despite insufficient financial support over the years, (4) introduction of shop-floor democracy in several local plants (which also contributes to improved labor relations), and (5) a network to support shared innovation and training among the participating firms (Hanlon and Williams, 1982). Among the factors contributing to JALMC's success were a clearly established focus on revitalizing existing plants, separation of collective bargaining issues from the JALMC agenda, early success, and skillful leadership from the mayor and a representative of the Machinists Union.

Collaborations Motivated by Shared Vision

Stakeholders' jointly recognizing a common problem and/or sharing an initial vision about desired changes does not ensure that collaboration under these circumstances will be conflict free. Although stakeholders may be joined by an overarching vision, such as increasing the number of employable youth or reducing the dependence of women on welfare, considerable controversy may arise over specific proposals for accomplishing these desired ends. Also, organizing initiatives like these not only involves coordinating the private sector but also requires building new working relationships across sectors and may require launching new referent structures (Trist, 1983). Clearly, these relationships depend on successful merger of different values and work cultures (Berger, 1986; Davis, 1986; Dimancescu and Botkin, 1986).

Because of these cultural and institutional barriers, managing the negotiation and implementation stages of these collaborative ventures can be especially difficult. There are no formal authority to induce compliance and standard operating procedures to ensure coordination. Parties must learn to share power and to coordinate information exchange in order to be successful. Overcoming these kinds of barriers to collaboration is a major practical consideration for organizing successful collaborations. This is the subject of Chapter Eleven.

This chapter has focused on two of the four general designs for collaboration, those created to solve shared problems. In the next chapter we turn our attention to collaborative designs for resolving conflicts.

9

Collaborative Designs
for Resolving Conflicts

*Where do you find common ground? At the point of
challenge.*

—Jesse Jackson

Conflict-Induced Collaborations

Chapter Eight identified four generic designs for collaboration
and took a close look at those intended to advance a shared vision. A second group of collaborative designs seeks to resolve
multiparty conflicts. Many multiparty conflicts take shape well
before they fall within the purview of a specific administrative
or judicial agency for resolution. Often conflicts of this type are
"tried" in the media, in local public meetings, and/or in legislative committees, but the parties themselves never meet for face-
to-face talks. Yet the opportunity to collaborate exists if the
parties could be convened. Others, including negotiated rulemaking and mini-trials, are proposed to augment administrative
or judicial proceedings in which it has been anticipated or already demonstrated that adversarial interaction will inhibit constructive resolution. The auspices for moving from conflict to
collaboration in these cases are provided by the court or an administrative agency.

A large number of multiparty conflicts arise over concerns about protection of the environment, neighborhood preservation, and land use. These are generally referred to here as environmental disputes. A study by Bingham (1986) examined more
than 160 environmental disputes mediated in the United States

197

between 1974 and 1984. In 1984 alone, close to forty such disputes were mediated, and the number continues to increase each year. The largest number of cases in the Bingham study dealt with land use, including such issues as sewage treatment and sludge disposal, housing and neighborhood impacts, highway and mass transit projects, and protection of wetlands. Land use issues accounted for 54 percent of the cases reported. Other categories of disputes included natural resource management and use of public lands, water resources, energy, air quality, and toxic chemicals. Of the 160 cases in the Bingham study, 45 addressed policy issues; the remaining 115 were site specific. The disputes were also classified according to who the parties were. For example, in the site-specific disputes, 35 percent of the cases involved environmental groups and 43 percent involved local citizens' groups. Private corporations participated in 34 percent of the disputes, while government agencies (either federal, state, or local) were included in 82 percent.

Several designs for addressing conflict-motivated collaboration are examined in this chapter. They are organized under two broad categories: dialogues and negotiated settlements, distinguished according to their expected outcomes. Dialogues are organized informally to promote the exchange of information among the stakeholders. They are designed to promote exploration and relationship building. If these objectives are achieved, the dialogue group may eventually produce proposals for policy changes. Negotiated settlements are expected to result in binding agreements over how to settle a conflict. Three designs for negotiated settlements are described in this chapter: regulatory negotiations, site-specific disputes, and mini-trials.

Dialogues

When parties to a conflict are convened for a dialogue, the primary objective is to clarify the issues in dispute. Just accomplishing this may prove to be a significant achievement. Sometimes the parties discover that their viewpoints do not differ as substantially as they had imagined. In other cases, the dialogue allows pent-up emotions to be expressed so that more constructive discussion of the important issues can ensue.

Dialogues can occur on several levels. They include formal or informal public meetings as well as policy dialogues sponsored by mediating organizations.

Public Meetings

Public meetings managed in a constructive manner provide an excellent opportunity to gather information about a problem. How the meeting is managed is important because public meetings can easily become one-way presentations or arenas for trading insults. Several steps can enhance the likelihood that a meeting will be constructive.

First, the purpose of the meeting should be made clear to everyone.

> Meetings that are open to the public are useful for gathering information, for identifying issues and interests, and for soliciting suggestions for alternatives. They are not effective for developing recommendations or reaching formal agreements, because there is no opportunity to develop ideas and adjust positions [Carpenter and Kennedy, 1988, p. 97].

For example, the purpose may be to inform the community of a plan for a proposed development and to acquaint the developer [and/or township officials] with citizen reactions to it. In this case, care should be taken to record the reactions and make sure that the parties understand one another. Ground rules to limit air time and to restrict debate will be useful to accomplish these ends and should be agreed upon before the discussion begins.

Public meetings are not arenas for resolving highly controversial issues. But, whoever is managing the meeting should be sure that they understand the concerns and clearly acknowledge their importance. Participants should also be made aware of subsequent plans for addressing their concerns. For example, representatives from the public meeting may be selected to investigate a negotiated settlement for the major issues which surface at the public meeting.

Follow-up meetings also provide a constructive vehicle at which to report back to interested parties about the results of any negotiated settlements which may have been agreed to. Representatives should revisit the original list of concerns at this time and show how each one was addressed in the negotiated settlement.

Policy Dialogues

The purpose of policy dialogues is largely to open up discussion among the parties, to identify and promote increased understanding of the issues that may be subject to debate, and to assess the extent of controversy that exists. Policy dialogues are intended to identify points of disagreement among the parties, to explore aspects of perceived risks and strength of commitment to various positions, and to search for shared interests as well as potential concessions. Often, to the surprise of all parties, shared interests are uncovered serendipitously during policy dialogues as the parties begin to reveal the background information that supports their public positions. Shared interests may initially be hidden by the hardening of public positions and restricted information exchange that typically characterize each side's public campaign to muster political support. For example, in a discussion over a resource management plan for steelhead fish in Washington State, sports fishermen and Indians discovered a common interest in protecting the native spawning grounds of the steelhead. The Indians favored this for reasons of cultural heritage; the fishermen benefited because native stock put up a more challenging fight. Discovery of this mutually desirable objective only emerged during mediation and eventually became the basis on which an agreement was crafted. Recognition of this common interest had been buried during years of antagonism and protracted legal battles among the parties over fishing rights (McCarthy, 1984).

Several organizations have been serving as conveners of policy dialogues on a national level in recent years. The Keystone Center in Keystone, Colorado, has sponsored policy dialogues on environmental issues for several years on topics ranging from groundwater contamination to biotechnology regulations. The Keystone Center was founded in 1975 to promote understanding of all aspects of the environment and natural resources and to develop consensus-based public policy in these areas. The center was a pioneer in launching policy dialogues.

> Since 1978, the Keystone Center has endeavored to provide a forum for communication, understanding and negotiations on public policy issues involving energy, science, technology and the environment. Through this forum, the Center serves as a neutral convenor of interested and affected parties, applying facilitation and mediation processes to resolve differences ["Keystone Center, Annual Report," 1986, p. 15].

In selecting participants for a dialogue, the center taps high-level representatives of business and industry, environmental and citizen groups, research and academic organizations, the science and labor communities, and government.

> It is the blending of scientific concerns and the formulation of innovative approaches to critical public policy concerns which characterizes the Keystone Policy Dialogue process. The process allows participants the opportunity to clarify and refine their positions, while at the same time increase their understanding of the goals and viewpoints of others ["Keystone Center, Annual Report," 1986, p. 16].

Typically a core group of twenty to twenty-five stakeholders is assembled. Because the topics under consideration are typically wide ranging and complex, the core group is augmented by experts who participate on a more limited basis.

Several examples serve to illustrate the scope and level of involvement in Keystone's dialogues. The Energy Futures Project was initiated in 1984 at the request of Donald P. Hodel, then secretary of energy, to identify critical energy issues and energy conditions in the future. It was chaired by Fletcher L.

Byrom, former chairman of the board of Koppers Company. During 1986 the work of the project was conducted by two working groups focusing on electricity policy and security of long-term liquid fuels. Among the policy considerations addressed by the liquid fuels group were proposals to eliminate several federal policies (such as the Windfall Profits Tax, the Federal Fuel Use Act, and incremental pricing legislation) and to create national standards for appliance efficiency. Consensus recommendations emerging from the Energy Futures Project have been presented to Congress, the federal Department of the Interior and Department of Energy, and industry and environmental groups.

Members of another Keystone dialogue organized in 1985 are deliberating about regulatory policies for the biotechnology industry. The diversity of interests represented in this dialogue include the Chemical Manufacturers' Association, the Environmental Law Institute, the Cetus Corporation, the National Academy of Sciences, Public Citizens' Congress Watch, the EPA, Mycogen Corporation, and the White House Office of Science and Technology Policy. In May 1987 a congressional briefing was held to present the first round of consensus recommendations that emerged from the dialogue. The recommendations propose reforms in the current regulatory framework for biotechnology research. The ongoing agenda of the National Biotechnology Forum includes concerns about U.S. competitiveness in biotechnology, implementation of regulation, the patenting of animal life, and the use of biotechnology in the Third World. New stakeholders will be added to the dialogue, and others will drop out as the topic area shifts.

According to John Erhlman, director of Keystone's Science and Public Policy Program, one of the most successful dialogues held under Keystone auspices was the Texas Waste Management Siting Process. In this dialogue (held in 1982 and 1983) approximately thirty participants designed a voluntary process for securing early community input into decisions about siting hazardous waste facilities in Texas. The consensus recommendations were originally proposed as voluntary, but after being adopted by several state agencies, the recommendations were incorporated into a solid and hazardous waste bill passed by the Texas legislature in 1985. The consensus group played an active role in promoting their recommendations once they were drafted by conducting regional workshops about waste disposal across the state. The legislation encourages applicants seeking a permit for disposal of hazardous waste to use the siting process. Applicants who do not adopt the process before permitting may be charged up to $25,000. The Gulf Coast Hazardous Waste Management Authority is currently reviewing a proposal for an incinerator in Texas City. Opposition to the proposal was considerably reduced through the use of the process. In this case, what started out as a policy dialogue in 1982 has led to a process for achieving negotiated settlements in subsequent site-specific cases.

Another organization that has convened a number of policy dialogues is the Conservation Foundation. The foundation is a leader in creating avenues for constructive exploration of differences and consensus building around environmental issues. In 1977 the foundation sponsored early discussions between environmental groups and chemical manufacturers about regulations to implement the Toxic Substances Control Act. Eventually this dialogue group (initiated and facilitated by Sam Gusman, formerly a governmental affairs representative for Rohm and Haas Corporation) assumed the role of a steering committee that recommended new topics for foundation-sponsored dialogues. One of the most recent dialogues facilitated by the Conservation Foundation addressed groundwater policy for the state of Tennessee. The impetus for the dialogue arose because groundwater issues affected several different state departments, but there was no unified plan for response within the state. A dialogue group including twenty-seven representatives from real estate, mining, pulp and paper industries, environmental groups, and federal, state, and local agencies was convened.

A third organization known for its facilitation of policy dialogues is the Institute for Resource Management (IRM), organized by Robert Redford. In 1985 and 1986 the institute guided a group of environmentalists and oil firms to an agreement about acceptable locations for oil drilling in the Bering Sea. The plan was then proposed to the U.S. Department of the Interior. As a follow-up the group established a referent organization known as the Bering Sea Advisory Committee to facilitate resolution of future leasing conflicts (Redford, 1987). More recently, a dialogue was initiated by the IRM to consider strategies for improving air quality through the use of alternative fuels. A preliminary conference for a wide array of stakeholders was held in December 1988 in New York City.

Other organizations involved in early initiatives to promote dialogue and information exchange on environmental issues include the Center for Negotiation and Public Policy (formerly the Center for Energy Policy) in Boston, ACCORD Associates (which operated from 1978 to 1988 in Boulder, Colorado), the Conflict Clinic (now at George Mason University), and the Mediation Institute (in Seattle, Washington). (See Bingham [1986] for a more detailed history of these early efforts as well as additional examples of policy dialogues.)

Negotiated Settlements

Negotiated settlements differ from dialogues in that the expected outcome of a negotiated settlement is a joint agreement among the disputants. Dialogue participants may also arrive at agreements, but they do not have the authority to execute them. They can only recommend to others (for example, to township supervisors or legislatures or regulatory agencies) that they adopt the recommendations of the dialogue's participants. Parties in a negotiated settlement, in contrast, are authorized to reach an agreement. Three kinds of negotiated settlements are described below: site-specific disputes, negotiated rulemaking, and mini-trials.

Site-Specific Disputes

Numerous site-specific environmental and development disputes have the potential to be resolved using collaborative approaches. There are already over a hundred examples of such disputes in which local, state, or federal government agencies, developers, environmental groups, and residents of local communities have come together with or without a third party to see if some accommodations could be reached to deal with mitigation of an existing hazard or with opposition to a proposed project (Bacow and Wheeler, 1984; Talbot, 1983; Susskind, Bacow, and Wheeler, 1983; Bingham, 1986). Government officials were common participants in these discussions; they were present at the table in 82 percent of the site-specific disputes studied by Bingham (1986).

Site-specific disputes have several key features that distinguish them from policy-level collaborations. These features are: (1) These disputes involve parties whose personal and economic well-being is directly tied up in (at stake) in the dispute. (2) These disputes frequently involve groups of stakeholders who are not formally organized and may not have identifiable leadership or "representative" spokespersons. (3) In addition, these disputes often involve very complex technical issues for which predictions of the risks involved turn on probabilities rather than facts. While this is also true of policy dialogues, stakeholders in site-specific disputes often lack knowledge of or background in the technical issues involved in the dispute. For example, if notice of a proposed waste incineration facility is released, local opposition to the proposed facility may arise overnight from previously unaffiliated community members whose major concern is potential threats to their health, safety, and economic viability. They are unlikely to have specific knowledge about waste incineration techniques or about the technical and economic suitability of one site over another. This may render them less-than-equal participants in a mediated negotiation. (4) Parties bring to the negotiation very different assessments of the risk associated with the proposals and different confidence levels about the possibilities of ensuring against risk. Differing perceptions of risk are not unique to site-specific cases, but their salience is often heightened in these cases because for some of the stakeholders the loss is personalized (Gricar and Baratta, 1983). Like many of the citizens in the Three Mile Island example in Chapter One, local stakeholders' computation of risks is directly calibrated to issues of personal safety. Thus, they are concerned with risks that may jeopardize their own and the

larger community's well-being, not with the technical and economic specifications of a proposed project. Because of these
concerns, some site-specific disputes, particularly those involving treatment of toxic or hazardous materials, must address very
delicate issues before ever getting to the table.

   "Not in My Backyard." Not the least of these is the
NIMBY ("not in my backyard") problem. The NIMBY problem
results from an unequal distribution of costs and benefits. For
example, while there may be general public acknowledgment
within a region or a state that additional waste treatment capacity is needed, this understanding rapidly changes to opposition
among residents of a specific community targeted for the facility. The targeted community objects to being one of a select few
who must bear disproportionately high costs so that widespread
benefits can accrue to many. The incentives to act under these
circumstances vary with the extent of the impact (Olson, 1965).
Persons receiving limited benefits are less likely to voice an
opinion than those for whom costs are concentrated. Often the
local opposition generated in this situation is so fierce that collaboration is not feasible. Local residents perceive that it is in
their best interest to block the proposed development. One way
to accomplish this is to prevent any negotiations from taking
place. In other cases opposition is utilized as a device to force
information exchange and increase community involvement in
decisions about the development and/or to guarantee that compensation is made for costs incurred by the local community if
they agree to support the project.
   Traditional efforts to address the conflicts associated
with site-specific disputes have focused on either the technical
or the legal aspects of these disputes. However, these approaches
fail to address the underlying reasons for the conflict and usually
prove to be stopgap measures rather than long-term solutions
(Bacow and Milkey, 1982; Bingham and Miller, 1984). Technical solutions (for example, more stringent licensing guidelines
or public education campaigns) often fuel the resistance that
stems from basic value differences and additional concerns not
answered by technical information alone (Gricar and Baratta,

1983; Elliot, 1988). Legal tactics (for example, state preemption of local authority) often generate legally motivated opposition such as lawsuits or administrative challenges to the permitting (Bingham and Miller, 1984). Traditional public hearing processes are also insufficient. They are designed to deal only with technical questions, are typically inserted too late in the process, and provide no guarantees that community concerns will be incorporated. In addition, they are not intended to address tougher political issues such as the viability of alternative sites or compensation to the local community.

Under these circumstances collaborative designs offer the most promise for resolving disputes fairly and wisely (Susskind and Cruikshank, 1987). They produce fair solutions by giving all the parties for whom costs and benefits can accrue equal access to the process. They generate wise outcomes also by searching for integrative solutions that allow all parties to satisfy basic interests by trading off small losses for more substantial gains. In addition, collaborative approaches are designed to maintain control over decision and implementation at the local level. Bingham (1986) has demonstrated the growing success of using mediation to solve site-specific disputes dealing with a host of environmental problems. Of the 115 cases she documented between 1974 and 1984, agreement was reached in 78 percent of the cases. Additionally, new centers offering mediation services (some specifically focusing on environmental and other public disputes) have opened in several states including Massachusetts, New Jersey, Wisconsin, Hawaii, and Minnesota. One of the primary functions of these state offices is the education of potential users both within and outside of state government to the benefits of collaborative resolution of disputes (Susskind and Cruikshank, 1987).

Siting Hazardous Waste Facilities. One of the most difficult but potentially most promising areas for the use of collaborative approaches is in the siting of hazardous waste facilities. The problems of distributing costs and benefits and the local opposition that results in these cases are serious but not insurmountable obstacles to reaching agreement. Collaborative approaches afford the best options to date, for several reasons. First, the legitimate interests of all parties are recognized and taken into consideration. Disproportionate costs to one set of parties can be reduced or alleviated through compensatory arrangements, thus producing more equitable outcomes (Bingham and Miller, 1984). Provisions for future negotiations can be built in to address new disputes that may arise during implementation.

Efforts to resolve siting of hazardous waste facilities have met with spotty success to date. Two short cases illustrate the multiple driving and restraining forces that operate in these settings. The first case, Hawkins Point, Maryland, was not a mediated negotiation. Instead, the negotiations took place in several stages. The case illustrates, however, the substantial costs incurred by a local community and the necessary steps taken to compensate the local residents for the costs imposed on them by the project. In addition, this case illustrates the various layers of opposition that developers may encounter during the siting process and how they were successfully resolved. A second case, from Canada, represents a successful siting attempt using a novel voluntary process.

Hawkins Point. (Data for this case were obtained from Bill Eichbaum, Massachusetts Department of Environmental Resources [formerly with Maryland Department of Environmental Resources], on January 19, 1988.) Facing the closure of its only hazardous waste landfill, the state of Maryland conducted a preliminary assessment of alternate locations. This analysis identified state-owned land at Hawkins Point that was already serving as a hazardous landfill and was adjacent to private landfill suspected of containing unidentified hazardous materials. Leachate from both these areas was contaminating groundwater nearby. The Maryland Environmental Service (MES), a unit of the state's Department of Natural Resources, was authorized to operate waste treatment facilities and was preferred by local residents over a commercial operator for the new site. MES conducted three sequential negotiations over the course of twenty-seven months to deal with opposition and to secure the necessary approvals. Initially MES had to deal with the local citizens' association, whose concerns included removal of heavy equipment and debris left by highway construction, investigation of the hazards posed by the existing sites, testing of local groundwater and garden soil for contamination from existing sites, royalty payments (one dollar per ton) to be paid to the residents, and access to employment at the facility. Since Hawkins Point was largely an industrial area, residential ownership in the area was sparse, with the exception of a small community of twenty-two homes and a church. Because the area was targeted for additional industrial development and largely unsuited to residential use, the state eventually agreed to buy out and relocate the community at a cost of $2 to $3 million.

A second level of negotiations was conducted with organized environmental groups including the Chesapeake Bay Foundation and Clean Water Action. These groups had a high level of concern but also were attracted to the proposed development because of the accompanying provisions to clean up existing sites. Eventually support from these groups was obtained. A third level of negotiations occurred with the city of Baltimore over a tonnage fee on the operation. The Hawkins Point hazardous waste landfill opened in July 1983 after incorporating several design changes that delayed construction and increased its operating costs. After an uneconomical year of operation, the facility was closed.

Observers consider the siting of the Hawkins Point hazardous waste landfill a success despite the short time it operated. Success is measured "in part because no extraordinary measures were required to overcome opposition . . . we would suggest that the ability to work out a solution with the host community, rather than appeal to a pre-emptive state authority, is a measure of the success of the effort" (McKewen and Sloan, 1986, pp. 250–251).

The Swan Hills Case. (Most of the data for this case were obtained during a telephone interview with Audrey Armour, faculty of Environmental Studies, York University, January 13, 1988.) Recognizing the critical need for public acceptance of hazardous waste facilities, Alberta, Canada, launched a unique approach to involving local communities in the siting process. In 1980 the provincial government initiated an intensive provincewide site selection and public information program. A preliminary mapping of areas according to their physical, biological, land use, and human characteristics was prepared by the government. Using a multilevel mapping technique, constraint-free areas were determined. Then, through a series of public forums conducted across the province by the Rural Education and Development Association (a grass-roots agricultural organization), public critique of and comment on the mapping procedure were invited.

> Public participation was encouraged in "building" the package and adding local refinements to the mapping. Attempts were made not to present perfect finished graphics to forums, but in fact to allow individuals to assist with development of draft mapping systems during the actual discussions [McQuaide-Cook, 1986, p. 32].

Communities were given a comprehensive picture of waste-handling procedures from doorstep to dump and of their own civic responsibility in preventing indiscriminate dumping. The province then sought volunteer communities for a proposed hazardous waste facility site. Five communities, all of which fit the preliminary selection criteria, volunteered. A downturn in revenues from the oil industry contributed to some communities' willingness to participate. After comparison of the volunteers, negotiations were conducted with Swan Hills, the community that was selected. The negotiations revolved around tax benefits, economic spinoffs, roadway improvements, employee housing, and employment priority for local township residents. Some exaggeration of the benefits during preliminary discussions raised expectations and forced subsequent renegotiation with the community. An agreement was reached and announced in March 1984; construction began in 1985. The plant is operated by a private contractor under the auspices of the Alberta Waste Management Authority, a crown corporation created to oversee the implementation of an integrated waste management system for Alberta.

The success of the Swan Hills siting is attributed to the extensive community outreach-and-education process that preceded site selection. Additionally, the province made it clear from the outset that no siting would occur without community assent. In late summer 1988 the Canadian cabinet created a mechanism for institutionalizing the voluntary site selection process.

Negotiated Rulemaking

Negotiated rulemaking brings together parties with a direct interest in a specific rule about to be promulgated by a government agency. The parties (usually including the agency) assay the relative merits of alternative rules until they reach agreement on a mutually acceptable version. The agency agrees up front to publish the negotiated version for review and comment (which is expected to be minimal if all the interested stakeholders were represented in the negotiations). Parties are offered the opportunity to review and sign off on the final version, which the agency then promulgates. Negotiated rulemaking has successfully produced several federal rules since 1983, when the first negotiated rulemaking was conducted. It was proposed to overcome problems inherent in the existing process of federal rulemaking.

Background. The process of rulemaking by the agencies of the U.S. government is itself governed by a set of rules embodied in the Administrative Procedure Act (APA) (Pub. L. No. 79-404, 60 Stat. 237 [1946], repealed and replaced by Pub. L. No. 89-554, 80 Stat. 378 [1966] [codified as amended at 5 U.S.C., pp. 551–559], 701-06 [1976]). These rules (most recently amended in 1976) together with supplements set down through more recent statutory and judicial decisions have created a very complex and time-consuming set of procedures that guide agency efforts to promulgate new rules (Harter, 1982; Perritt, 1987). These procedures are based on the concept of hybrid rulemaking. The latter seeks to strike a compromise that affords agencies broad discretion (based on technical expertise) over the regulatory domain while ensuring adequate participation of regulatees in the rulemaking process.

The volume of new regulations enacted during the 1970s and provisions for increased congressional oversight during the late 1970s added further complexity to rulemaking procedures. The net result of these changes was "to convert the agency from an expert guardian of the public interest to a form of 'umpire' albeit an active one" (Harter, 1982, p. 14). Balancing these competing mandates became increasingly difficult. As a result, criticism of the expense, the delays, and the legitimacy of regulatory decision making mounted (see Chapter Two for details). Regulatory negotiations were proposed in response to these criticisms.

In 1980 bills proposing regulatory negotiation were introduced in Congress and were the subject of hearings before two Senate committees (see Joint Hearings Before the Select Committee on Small Business and the Subcommittee on Oversight of Governmental Affairs on Regulatory Negotiation, Ninety-sixth Congress, 2nd Session 7 [1980]). In 1982 the Administrative Conference of the United States adopted a set of recommended procedures for negotiated rulemaking (see "Procedures for Negotiating Regulations," APA Recommendation No. 82-4, 47 *Fed. Reg.* 30, 701-730, 170 [1982]). The EPA was one of the first federal regulatory agencies to experiment with regulatory negotiation. The EPA designated authority for negotiated rulemaking to its Office of Program Planning and Evaluation. In early 1983 the EPA solicited proposals from interested parties for possible rules to negotiate. Of the approximately fifty suggestions, only a few satisfied EPA's basic criteria. The criteria included:

1. Rules had to be in a "middle range" of development, neither near to final promulgation nor years from initial proposal.
2. Rules could not involve too many parties or issues. Regulations affecting large, unsettled questions of science were rejected.

3. Rules representing distinct regulations were favored over generic "groups" of rules or policy issues (Fiorino and Kirtz, 1985, p. 31).

Advantages. According to Harter (1982), regulatory negotiations were designed to alleviate several problems inherent in the hybrid rulemaking process. For example, APA procedures required agencies to substantiate for the record the factual bases for their decisions. Often, however, the necessary scientific and technical evidence for agency decisions is unavailable, incomplete, or extremely burdensome for an agency to recover. Decisions often turn on political or subjective judgments involving the estimation of future risks rather than on hard facts.

Disputes over standard-setting arise in large part because traditional approaches to regulation, and the administration of regulation, do not work as intended. In theory, experts or specialists are supposed to set guidelines based on objective scrutiny of the best scientific information available to them. Yet, every standard also involves an assessment of risks and a decision about the distribution of costs and benefits. Although the process of setting environmental quality standards involves technical analysis, it also involves subjective or political judgments [Susskind, 1981, pp. 1, 13].

Resolution of these political issues is left to the agency. As Stewart (1975, pp. 1683–1684) observes:

The ideal of rational decision assertedly consists in the best resolution and harmonization of conflicting interests, but since there is generally no agreed-upon criterion of what constitutes a "best solution," decision making will normally be a question of preferring some interests to others. After even the most attentive consideration of the contending affected interests, there is still the inescapable question of the weight to be accorded to each interest and the values invoked in its support.

Thus agencies are subject to criticisms about legitimacy when they make political choices. Regulatory negotiation is designed to build in legitimacy by asking the stakeholders to make the political decisions by reconciling competing interests among themselves.

Regulatory negotiation also encourages more rapid identification of the parties' real interests than occurs in the traditional process, in which interests are undifferentiated, exaggerated, and often distorted through legal intermediaries (Harter, 1982; Reich, 1981). When the stakeholders present their own issues face to face, they must establish priorities and determine what trade-offs they are willing to make. The nature of the trade-offs facing parties in a rulemaking negotiation is illustrated by these comments from an auto industry executive who participated in EPA's first regulatory negotiation:

> For the first time my competitors and I were part of a team. Rather than trying to outsmart each other, we had to consider each other's needs as part of an industry group. I had to balance priorities—the possibility that my company may need to use nonconformance penalties versus the likelihood that a competitor, possibly a new foreign competitor, would use or abuse nonconformance penalties [*Regulatory Negotiation: Four Perspectives*, 1986, p. 9].

As Harter notes, making trade-offs face to face is particularly beneficial when issues are being juggled among multiple parties. In such cases a series of sequential, bilateral decisions is likely to produce suboptimal solutions.

A final advantage of regulatory negotiation is that it offers a less expensive method of rulemaking. This is possible because parties need to spend less time devising elaborate position statements and supporting evidence and introducing these into the public record for the agency to consider. "It reduces the need to engage in defensive research in anticipation of arguments made by adversaries" (Harter, 1982, p. 28). Instead, the parties agree on neutral experts to conduct jointly determined research supported by a resource pool provided by the agency (often with the help of outside funds).

Design Features. Several features of the negotiated rule-making process are noteworthy. First, once a candidate rule passes preliminary screening, a convener is appointed to identify stakeholders and to determine the feasibility of negotiations. Usually, the convener interviews potential participants, including that of the respective program office within the agency, to glean the scope of the issues and to test the parties' willingness to participate in negotiations. Following a positive recommendation from the convener, the agency must publish a notice of intention to negotiate in the *Federal Register.* The convener plays a pivotal role in problem setting for it is the convener's task to determine the parties' commitment to negotiate. This determination is crucial to the future success of the negotiations, as the following decision about whether to negotiate standards for low-level radioactive waste illustrates:

> Initial reactions from industry and state and local contacts were positive. The Nuclear Regulatory Commission (NRC) and the Department of Energy (DOE) were key stakeholders in any program involving radioactive waste, so their participation was essential. Both entities agreed to participate. . . . The initial response from environmentalists was mixed, but there seemed to be sufficient interest to suggest they would participate. As the conflict assessment proceeded, however, major reservations from the environmental groups and the NRC emerged. Environmentalists were concerned, first, about whether one or two environmental groups could effectively represent the environmental community on this issue. They also doubted that their resources were sufficient to participate effectively on a rule of this scope and complexity. Third, environmentalists were concerned about the highly controversial data that would be at issue. The NRC was apprehensive about any EPA actions that could slow down state efforts to develop disposal sites. In light of

these concerns, EPA decided to drop the rule from further consideration for negotation [Fiorino and Kirtz,
1985, p. 32].

Clearly, in this case the incentives to negotiate were insufficient
to proceed.

The next step in convening a negotiated rulemaking is
formal chartering of the group as an advisory committee under
the Federal Advisory Committee Act (FACA). FACA requires
approval of committee membership by the Office of Management and Budget (OMB), announcement of plenary meetings in
the *Federal Register,* openness of plenary meetings to the public, and detailed records of all meetings. While these requirements have not unduly restricted regulatory negotiations to
date, some speculate that they may pose practical impediments
to more widespread use of negotiations for rulemaking (Perritt,
1987).

In addition to hiring a convener, agencies engage a mediator or facilitator to assist the parties during the deliberations.
Usually the mediator helps to establish the agenda, ensures that
parties are heard, keeps minutes, and assists in formulating information requests and arranging trade-offs. Conveners and mediators are generally external to the agency. In some cases, conveners have also served as mediators for the rulemaking negotiations.

With the exception of one early regulatory negotiation
conducted by the Occupational Safety and Health Administration (OSHA), agency personnel have participated in the negotiating group. The benefits of this are several: Greater access to
the agency is afforded than in hybrid rulemaking; stakeholders
do not need other avenues to influence the agency; the agency
understands the basis for the final agreement; the agency, like
any other member, can exercise veto power during the negotiations; and stakeholders learn agency interests and can adjust
their own accordingly (Perritt, 1987). Similar arguments can be
made for participation by OMB staff, but since the first two
regulatory negotiations within EPA, OMB has not participated
in the negotiations.

Agency Experience with Regulatory Negotiation. OSHA's first negotiated rulemaking addressed a permanent standard for occupational exposure to benzene. OSHA's previous efforts to promulgate a benzene standard had been rejected by the courts. The committee consisting of representatives from four unions and four industries came close to reaching agreement but in the end was unable to do so. The lack of agency involvement and efforts to second-guess OSHA's and OMB's actions should the negotiations collapse contributed to the failure to reach agreement (Susskind and McMahon, 1985; Harter, 1986a; Perritt, 1987). In addition, the ground rules prevented the committee from transmitting its findings to OSHA unless agreement was reached on all issues.

In July 1986 OSHA began its second regulatory negotiation, seeking to establish a standard for exposure to a chemical called methylene dianiline (MDA). OSHA actively participated in these negotiations, including the preparation of draft language for the proposed rule. The agency's promise to promptly issue a regulation of its own if the committee did not reach consensus also facilitated agreement (Perritt, 1987).

Two rules were selected by EPA for negotiation during 1984. One dealt with penalties for manufacturers of diesel engines that did not meet federal clean air standards (Section 206 of the Clean Air Act). The second addressed procedures for granting emergency exemptions for pesticide use under Section 18 of the Federal Insecticide Fungicide and Rogenticide Act (FIFRA). In both cases the groups reached consensus, and the rules were promulgated after only minimal comments were received during the public comment period. Since then EPA has conducted five other regulatory negotiations. Three of these were successfully negotiated, and final rules have been issued. The other two failed to produce consensus. Still, the attempts at collaboration produced some positive outcomes. In EPA's negotiation over hazardous waste injection wells, the parties reached agreement on two of the three main areas of contention. Despite irreconcilable disagreement on the third issue, several parties concluded that the "negotiations produced a more informed, specific and workable rule than the one they would have expected from a conventional rulemaking" (Fiorino, 1988, p. 23). Table 8 summarizes all the regulatory negotiations conducted to date by several U.S. regulatory agencies.

Two other agencies have experimented with regulatory negotiations and three others are considering doing so. The FAA and the FTC have each conducted one. The former considered revised specification for flight and duty time for pilots. Although the committee could not reach 100 percent agreement, they passed on to the agency areas of agreement as well as disagreement, which the agency then resolved to the committee's satisfaction (Harter, 1986a). A rule was issued in March 1984. The FTC initiative invited revision of its procedures for informal dispute settlement. In this negotiation, three initial stakeholders agreed not to participate in order to keep the group to a manageable size (Perritt, 1987). Despite several attempts at consensus, no agreement was reached in this dispute.

For several of the regulatory negotiations, a resource pool was set up to assist the participants in securing scientific information and expert consultation if any stakeholders desired them. The funds also covered travel expenses for those stakeholders who needed such assistance. Contributions to the resource pool often came from corporate participants and from private foundations. Foundation contributions were essential to securing the participation of some environmental groups, because these groups could not accept "subsidization" from the corporate interests they opposed.

Overall, several authors have concluded that regulatory negotiations offer outcomes superior to conventional procedures (Susskind and McMahon, 1985; Perritt, 1987; Fiorino, 1988). Benefits acknowledged by the parties have included exposure to a wider range of information, opportunities to educate opponents, and improved agreements reached by parties trading off interests of differing value (Fiorino, 1988). A bill currently in Congress would strengthen the practice of negotiated rulemaking by resolving any lingering questions of administrative law regarding the Administrative Procedures Act and the Federal Advisory Committee Act (Bureau of National Affairs, 1988). The bill would also authorize the chairman of the Administrative Conference of the United States to fund agency costs for use of the process.

Mini-trials

One form of dispute resolution that has proved particularly useful for resolving multiparty disputes (primarily among corporations) is the mini-trial. Mini-trials are structured, nonbinding proceedings in which the principals themselves negotiate a settlement after hearing summaries of the evidence from all sides. More specifically, attorneys for each side present condensed versions of their case before a panel of authorized representatives of all the parties (usually a high-ranking executive from each organization is involved). The idea is for each attorney to engage in limited discovery (investigation of the case) and to provide a short argument summarizing her or his best case to the principals. The principals then meet informally and, based on the appraisals they have collectively heard, try to formulate an acceptable settlement.

The advantage of the mini-trial is that it avoids extended pretrial preparation and protracted evidentiary hearings on the legal and technical details of the case. Witnesses are not usually involved, but the principals can query the attorneys if they choose.

> The theory behind the mini-trial is that the party representatives, armed with a crash course on the merits of the dispute (but without any emotional or face-saving motivations) and aware of the larger interests of their side, will be better able than the advocates or lower-level party representatives to appraise their positions and negotiate a mutually beneficial settlement [Green, 1986, p. 241].

Mini-trials are often initiated after litigation is under way and early efforts at settlement have proved unsuccessful. Mini-trials increase the incentives to settle by shifting the principals in the

Table 8. Summary of Regulatory Negotiations.

Agency	Rule Negotiated	Notice of Intent	Agreement Reached	Rule Issued	Number of Participants	Agency Participation	Convener/ Mediator
FAA	Flight and duty time for pilots	Spring 1983	Yes[a]	March 1984	Not available	Yes	Nicholas Fiardis (Fed. Med. and Conc. Service)
OSHA	Benzene standard	April 1983[b]	No	—	8	No	Harter/Cormick
EPA	Nonconformance penalties for diesel engine manufacturers (under the Clean Air Act)	April 1984	Yes	August 1985	22	Yes	McGlennon
EPA	Emergency exemptions for pesticides (Section 18 FIFRA)	August 1984	Yes	January 1986	22	Yes	McGlennon/Wilcher (EPA)
EPA	Farmworker protection from pesticide hazards	September 1985	No	July 1988[c]	23	Yes	Harter
EPA	New source performance standards for residential wood combustion units (Section III Clean Air Act)	August 1985	Yes	February 1987	17	Yes	Harter and Hirsch

FTC	Informal dispute settlement rules (Rule 703 Magnuson-Moss Warranty Act)	February 1986	No	—	25	Yes	McGlennon/Bingham
EPA	Resource Conservation and Recovery Act permits	July 1986	Yes[d]	September 1987	21	Yes	McGlennon and Schneider
EPA	Hazardous waste injection wells (Hazardous and Solid Waste Amendments of 1984)	July 1986	No	August 1987[c]	19	Yes	McGlennon/Harter, and Bingham
EPA	Asbestos Hazard Emergency Response Act	October 1986	Yes[e]	April 1987	28	Yes	Carpenter and Tyson/Olpin and Hoffman
OSHA	Methylene dianiline	October 1985	Yes	May 1987	14	Yes	Federal Mediation and Conciliation Service

[a] Committee failed to reach consensus but endorsed agreement prepared by FAA.
[b] Planning time, no formal notice of intent issued.
[c] Rule issued by EPA on its own.
[d] Agreement endorsed by 20 of the 21 parties.
[e] Agreement reached among 20 of the 24 parties. Published rule used agreement as basis.
— indicates that no rule has been issued by the agency.

case from legal to management representatives, by focusing the negotiators on the essential issues in the case, and by allowing them to make a realistic appraisal (on the basis of the summary arguments) of the strength of their own case vis-à-vis the others. Often this appraisal is aided by the presence of a neutral third party who also hears the evidence and, if invited to do so, renders an opinion about the likely outcome were the case to be litigated.

The mini-trial was first used in 1977 in a technically and legally complex case dealing with patent infringement. According to Green (1986, p. 242), mini-trials are most effective for cases characterized by "complex questions of mixed law and fact." Mini-trials have been used successfully in cases involving product liability, contracts, patents, antitrust actions, insurance, toxic torts, employee grievances, and trade secrets. Most mini-trials deal with multiparty disputes; some have been international and some have involved government agencies (Center for Public Resources, 1986; Green, 1986).

Once the parties agree to utilize a mini-trial, they must agree on a procedure for conducting it. Because the procedure is private and not binding, the parties may adopt any guidelines they prefer. However, some suggested procedures are available. The Center for Public Resources, a New York–based organization that has considerable experience facilitating intercorporate disputes, has published the Mini-Trial Handbook (Green, 1982) with suggested procedures and case examples. For example, in preparing the initial agreement to conduct a mini-trial, the following issues should be stipulated:

- what to do about the status of pending litigation, if any
- issues to be discussed at the mini-trial
- discovery required for the mini-trial
- identity and roles of participants at the mini-trial, especially the business executives with settlement authority
- selection and role of the neutral adviser, if one is to be employed
- when and where the mini-trial will take place, and a schedule for case presentations and postmini-trial negotiation sessions

- identification of documents (including brieflike statements) to be exchanged in advance and submitted at the mini-trial
- confidentiality and inadmissability of mini-trial statements, submissions, and outcomes
- apportionment of mini-trial costs (Center for Public Resources, 1986)

One important provision of this agreed-on protocol concerns inadmissibility of evidence. Usually, in a mini-trial it is understood that all evidence is confidential and cannot be admitted in subsequent legal proceedings. Failure to reach agreement, however, does not preclude either party from pursuing litigation. Mini-trials are often initiated after a lawsuit has been filed and preliminary discovery has occurred. A mini-trial can look particularly attractive to all parties when the costs (in time and money) of preparation for a trial are prohibitive.

For example, in a breach-of-contract suit filed by Bordon Inc. against Texaco Inc., the latter had only completed 30 percent of the data it needed after two years of evidence gathering and over $250,000 in copying costs alone. A three-week mini-trial involving the executive vice-presidents of both firms produced a novel settlement (a renegotiated contract) instead of the more traditional monetary award to one party ("Use of Mini-Trial . . . ," 1985). Such an agreement was possible because the negotiators could reconvert the case into a business problem. According to Green,

> this reconversion is achieved by bringing in new negotiators . . . who are not emotionally involved in the dispute, but who have authority to settle the case and who can view the dispute in a broader context in which imaginative, integrative solutions are more likely to be found. The presence of these nonlegal representatives of the clients also brings together the true parties in interest, who often are better able than the legal representatives to assess the strategic risks and overall importance of the case to the client [1986, p. 238].

A multiparty suit between the National Aeronautics and Space Administration (NASA) and two of its contractors was settled

by a mini-trial. The case involved technical contract provisions
for the Tracking and Data Relay Satellite System (TDRSS), a
communications system for the space shuttle. The contractor,
Space Communications Company (Spacecom, a partnership
among three companies), and its subcontractor, TRW Inc., had
filed a claim with NASA's Board of Contract Appeals because
NASA had added directions to the contracts three years after
they were let. Not only did the new technical directions generate disputes, but the question of who should pay for the multi-
million-dollar change was also unresolved. Additionally, the dis-
position of the case had implications for other government
contracts. Discovery for the case was extensive because the issues involved complex technical uncertainties. After a year of
litigation, both sides agreed to try a mini-trial. The negotiators
included the director of Goddard Space Flight Center, an associate administrator for TDRSS from NASA, the president of
Spacecom, and a TRW executive. Attorneys for each side had
two and a half hours each to present evidence. After a few days
of negotiations, agreement was reached on the principal case
and on some other contract issues as well. (This case is discussed
in more detail in Eric S. Green, "The Mini-Trial Handbook," in
Center for Public Resources [1982], MH45–MH48.) Had this
case gone to trial, presenting the evidence and weeding through
the facts would have been a technical nightmare. The mini-trial
expedited a settlement because the principals were already familiar with the technical issues.

Resolving Future Conflicts

Clashes over growth, development, new technologies, distribution of scarce resources, the preservation of existing cultures,
environmental quality, and cherished ways of living are inescapable in the world in which we live. Yet our experience with effective ways to tackle the complex trade-offs involved in these
decisions falls far short of the need. Collaboration offers some
clear although not simple alternatives. Despite the wide array of
examples presented in this chapter, our experience with collaborative designs for resolving conflicts is still quite limited. Some
powerful precedents have been set; we still have much to learn.

Collaborative processes are not yet well-accepted practice for addressing complex multiparty disputes. Just as in collaborative designs for addressing shared problems, institutional and cultural barriers often impede using collaboration to resolve conflicts. In part this is because collaboration requires fundamental shifts in our thinking about how to organize ourselves to share power. We need a conceptual foundation for this activity as well as practical skills for how to make collaboration work. Developing this conceptual and practical wisdom poses a considerable challenge for us. Much work is therefore yet to be done if we are to learn just how effective collaborative designs can be.

In the final section of this book, the question of these challenges of organizing is explored from both conceptual and practical perspectives.

10

Developing a Theory
of Collaboration

*Constructive responses to emerging problems depend on
the degree to which different appreciative judgments can
be interpreted within a shared organization culture.*
                                                    —Vickers, 1965

Preamble

So far we have provided a rationale for collaboration from a historical perspective, examined the dynamic process of collaboration as it unfolds in practice, and observed the increasing pursuit of collaborative processes by private- and public-sector
organizations. We have reviewed the concatenation of factors
that provide a historical explanation for the rise of collaboration. Collectively, these factors point to collaboration as an essential response if we are to achieve constructive and timely
resolution of critical problems that range from local to international in scope. Overall, we have been building a case for why
and how collaboration enables us to manage the increasing
interconnectedness of our world.

    Some readers (particularly social scientists) will want a
more theoretical perspective on collaboration than I have provided so far. This chapter is for them. Since it is not possible to
brand this chapter with a "beware of theory" sign or an other-
wise appropriate omen to warn readers of a more practical bent,
this preamble will have to suffice. The intent in this chapter is
to examine collaboration from the perspective of organization
theory and to propose changes to the traditional model of interorganizational relations that dominates the literature. In its place

I argue for a more dynamic, process-oriented theory of how organizations interact. In particular, the potential of collaboration to introduce a new negotiated order among the stakeholders is emphasized. In simpler terms, the process of collaborating creates changes in the patterns of interaction among the parties. Those readers who do not find these issues particularly tantalizing may want to proceed directly to Chapter Eleven.

This chapter advances a theory of collaboration as an emergent interorganizational process. Recent conceptualizations of interorganizational relations have been criticized for emphasizing transactional patterns and structural arrangements among established networks of organizations (Laumann and others, 1978; Rogers and Whetten, 1982; Fombrun, 1986). In doing so, they underrepresent the dynamic, emergent, and mutable character of interorganizational relationships. By focusing on established patterns of interaction, past studies have discounted how coalitions of stakeholders are formed and changed amid a dynamic interorganizational field, how diverse interests are forged into collective action, and the temporary character of many interorganizational alliances. Studying collaboration offers a window to these processes, thereby contributing to the development of a more dynamic, process-oriented theory of interorganizational relations.

In Chapter One collaboration was defined as a process of joint decision making among key stakeholders of a problem domain about the future of that domain. Five key aspects of this definition were also presented.

1. The stakeholders are interdependent.
2. Solutions emerge by dealing constructively with differences.
3. Joint ownership of decisions is involved.
4. Stakeholders assume collective responsibility for the future direction of the domain.
5. Collaboration is an emergent process.

In this chapter, these five points are examined more fully within the context of negotiated order theory. Collaborations can be thought of as negotiated orders created among stakeholders to control environmental turbulence by regulating the exchange relationships among them.

Collaboration as a Negotiated Order

Collaboration is conceptualized here as a mechanism by which a new negotiated order emerges among a set of stakeholders. Other studies of interorganizational networks have characterized them as either transactional (focusing on the exchange of resources between the members) (Levin and White, 1961; Galaskiewicz, 1979; Fombrun, 1982) or as attribute networks (such as industry groups linked by similar characteristics) (Fombrun, 1982). These perspectives emphasize the objective and instrumental rather than the cognitive and expressive character of these relations (Fombrun, 1982). Viewing collaborations as negotiated orders emphasizes instead the cognitive and expressive character of these relations.

Negotiated order refers to a social context in which relationships are negotiated and renegotiated. The social order is shaped through the self-conscious interactions of participants. Negotiated order theorists (Strauss and others, 1963; Strauss, 1978; Goffman, 1973; Day and Day, 1977) focus on social processes by which intraorganizational order is negotiated.

> The negotiated order theory downplays the notion of organizations as fixed, rather rigid systems which are highly constrained by strict rules, regulations, goals, and hierarchical chains of command. Instead, it emphasizes the fluid, continuously emerging qualities of the organization, the changing web of interactions woven among its members, and it suggests that order is something at which the members of the organization must constantly work. . . . Organizations are thus viewed as complex and highly fragile social constructions of reality which are subject to the numerous temporal, spatial, and situational events occurring both internally and externally [Day and Day, 1977, p. 132].

In this analysis negotiated order theory is applied to interorganizational transactions. That is, a set of organizations can collectively negotiate agreements to govern their interactions. Collaboration provides a mechanism by which information can be exchanged in order to create those agreements (Emery and Trist, 1972; Trist, 1983). The term *negotiated information order* can also be thought of as an institutionalized thought structure among a network of organizations (Warren, Rose, and Bergunder, 1974).

As noted in Chapter One, however, collectively establishing an agreement that satisfies multiple stakeholders involves considerable negotiation. Not only do the stakeholders need to appreciate the necessity of joint activity in order to join together, but also they must delimit the problem domain and reach agreement on how they will collaborate before they can even begin to address the substance of any transactions. They must also agree on the scope and the quality of information they will exchange. Once negotiations are under way, the parties continue to assess whether the information they exchange is technically and socially sufficient (Heimer, 1985). Often critical junctures turn on whether the parties can agree on the validity of technical or scientific data and their interpretation. "When a system of criteria for the social sufficiency of information is worked out by a group of interrelated organizations, we speak of a 'negotiated information order' in which the kind of information and its priority have been agreed upon by all parties" (Heimer, 1985, p. 397).

Essentially, the negotiated order evolves through the process that Trist (1983) refers to as joint appreciation. Appreciation involves assessing a current course of activity in light of current norms and beliefs about what is possible and desirable for the future (Vickers, 1965). Building a joint appreciation, then, means sharing these appraisals of the domain and trading individual and collective perceptions of what is and what is not possible. Thus, "appreciating" involves making judgments of fact as well as value judgments about how things should be (Vickers, 1965). "The most important issue is that if they do not see a sense of positively correlated fate, the only reason for the network being an entity, there will be no agreed task" (Boje, 1982, p. 13).

Based on this joint appreciation, the stakeholders craft agreements by which to regulate their future interactions. These agreements may include rules governing future interactions among stakeholders, redesign of roles and responsibilities among the stakeholders, or recommendations to policymaking bodies about the domain. Essentially, these agreements constitute a normative framework through which members correlate their activities with respect to the problem. In so doing, they establish a temporary order for the domain.

Conceptualizing collaborations as negotiated interorganizational orders emphasizes several points. First, collaborations involve strategies collectively constructed by the stakeholders to cope with exogenous environmental pressures. Second, this conceptualization captures the imprecise, emergent, exploratory, developmental character of these interorganizational arrangements. Collaborations are dynamic negotiations that may eventually lead to some form of institutionalized agreement. Third, collaborations serve as quasi-institutional mechanisms for accommodating differing interests within society and for coordinating interorganizational relations. Collaborations perform a norm-setting function at the domain level. Thus, they represent a nascent institutional form whose legitimacy as an institution is still being negotiated. Fourth, collaborations serve as vehicles for action learning (Ramirez, 1983; Morgan and Ramirez, 1984).

Collectively Devised Strategies for
Responding to Environmental Turbulence

Traditionally, organization theorists have focused on the efforts of individual organizations to negotiate stable environments for themselves through contracting, industry agreements, and standardizing internal procedures (Cyert and March, 1963). Others have described individual firms' strategies for reducing dependence on other organizations (Pfeffer and Salancik, 1978) and for managing external demands (Ansoff, 1965; Mason and

Mitroff, 1981; Freeman, 1984). Still others have stressed iso-morphic response to the environment (Lawrence and Lorsch, 1967; Meyer and Scott, 1983; Scott and Meyer, 1987). All of these approaches stress adaption to environmental uncertainty at the level of the individual firm. In the face of turbulence, however, individual strategic adaptation is insufficient. As dis-cussed in Chapter Two, changes in the economic infrastructure, associated with the information explosion and globalization of economic, social, and political interests, necessitate the evolu-tion of new organizational forms (Trist, 1983; Williams, 1982; Perlmutter and Trist, 1986; Peters, 1988). Individual organiza-tions can no longer accurately forecast or regulate the complex transactions that occur among an increasingly interdependent set of stakeholders.

Let us look more closely at why collaborative interorga-nizational arrangements offer an advantage over individual ef-forts to adapt. The theoretical argument supporting collabora-tion derives from Ashby's (1960) concept of requisite variety. Requisite variety refers to the match between the internal com-plexity of a system's adaptive planning capacity and the com-plexity of the environment to which it is trying to adapt. Ashby contends that in order to control its environment, an organiza-tion needs to build a level of internal complexity commensurate with the complexity of its environment. Meyer and Scott (1983) and Scott and Meyer (1987) provided empirical evidence for this incorporation of external complexity by administrative units within schools. Similarly, Kriger (1988) describes the cre-ation of subsidiary boards by multinational firms to respond to the increased complexity of managing in a global environment. Without embodying this variety, single organizations are hard pressed to identify as well as to respond to the myriad of stim-uli creating potential threats and opportunities for them.

In the face of turbulence, however, individual organiza-tions lack the requisite variety to provide successful adaptation at the domain level. In turbulent conditions "the emergence of interrelated, rapid outcomes exceeds the existing organizational matching capabilities," rendering the environment "increasingly uncertain and unmanageable for the organization" (Ramirez,

1983, p. 729). /The increasing interdependence of public and private organizations and the interweaving of local, national, and global interests has reduced the capacity of any organization to act unilaterally.\ "No agency controls the essential elements of a policy making system that is now intergovernmental and intersectoral. The existence, intentions and jurisdictions of other actors substantially reduces functional autonomy and often creates a strong sense of powerlessness. . . . Policy formulation and implementation require multilateral cooperation and shared power across traditional boundaries and jurisdictions" (Luke, 1984, pp. 16–17). Thus, the paradigm of individual strategic response to global change is giving way to collectively crafted strategies (Perlmutter and Trist, 1986).

Powerlessness to take effective action in the face of turbulence is not limited to individual firms. As noted in Chapter Two, state-sponsored interventions have also failed to redress critical economic and social problems. Neither incrementalist nor large-scale centralized planning efforts (such as Model Cities) have been effective in dealing with urban decay, inadequate housing, or needs for educational reform (Ackoff, 1974; Rittel and Webber, 1973). Efforts to introduce interactive planning (Ackoff, 1974, 1981; Ozbekhan, 1971), which stresses incorporating wider participation and continual learning, have been proposed as alternatives to traditional goal-oriented and postfigurative planning (Mead, 1978). Such processes are becoming increasingly important to move decisions through the bureaucratic morass created by overlapping discretion among governmental units (Agranoff and Lindsay, 1983; Wright, 1983). Plans are also frequently thwarted by political stalemate or are stalled in implementation by protracted legal challenges.

The adoption of "collective strategies" offers a viable antidote to turbulence. For example, private-sector firms that cannot incorporate sufficient operational flexibility in their own organizations to address changing technology and global competition have established collaborative arrangements such as joint ventures, licensing agreements, and R&D partnerships with other organizations to compensate for loss of this flexibility (Astley and Brahm, 1988; Perlmutter and Heenan, 1986). Similarly, hospitals have formed consortia for coordinating local services and purchasing expensive new technologies. Arrangements of this type have been called "collective strategies" because they represent strategic initiatives to increase the competitive advantage of the participating firms by pooling resources and sharing the risks associated with certain ventures (Astley and Fombrun, 1983).

The development of collective strategies among third-sector organizations for client referrals, comprehensive service delivery, and resource procurement has been common among these kinds of organizations for several years. In fact, these inter-organizational systems have formed the basis for much of the existing literature on interorganizational relations (Warren, Rose, and Bergunder, 1974; Van de Ven, Emmett, and Koenig, 1975; Hall and others, 1977; Van de Ven, Walker, and Liston, 1979; Provan, Beyer, and Kruytbosch, 1980; Schermerhorn, 1975, 1979; Whetten and Leung, 1979; Whetten and Aldrich, 1979). (See Rogers and Whetten [1982] and Galaskiewicz [1985] for extensive reviews of this literature.) Despite the major contribution of these theories to an understanding of the cross-sectional dynamics of resource exchange among existing networks and their structural characteristics, they provide little insight into the evolution of these interorganizational relationships. (See Trist [1983], McCann [1983], Gray [1985], Van de Ven and Walker [1984], and Cummings [1984] for efforts to conceptualize interorganizational systems longitudinally.) Indeed, several authors have pointed out the need for a more dynamic, process-oriented model of interorganizational relations (Rogers and Whetten, 1982; Gamm, 1981; Fombrun, 1986) focusing on how and why coalitions mobilize (Laumann and others, 1978) and the negotiation processes that lead to collective action (Gricar and Brown, 1981; Gray, 1985).

Collaboration as a Temporary and Emergent Organizational Form

Viewing collaboration as the unfolding of a negotiated order emphasizes its temporary and emergent character. A theory of collaboration must account for how these processes organize a previously unconnected set of stakeholders to address common problems. In the problem-setting phase of collaboration, for example, the stakeholders of a domain usually either have no formal connections to one another (although they may be affiliated through other networks) or are interdependent players in an adversarial game. Stakeholders are considered "unorganized" if they have virtually no connections with each other or "underorganized" if their interactions are largely unregulated (Brown, 1980). The Committee on Residential Lending (discussed in Chapter Four), began as an underorganized system, since the parties did not collectively undertake any joint activities. Nonetheless, some fundamental bilateral interdependencies *did* exist among stakeholders. The municipality deposited tax receipts into local banks. Individual citizens and individual lenders had a symbiotic dependence on each other with respect to financing of mortgages. Their collective vulnerability to the loss of these economic transactions, however, was not consciously appreciated. A collective consciousness about these interdependencies was not evident. At this stage the relationships among the parties were clearly "underorganized" (Gricar and Brown, 1981, p. 886). During the problem-setting phase the citizens' group engaged in mobilizing tactics and attempted to meet with the lenders and the city government. Interorganizational interactions heated up considerably during this time, although they continued to be largely unregulated, conflictual, and dyadic in nature. According to Brown (1980), underorganized systems are prone to either suppression of conflict or escalated conflict, since they exhibit neither a clear power structure nor strong inhibitions on dissent.

Collaboration, then, establishes a process by which the domain can become more organized. At a minimum, through collaboration, stakeholders acknowledge the fact that their efforts to influence the domain are interconnected. If they proceed through the direction-setting and implementation phases, potential outcomes include proposals to regulate certain activities within the domain and/or to take collective action. The extent to which these proposals are generated and become institutionalized will vary with the nature of the issues and the design of the collaborative efforts. This will be explored further below in the section on collaborative arrangements and their functions.

Collaboration as Quasi-Institutional Mechanism for
Accommodating Differing Organizational Interests

A theory of collaborations as negotiated orders emphasizes the temporary and dynamic character of these interorganizational interactions./While most collaborations are temporary and exploratory ventures, they often produce lasting normative agreements among the stakeholders, and some even evolve into more enduring institutional forms Therefore, consideration of the institutional aspects of collaborations is also warranted.

Selznick (1957) introduced the notion of institutionalization as a process. More recently, institutional theorists have focused on the socially constructed character of organizations (Zucker, 1977, 1983; Meyer and Rowan, 1977). However, these conceptualizations emphasize the adoption and maintenance of formal institutional arrangements through the operation of widely accepted societal norms that govern interorganizational relations (Meyer and Rowan, 1977; Zucker, 1977, 1983; Tolbert and Zucker, 1983; DiMaggio and Powell, 1983). Institutional theory, for instance, contends that institutionalized agreements sanction which negotiations between organizations are permitted to occur, what can be subject to negotiation, and how such negotiations are to be conducted (Tolbert and Allen, 1987). The regulations of the Securities and Exchange Commission are a good example of how negotiations are prescribed and sanctioned. Other dispute resolution mechanisms, such as collective bargaining, litigation, and arbitration, can also be explained by institutional theory as legitimate institutional processes characterized by rules and precedents to delimit which issues can be negotiated and by what rules. These rules are legitimated within an overarching societal paradigm. According to Perlmutter and Trist (1986, p. 2), such paradigms "determine the modes of managing change and types of negotiation between different organizations and their spokesmen."

Because collaboration represents a nontraditional process for dispute resolution and social planning, until recently there have been no paradigm for invoking its use and few rules and precedents by which to implement it. Over the last ten years, however, collaboration has been increasingly adopted as a method of multiparty dispute resolution. Institutional theory does not help explain the growing interest in alternatives to these traditional methods of negotiation or how these alternatives evolve. For this a negotiated order perspective, rather than an institutional one, is most beneficial, because the former addresses how the processes of deinstitutionalization and reinstitutionalization come about through negotiation. That is, negotiated order theory applied to interorganizational relations is concerned with change in the institutionalized order as constituted and with how such changes emerge.

As collaborative processes continue to gain acceptance, they are beginning to have the cumulative effect of changing some institutionalized structures (Strauss, 1984). For example, multiparty mediation clauses have been written into land use legislation in several states (Bingham and Meely, 1988), and there is an increasing use of collaboration among business organizations to minimize the risk of new ventures (Astley and Fombrun, 1983; Perlmutter and Heenan, 1986; Dimancescu and Botkin, 1986; Holusha, 1988).

Thus, collaborative initiatives can be understood as emergent interorganizational arrangements through which organizations collectively cope with the growing complexity of their environments. Collaborations typically augment (and sometimes substitute for) the more traditional administrative or judicial decision-making apparatus in our society. Lawrence Susskind describes multiparty negotiations as "adding a step" in the traditional public policy process because they are usually inserted prior to the conduct of legally required legislative, administrative, and judicial proceedings (Personal Communication, October 14, 1987).

In summary, then, collaboration is conceptualized as a negotiated order, and collaborative negotiations are one mechanism through which existing normative policies can be changed (Giddens, 1979). The emergence of collaborative processes poses challenges to the legitimacy of traditionally accepted mechanisms for social integration (for example, centralized planning, litigation, individual competitive strategy). Increasing turbulence provokes reexamination of our reliance on certain institutions, because they no longer provide sufficient adaptive responses at the individual or the societal level. Collaboration provides an alternative consensus-building or integrating mechanism for society. Interestingly, the legitimacy of collaborative processes to serve this integrating function must be renegotiated in each setting where it is applied. In addition, the evolution of norms to guide the process and stakeholders who will adopt it must be identified and mutually sanctioned.

Collaborations as Vehicles for Action Learning

The need for such change has been explained in recent theories that describe organizations as undergoing evolutionary metamorphoses to correspond to changes in their environments. These theories suggest that systems and their environments are so interdependent that as one changes it creates the need for change in the other. Hence, the need for mutual learning and continual readjustment is created (Michael, 1973; Schön, 1980; Morgan, 1982). Ramirez (1983) characterizes the process of collaborating as action learning.

> Action learning reframes management from the traditional function of control to one in which the main concern is to facilitate the colearning process (Morgan, 1982). . . . The emphasis that action learning places on learning involves a recognition that how we go about dealing with the unpredictable, uncertain futures that turbulence entails is increasingly important in terms of what it is that we do [Ramirez, 1983, p. 726].

Central to the learning process is the notion of reframing or redefining the problem domain. The potential for reframing afforded by collaboration, and the blinders that prevent us from achieving it, can be graphically appreciated by the now familiar exercise of the nine dots (see Figures 3 and 4).

To complete the exercise, it is necessary to connect all nine dots with four straight lines without lifting pen from paper. Most people who try to solve this simple problem are

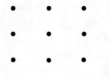

Figure 3.   The Nine Dots Exercise.

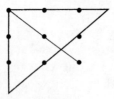

Figure 4.   Solution to the Nine Dots Exercise.

blinded from doing so by the powerful image of a square that they impose on the collection of dots. Their mental preoccupation with the square restricts the range of solutions they can envision. Thus, they are precluded from seeing the feasibility of the solution—extending a line outside the boundaries of the imaginary square (illustrated in Figure 4). The inability to see the larger picture in this case is caused by a feasibility preoccupation with another more salient and more restrictive image. Because individual organizations are likely to bring their own feasibility preoccupations to problems, the range of options such a firm could envision is a restricted set, within which its self-interest undoubtedly figures prominently. Moreover, it is likely that this set may not include options that another organization, with its own feasibility preoccupations, would propose. Hence, the parties are in conflict over a possible solution and perhaps over the very definition of the problem. Yet initial definitions of the problem and feasibility preoccupations regarding solutions can greatly constrain possibilities for resolution. This occurs because each party develops a position from within its own feasible set of options. Furthermore, traditional bargaining processes (referred to as position bargaining by Fisher and Ury, 1981) lock the parties into incompatible positions. This prevents them from exploring the interests underlying their positions, because they assume that incompatible positions mean incompatible interests (Fisher and Ury, 1981).

Collaboration enables the parties to identify these underlying interests and to reframe the problem and search for a solution that addresses as many of these interests as possible. The potential afforded by using a collaborative process is that the parties will search for a common definition of the problem and then generate a wide enough set of possible solutions to find one that incorporates at least some of the interests of each of the stakeholders. It is precisely through this process of searching together that the negotiated order is created (Emery and Emery, 1978).

As stakeholders share their individual appreciations about the problem, a more comprehensive understanding of the problem emerges. Thus, collectively the stakeholders can create an appreciation that is rich enough in variety to represent the complexity of the problem itself and robust enough to withstand buffeting from the environment. In the face of appreciations that differ from their own, individual stakeholders have the opportunity to expand and revise their own interpretations and to escape from the blinders imposed by their own feasibility preoccupations.

Organizing a collaborative venture requires establishing a basis for shared organization. Once this basis is established, the stakeholders can formulate a collective strategy for the domain. This means collective mobilization of action and resources ori-

ented toward the achievement of ends shared by the stakeholders (Astley and Fombrun, 1983). This does not mean that all
parties are equally interested in all parts of the agreement or
that their motivations for adopting an agreement are identical
(Donnellon, Gray, and Bougon, 1986). Reaching agreement
usually involves delicate trade-offs in which minimal concessions by one party permit another to satisfy its primary interest,
and vice versa.

Collaborative Forms and Expected Outcomes

It has been repeatedly suggested that, despite being characterized as generic, collaborative designs differ from one another in
practice in several substantive ways. Some are initiated in the
context of ongoing litigation; others are efforts to preempt litigation. Some arise out of pessimism, as last resorts to settle bitter, protracted conflicts; others emerge out of optimism, as
visionary explorations for new possibilities. Depending on the
context, collaborations also produce different outcomes, ranging from increased appreciation and better understanding of the
domain to policy recommendations to contractual agreements.
Table 9 depicts four types of collaborative arrangements distinguished according to functions and outcomes. Proceeding from
top to bottom, the interorganizational associations between the
parties become progressively more institutionalized.
    Other organization theorists have proposed typologies of
interorganizational structures that reflect some of the characteristics of those in Table 9. In distinguishing three kinds of alliances ("efforts to coordinate autonomous organizations without the authority of a formal hierarchy"), Whetten and Bozeman (1984, p. 21) identify federations, councils, and coalitions.
The least organized of these are coalitions, in which power is
shared among the member agencies because they do not dele-
gate authority to a central administrative unit. This form may
be most like the confederative form in Table 9. Mulford and

Table 9. Collaborative Arrangements and Their Functions.

Type	Function	Possible Outcomes	Examples
Exploratory	Acknowledge interdependence Establish trust Clarify parameter of problem domain	Shared problem definition Preliminary policy analysis Narrowing/broadening of the issues	Search conference Policy dialogue Fact finding
Advisory	Analyze problem Draft recommendations to administrative, legislative, or judicial body	Policy recommendations	Regulatory negotiation Advisory committees
Confederative	Draft and adopt recommendations for ongoing interaction	Operational agreements Resource exchanges Nonbinding agreements Self-regulations	Jamestown labor-management committee Public-private partnerships
Contractual	Formally coordinate or regulate interactions Institutionalize relationships	Contractual/legal agreements Binding agreements	R&D consortia Campbell Soup labor contract Mini-trials

Rogers (1982) propose three strategies for managed coordination: mutual adjustment, alliance, and corporate. These are distinguished on the basis of whether individual agency or collective goals are emphasized, on the extent to which power is centralized, and on the degree of formalized decision rules. They also attempt to distinguish coordination from cooperation along these same dimensions (p. 12). Cooperation is accordingly characterized by no formal rules, pursuit of individual goals, few linkages, and involvement of low-level members. All of these typologies tend to presume an ongoing network of existing organizations, thereby excluding more temporary and loosely organized forms of association from consideration. They also do not explain how linkages are formed initially or how they intensify.

Astley and Fombrun (1983) distinguish four classes of collectives, based on type of association (direct or indirect) and form of interdependence (commensualistic or symbiotic). (Commensualistic organizations represent the same species [that is, are members of the same industry or service area]. Symbiotically interdependent organizations are linked by resource transactions [for example, coal and steel companies].) Their description of organic collectives comes closest to capturing the loose association of some collaborative designs. Organic collectives are held together by a kind of political constitution in which bargaining and influence processes are "conducted within an institutionalized normative framework that prevents disintegration of the network" (Astley and Fombrun, 1983, p. 585).

Table 9 identifies four categories of collaborative arrangements: exploratory, advisory, confederative, and contractual. The function of exploratory forms of collaboration is to heighten stakeholders' awareness of their interdependence. Ackoff (1974) calls this formulating the mess. Where antagonism between the parties is high, initial efforts to acknowledge interdependence may dwell on the inability of each group to act unilaterally and the losses accruing to all parties from inaction. For example, protracted inaction by the United States and other nations in dealing with the degradation of the ozone layer increases the risk of skin carcinoma for people across the globe.

A related function of exploratory collaborations is the establishment of trust among the parties. Especially where trust has been eroded through years of adversarial relations or recent escalation of hostility, rebuilding an atmosphere of trust requires time, initiative by at least one party, and good-faith efforts and confirmatory behavior by all participants. The establishment of ground rules and the presence of a neutral third party to ensure and maintain a fair and constructive process can be especially helpful to infusing a climate of trust in the proceedings (Carpenter and Kennedy, 1988).

Clarifying the parameters of the problem domain is another function of exploratory collaborations. Frequently, parties have different and often ambiguous conceptions of the problem. Informal negotiations allow parties to hear other stakeholders' conceptions of the problem domain and to clarify its scope and dimensions. This may mean agreeing on a more comprehensive definition or setting priorities on a few of the most critical issues or redefining the problem in a way that incorporates the multiple concerns of all the stakeholders.

Collaborations characterized as "advisory" incorporate and extend these exploratory functions to analyze and agree on options for dealing with the problem. A likely outcome of advisory collaborations is the drafting of policy recommendations for adoption by a legislative or administrative body. Regulatory negotiations exemplify this type of collaborative arrangement.

Confederative collaborations assume the added function of adopting and implementing the consensual agreements reached by the stakeholders. Implementation may take the form of cooperative exchanges of resources, normative rules (such as codes of ethics), or ongoing efforts to coordinate behavior among the stakeholders. Public-private partnerships embody implementation agreements of this type in which corporations agree to sponsor programs in the public schools, for example.

Contractual arrangements are the most institutionalized form of collaboration. Stakeholders in contractual collaborations establish contractual agreements enforceable by law or other authority. These serve to regulate the stakeholders' interactions and provide formal means of coordinating the transactions among them. In the negotiations between Campbell Soup Company, farm workers, and growers, contractual agreements governing wages, working and living conditions, and volume of purchases were adopted for a three-year period. Similar formal agreements are established within R&D consortia with respect to the dollar investment and patent rights of each participating member.

Toward a Dynamic Theory
of Interorganizational Relations

Negotiated order theory has been used to explain the internal dynamics of groups and organizations. We believe it also has much to contribute to understanding interorganizational phenomena. Because of the theory's focus of emergent dynamics, it has the potential to inform a much-needed dynamic, processual theory of interorganizational relations. The limitations of prevailing theories of interorganizational relations to go beyond current static, context-independent explanations have been extensively documented (Rogers and Whetten, 1982; Fombrun, 1986). A similar critique of research on bargaining and negotiation has been provided by Strauss (1978).

The theory views collaborations as negotiated interorganizational orders created by the stakeholders. This perspective presents a dynamic, process-oriented theory of interorganizational relations and accounts for the contextual influences on interorganizational dynamics.

Several interorganizational theorists have pointed out the need for a dynamic, process-oriented theory of interorganizational relations (Rogers, 1982; Gamm, 1982; Motamedi and Cummings, 1984). The focus of the negotiated order perspective is on change rather than on permanence. Thus, it can enrich our theory of interorganizational forms and the temporary nature of many interorganizational arrangements. The study of collaboration offers a unique vantage point from which to merge the negotiated order perspective on negotiations advanced by Strauss

(1984) with a dynamic, context-inclusive view of interorganizational relations. It is critical that organization theory pay attention to institutionalization of these collective allegiances, because they play an increasingly important role in today's global society (Astley, 1984, p. 533).

11

Overcoming Obstacles
to Successful Collaboration

*People can agree if they don't agree on why they are
agreeing.*
—Harland Cleveland, May 10, 1984

Often critics of collaboration assail it as idealistic and naive.
Hopefully, the examples of collaboration examined throughout
this book have conveyed a different image: one of realistic potential and challenge. For indeed, the track record of multiparty collaboration to date is both encouraging and sobering.
And, just like other methods of problem solving or conflict
resolution, collaboration needs to be evaluated on its track
record.

In some instances, such as the Storm King negotiations,
collaboration has reversed a seemingly hopeless stalemate. In
many instances, the outcomes of collaboration have often far
exceeded the expectations of any of the parties. Follow-up
interviews with participants have revealed several positive outcomes of collaborating. These include access to information,
greater flexibility in inventing solutions, greater perceived influence over decision making, opportunities to educate other
stakeholders, improved communication among the parties, and
higher-quality solutions than those expected from conventional
processes (Bingham, 1986; Fiorino, 1988).

In other cases, however, considerable effort was expended
with disappointing results. Frequently, hard-fought agreements
were never implemented or became stalled interminably during
implementation. Omission of key stakeholders occasionally
sabotaged agreements. Perhaps the most bittersweet experiences

246

involve successful negotiations whose results are too long in coming (as in the transformation of labor-management relations at Eastern Airlines, which occurred too late to improve economic performance enough to avert a hostile takeover of the company). Both the successes and the failures provide important sources of learning about when collaboration can fruitfully be used and how it can be most constructively accomplished. Many obstacles to successful collaboration have been alluded to in previous chapters. The most serious obstacles are reviewed here, and consideration is given to circumstances in which collaboration is not recommended. Following this is a discussion of criteria for judging success and a review of the track record to date. The last section offers advice to conveners on how to organize for successful collaboration.

Obstacles to Collaborating

Despite the compelling incentives to collaborate (described in Chapter Two), there are many reasons why collaborative attempts fall short of the ideal or are never even initiated. Many obstacles to collaborating are embedded in the philosophy and patterns of activity associated with the management era. Despite their inappropriateness in a global environment, old practices do not change overnight, and resistance to changing established practices is a predictable human response (Klein, 1976; Lorsch, 1986). People resist change for several reasons: they do not like the uncertainty associated with change; they feel insecure or afraid of expected consequences of the change; they have an investment in the status quo; or they do not understand or agree with the consequences of the proposed changes. A critical tool for dealing with resistance is understanding what causes it. Conveners of collaborative endeavors should realistically expect resistance to collaboration and be prepared to cope with the obstacles. Several obstacles are described below.

Institutional Disincentives

Certain institutional commitments create disincentives to collaborate. Environmental groups, for example, express concerns that mediated negotiation will dilute their mission of championing environmental protection. As advocacy organizations, these groups see their role as public education and advocacy to increase environmental protection of natural resources. Collaboration is viewed as short-circuiting these campaigns by removing the discussions from the public eye. In the words of one environmentalist:

> Some groups pride themselves on including all sides from the start in their deliberations, and that usually results in such a watered down environmental position that it is not worth the time and effort. It has led to the belief among environmentalists that their job should be to formulate clear environmental objectives, advocate those objectives, participate in major decision-making processes with as much persistence and vigor as their opponents, and forge compromises if necessary at the end rather than at the beginning [Hayes, 1988, p. 2].

Strong advocacy also serves the institutional needs of these organizations since they depend on support from membership contributions to sustain their work. Litigation represents a highly visible form of commitment to environmental objectives.

> The environmental community is typically represented by national public-interest law firms. These firms, such as the Natural Resources Defense Council, the Sierra Club Legal Defense Fund, and the Environmental Defense Fund, are conspicuous in their lack of interest in mediation as an alternative to litigation. . . . The visibility of these organizations and their ability to raise funds to support their continuing legal efforts is based on a record of successful litigation. Participation in mediation activities would draw time and energy away form their primary mission and does not attract the level of attention that a favorable legal judgment does [McCarthy, 1984, p. 78].

These institutional disincentives represent investments in established ways of conducting business that allow stakeholders to satisfy certain interests. Therefore, stakeholders are reluctant to abandon them in favor of more uncertain outcomes of collaboration. Overcoming these obstacles may mean delaying initiation of collaboration until stakeholders concerned about the issue are well defined and organized. Alternately, periodic opportunities for public education and comment can be designed into the collaborative process from the outset.

Limited resources are also an issue for many public interest groups since much of their work at the local level is done by volunteers. Participation in collaborative endeavors is seen as a drain on time and financial resources (McCarthy, 1984; Hayes, 1988).

McCarthy (1984) also points out the institutional disincentives for law firms of recommending collaborative approaches to their corporate clients. Assessing the merits of a case for litigation, gathering evidence, taking depositions, and preparing witnesses form the backbone of litigation analysis but are unnecessary steps if a collaborative process is used. Some corporate clients, however, are looking favorably on mediated settlements because of their potential to reduce legal expenditures. Thus, collaborative initiatives can work against the interests of the legal profession. As a result, some law firms are expanding their practice to also offer alternative dispute resolution options for their clients.

Historical and Ideological Barriers

Historical relationships characterized by long-standing bitter adversarial interactions among parties often create insurmountable obstacles to collaboration. Conflicts stemming from deep ideological differences or in which violence has been prevalent are more suited to shuttle diplomacy or to intervention by a judiciary than to face-to-face collaboration.

When questions of constitutional law are at stake or parties wish to establish a general legal precedent or to achieve statutory reform, collaboration is also not an appropriate vehicle. In these cases, litigation is necessary to bring the force of law behind a decision to ensure action and to establish precedent for future cases.

Power Disparities

Concerns about preserving an institutional power base also pose
real obstacles to collaboration. Parties will be understandably
reluctant to collaborate if they are at a disadvantage to adequately represent their interest or if they believe their interest
will be deemed secondary to more powerful ones.

> Those who represent minority or less powerful interests
> may see little value in a negotiated solution to a dispute
> because they believe that the only possible outcome will
> be an appeasement that could blunt attempts to raise
> more fundamental issues, more pervasive problems, or
> new principles. For some parties in some instances, the
> public awareness created by continued conflict may have
> greater value than the benefits to be gained by resolving
> a particular dispute. Thus, resolving that specific dispute
> without achieving more sweeping change in precedent
> or policy may be viewed not as a success but as a failure
> [Bingham, 1986, p. 66].

Obviously, in these circumstances, some parties believe they
have much more to gain by not collaborating. Once the issues
have received a more public airing and the balance of power
changes, reintroduction of proposals for collaboration may be
received more favorably.

Societal-Level Dynamics Creating Obstacles
to Collaboration

Certain societal-level characteristics also present obstacles to
collaborating. Cultural norms in the United States are rooted in
a strong sense of individualism (Hofstede, 1980), more so than
in most other cultures. This orientation toward self rather than
community encourages people to view collaboration with skepticism, seeing such negotiating as a sign of weakness rather than
as the challenge that it is.

Collaborative approaches are more difficult during periods

of zero sum growth or when the policy under consideration concerns allocation of scarce resources (Whetten and Bozeman, 1984). Division of resources among many competing for their share is difficult enough, but when allocations require cuts or involve assignment of proportional liabilities, achieving agreement is particularly difficult. For example, at Superfund sites, where the federal government is overseeing the cleanup of toxic waste dumps, decisions about proportional liability for costs need to be reached among the potentially responsible parties (firms who used the sites for dumping) before cleanup can begin. Collaborative methods for allocation in these circumstances are being developed, however (Center for Public Resources, 1985; Bureau of National Affairs, 1987; Susskind and Cruikshank, 1987).

Differing Perceptions of Risk

One of the fundamental tenets of collaborative designs for addressing disputes is acknowledging the legitimate differences in how parties perceive a problem. In environmental disputes differing perceptions of risk between proponents of a project and other stakeholders are often at the heart of the dispute. Depending on how one visualizes the risks involved, very different conceptions of the problem arise and different solution preferences emerge. Perceptions of risk cause us to focus our attention on some problems and ignore or deemphasize others (Elliott, 1988). Usually, however, neither side accepts the problem conceptualization of the other as legitimate (Gricar and Baratta, 1983).

For example, project proposers and government regulators typically adopt a very technical view of the issues. They use existing knowledge to predict the probability of certain hazards (based on statistical averages) and design solutions to prevent mishap based on those probabilities. According to Elliott (1988), they operate with a prediction/prevention model of risk. Within this model, risks can be ranked according to their expected outcomes. Risk management consists of anticipating and devising strategies to prevent or contain these risks. Despite their reliance on precision, technical models of risk are subject to disagreement among experts. This, and the fact that they are often based on estimates and extrapolations rather than direct experience, are the bases on which technical models are criticized and mistrusted.

Alternate models of risk (which Elliott dubs "lay conceptions") (p. 6) focus attention on the extreme possibilities rather than on statistical averages. Risk management from this perspective involves controlling for the extreme cases. Risk management strategies require detection systems and the capability to mitigate the effects of hazards that are detected (Elliott, 1988). Thus, it implies constant monitoring and an ability to respond to change. The most extreme form of risk management from this perspective, of course, is to block the project completely.

Elliott (1988, p. 9) has classified lay publics according to three perceptions of risk: sponsors, guardians, and preservationists. Sponsors believe risks will be minimal if the appropriate technology is utilized and regulatory agencies enforce the rules. Guardians do not trust technology per se or its operators. They prefer to enlist community participation in managing the risks (for example, by requiring independent monitoring). Preservationists mistrust even detection and mitigation systems and prefer the certainty of the present to uncertainty associated with the proposed project. In the absence of compelling reasons to proceed, they prefer that no action be taken.

A collaborative process requires building an agreement that responds to all three of these perceptions of risk. A proposed project that does not respond to all three is destined to generate opposition. How can an effective response be crafted? To satisfy the sponsors, a sound technical proposal is needed. To satisfy guardians, future plans for mitigating risk must be built into the agreement. For preservationists, the incentives to go forward must be increased (perhaps by demonstrating insufficient control in the current situation or by offers of compensation) and/or by ensuring a sense of local control in the future. One way of framing such a discussion is to explore the terms under which the community might accept the facility (Bacow and Milkey, 1982). For example, opponents to the venting at Three Mile Island eventually agreed to it when they recognized that the current state of affairs (prior to venting) was potentially more hazardous because of the potential of an unregulated leak. In addition, the monitoring program afforded them an opportunity to make their own judgments about the necessity for evacuation during the purge. The local residents of Swan Hills saw the proposed waste-treatment facility as an opportunity to improve the economic well-being of their community.

Technical Complexity

The technical complexity of many multiparty disputes (especially environmental and development ones) generally poses additional obstacles to successful collaboration. Technical responses to environmental problems are based on knowledge of how ecosystems will evolve if no changes are made and knowledge about how they will change if the proposed development is introduced (Bacow, 1980). In designing a system to evaluate these changes, however, scientists introduce value judgments.

> Even the simple task of measuring change in the environment forces the analyst to make judgments about the relative importance of the different components of the change. Moreover, these are not trivial decisions: different indices can lead to different conclusions [Bacow, 1980, p. 118].

Parties in environmental negotiations often find themselves in dispute over the accuracy of various technical reports and expert witnesses. As Bacow (1980) suggests, these differences cannot be resolved at the technical level but are rooted in the value premises embedded in each piece of research. In order to reach agreement on the acceptability of technical input, the parties will need to agree on the underlying value premises. To do this often requires making predictions about the future as well, since predicting natural evolution of the environment depends on what actions are taken by human agents with respect to regulation, new technology, and the like.

Collaborative designs, then, must include some bases for

the parties to explore the common value premises against which they would like technical assessments to be judged. Designs need to build in methods for exploring mutually desired futures (Emery and Emery, 1977) against which technical projections of change can be compared and evaluated. Some preliminary experiments with computer-assisted negotiations to deal with extremely complex technical projects have been attempted (Raiffa, 1982; Susskind and Cruikshank, 1987). This technology allows negotiators to collectively experiment with different scenarios and to project the impact of various options on the situation of interest.

Political and Institutional Cultures

Institutional cultures within organizations also pose formidable obstacles to the wider acceptance and use of collaboration. Here the inertial forces of institutional culture come into play. Getting a government agency to see negotiation as a feasible and desirable alternative requires (1) education about the advantages of and the skills needed for collaboration, (2) agency guidelines for when and how collaboration can be deemed useful, and (3) reward systems that encourage agency officials to participate. Current administrative systems often provide disincentives to search for negotiated settlements because administrators are judged on how efficiently, not how creatively, they dispense with cases. "Although mediation enlarges the options available for resolving disputes, it would require an extensive redirection of established procedures" in most agencies (McCarthy, 1984, p. 77). Agencies generally do not have formal provisions for collaborative dispute resolution processes. Even where these practices are encouraged, budget constraints and reward structures often serve as powerful disincentives. Reflecting on the situation at EPA, McCarthy (1984) writes:

> One kind of encouragement that could be persuasive is the inclusion of the number of cases brought to mediation as a positive factor in evaluating personal performance. For this to occur, there would have to be a

> greater understanding of mediation among agency staff.
> Thus, the use of mediation as an alternative dispute
> settlement mechanism will involve a substantial commit-
> ment to educating EPA case administrators and the
> provision of incentives to spur the use of the process
> [p. 77].

Budget cycles also discourage using collaborative approaches because resources need to be projected well in advance of opportunities for collaboration, which cannot necessarily be anticipated
in advance.

Institutional cultures also often inhibit effective implementation of agreements. Partners in public-private partnerships
and in cross-cultural joint ventures experience considerable difficulties reconciling specific expectations about how implementation activities should be managed. For example, in meetings
of President Reagan's Task Force on Private Sector Initiatives,
public- and private-sector participants had differing expectations about the amount of group debate, and the chairperson's
designs for managing the task force's data bank engendered
similar controversy (Berger, 1986). In joint ventures, disputes
arise over the design of management systems to oversee the
jointly sponsored operations (Holusha, 1988).

When Not to Collaborate

Not all the obstacles discussed above are insurmountable in
every situation. Still, negotiators and conveners attempting collaboration need to anticipate and to make a realistic evaluation
of their ability to overcome real and potential obstacles. In
some cases the wisest course is not to collaborate. The prognosis
for launching a successful collaboration is poor when:

- The conflict is rooted in basic ideological differences.
- One stakeholder has the power to take unilateral action.
- Constitutional issues are involved or legal precedents are
  sought.
- A legitimate convener cannot be found.

- Substantial power differentials exist or one or more groups of stakeholders cannot establish representation.
- The issues are too threatening because of historical antagonisms.
- Past interventions have been repeatedly ineffective.
- Parties are experiencing perceptual or informational overload and need to withdraw from the conflict.
- Maintenance of interorganizational relationships represents substantial costs to the partners (Whetten and Bozeman, 1984, p. 31).

Factors for Judging Success

Most of the evidence to date on the success of multiparty collaboration is in the form of individual or comparative case studies (Bingham and Miller, 1984; Brooks, Liebman, and Schelling, 1984; Emery and Emery, 1978; Fiorino, 1988; Tabor, Walsh, and Cooke, 1979; Talbot, 1983). Several criteria on which the success of collaboration can be judged can be derived from these case studies. Two obviously objective criteria are whether or not an agreement was reached and whether it was implemented. Many other interim criteria involve more subjective standards that reflect the participating stakeholders' assessments of the outcomes. The importance of succeeding with respect to these subjective standards is often just as critical as achieving objective success because, if the parties are unhappy with the process of collaborating, they are unlikely to accept the outcome. If the parties do not believe that the real issues were addressed and their own interests were satisfied, then the collaboration has not been successful. In dialogues and appreciative planning processes, where reaching agreement is not the stated objective, subjective assessments of success may be all that is possible.

The following list summarizes several subjective and objective criteria for judging the success of collaboration:

- Does the outcome satisfy the real issues in dispute?
- Do the parties feel they affected the decision?

- Are the stakeholders willing and able to implement the decision?
- Does the agreement produce joint gains for the parties?
- Were communication between the parties increased and the working relationships improved?
- Has the agreement held up over time?
- Was the process efficient in terms of time and resources?
- Does the solution conform to available objective standards?
- Do the parties perceive the procedures were fair?
- Did the procedures conform to accepted standards of procedural fairness?

Realistically, a successful collaboration will satisfy several, if not all, of these criteria. A collaboration that produced a fair and lasting agreement should likely be judged a success, even if the process of achieving it was grueling and inefficient.

For collaborations in which specific agreements or recommendations are sought, objective standards for judging outcomes and procedures, when available, should not be overlooked. Where possible, agreement about what constitutes a fair and just agreement should be settled early on in the process (Fisher and Ury, 1981).

The Track Record So Far

Bingham (1986) has provided some aggregate analyses of case study data that provide insight about success. She has amassed data on 132 environmental disputes in which agreements were sought through mediated negotiation. Of these cases, ninety-nine were site-specific disputes, and thirty-three were policy dialogues. (Bingham uses the term *policy dialogues* to refer to several collaborative initiatives that dealt with policy issues. In four of these, the objective was to reach a decision. The objectives of the other twenty-nine were to agree on recommendations.) "In 68 of the agreement-oriented cases, the parties [organizations] at the table had the authority to make and implement the decisions; in the other 64, the participants helped to agree on recommendations to a decision-making authority that did not participate directly in the negotiations" (Bingham, 1986, pp. 72-73). Success was measured according to (1) whether a decision or an agreement on recommendations was reached and (2) to what extent the agreements or recommendations were implemented if they were reached. The results of this analysis appear in Table 10.

Little difference in reaching agreement was found between site-specific disputes and policy dialogues. Parties came to agreement in 79 percent of the site-specific cases and 76 percent of the policy dialogues. Reaching agreement meant unanimous support for the agreement by all the parties. Counted among failures to reach agreement were those cases in which the negotiations were terminated because the parties were unable to persuade their constituents to ratify the agreements.

Not surprisingly, implementation of agreements was higher for site-specific disputes than for policy dialogues. Parties in a policy dispute have little or no authority to carry out any agreements they reach. They are dependent on persuading legislative or administrative agencies to adopt their recommendations. As in the National Coal Policy Project, representatives of these agencies may not even have participated in the dialogue.

> Once agreement has been reached in a policy dialogue, implementation can be particularly difficult. In early policy dialogues, it was assumed that a broad consensus among private parties at interest would be sufficient to persuade public officials to adopt suggested policy options. Except in a few cases, the complexity of the policy-making process has proved this assumption wrong [Bingham, 1986, p. 80].

Furthermore, the agreements reached in policy dialogues are often at the level of general principles rather than concrete action steps that are readily implementable (Bingham, 1986). An additional factor that makes implementation of policy recommendations more difficult is the changing character of the public policy arena, in which public opinions and legislative priori-

Table 10. Track Record for Mediated Negotiations of Environmental Disputes.

		Site-Specific Disputes (n = 99)			Policy Dialogues (n = 33)		
	Total cases	To reach a decision	To agree on recommendations	Total	To reach a decision	To agree on recommendations	Total
For all cases (N = 132)							
Agreement	78% (103)	81%	74%	79%	100%	72%	76%
No agreement	22% (29)	19%	26%	21%	0%	28%	24%
For cases in which an agreement was reached (n = 103)							
Agreement fully implemented	70% (50)	85%	64%	80%	0%	50%	41%
Agreement partially implemented	14% (10)	7.5%	29%	13%	100%	0%	18%
Agreement not implemented	15% (11)	7.5%	7%	7%	0%	50%	41%
Success of implementation unknown	(32)	(12)	(12)	(24)	(1)	(7)	(8)

Source: Bingham, 1986, pp. 73 and 78, Figures 5 and 6.

ties shift and public officials come and go (Horowitz and Prahalad, 1981; Gray and Hay, 1986; Bingham, 1986).

Assessing the success of search conferences and collective
strategies presents considerably more difficulty than evaluation
of conflict-induced collaborations. Systematic analyses comparing the success of public-private partnerships, for example, are
difficult to generate since the objectives and conditions within
which these voluntary efforts are undertaken are not controlled.
Furthermore, the number of actors in these partnerships is
often extensive and changing, and comprehensive documenta-
tion of processes and results is either not available or is buried
in the personal archives of the participants. Anecdotal case
analyses, however, have suggested some bases for evaluation.
For example, where specific initiatives were launched to address
a specific social problem, a basic measure of success is whether
any programs were initiated. Partnerships point to concrete evidence, like the number of new low-income housing units built
or the number of summer job placements. More compelling evidence, of course, is whether the new programs helped to alleviate the underlying problems.

Anecdotes also provide insight into some of the difficulties encountered by collective strategies. Sustaining the programs
between conception and implementation appears to be a particularly difficult problem (Gray, 1988; Doyle, 1988). Implementation is also plagued with difficulties derived from the merger
of different institutional cultures (Berger, 1986; Holusha, 1988;
Gray, 1988) and concerns about usurping the traditional terri-
torial prerogatives of the other partners (Otterbourg and Timpane, 1986).

Clearly, the record of collaborations to date is a checkered
one. Many experiences contain aspects of both success and failure. While the evidence is not 100 percent favorable, it is heartening. For example, even when parties do not reach agreement,
they frequently applaud the process. Moreover, the number of
disputes and problems for which collaboration is a possible
alternative is growing. Finally, as we learn more about what
works and what does not, the number of successes should increase. We turn now to factors enhancing success.

Organizing for Successful Collaboration

Research has addressed several crucial factors that influence the success of collaborative initiatives. Conveners who are initiating collaborative ventures and stakeholders who will be participating can enhance their chances of success by incorporating these factors into their designs.

First, potential conveners contemplating a collaboration must thoroughly diagnose the domain-level dynamics, including the history of the problem and prior relationships between the stakeholders. This preliminary diagnosis often provides some organization to the domain and influences whether parties will agree to participate. In order to approach stakeholders, conveners must provide a preliminary articulation of the problem of concern and an identification of who the other participants will be. Conveners need to learn the extent to which each stakeholder is impacted by the problem, their access to other alternatives, and whether they have the power to advance or block a negotiated solution. Effective diagnosis involves prudent analysis of the nature and strength of the underlying interdependencies and power dynamics among the stakeholders (Gray, 1985). Domains in which one or more key stakeholders discount their dependence on other stakeholders and overestimate their individual capability to influence outcomes affecting the domain may be unlikely candidates for collaboration unless a convener or mediator can reframe their incentives.

If a preliminary diagnosis suggests that collaboration is possible, careful attention should be given to both member factors and process factors as the design of the collaboration unfolds. Some important factors in organizing for a successful collaboration are:

Member Factors
- inclusion of all affected stakeholders
- sufficient stakeholder incentives

Process Factors
- agreement on the scope of the collaboration
- ripeness of issue(s)

- timing
- negotiating in good faith
- maintaining good relationships with constituents

Member Factors

Member factors include who is invited to participate in a collaboration and their willingness to participate. Conveners and mediators can exercise some influence over each of the factors in the design of the collaborative process.

   Inclusion of All Affected Stakeholders. One of the most serious limitations is not involving key stakeholders. While it is difficult to assess the specific impact of stakeholder selection without a control group, evidence from cases in which key stakeholders were left out or not represented directly suggests that implementation was more often impaired (Bingham, 1986). A successfully negotiated agreement between a local community and the Department of Energy to site a nuclear waste storage facility in Roane County, Tennessee, met with intense opposition from environmental groups, state agencies, and the state legislature after it was announced (Peelle, 1987). While several factors (including the general volatility of the issue and a past history of distrust of the Department of Energy) kindled the opposition, it is noteworthy that the opposition groups were not seated at the negotiating table.

   The most compelling evidence about omission of stakeholders deals with the absence of those with the power to implement the decisions. Failure to include these stakeholders greatly reduces the extent of implementation of agreements (Bingham, 1986; Gray and Hay, 1986). A youth employment project initiated by a public-private partnership graphically illustrates this. Elite planners from several major corporations and the city school system were unable to solicit the participation of principals and counselors in the project, largely because these "lower-level" stakeholders were not included in designing the program (Gray, 1988). The lesson is simple: Enhanced commitment to plans emerges from participation in their design (Delbecq, 1974).

Stakeholders Must Have Sufficient Incentives.   Individual stakeholders must see a compelling reason to try collaboration. They must believe that their interests will be protected and advanced throughout the process. During problem setting, conveners and mediators can do much to help parties appreciate their stake in the domain. They can clarify and prioritize stakeholders' most important concerns and evaluate their options for advancing their interests outside of a collaborative process. Stressing the costs of taking no action can often increase incentives to collaborate. Additionally, the danger of a higher authority imposing a solution if one is not developed collaboratively may induce some stakeholders to participate to ensure that their interests are incorporated in the solution.

Incentives are heightened when parties see a direct opportunity to pursue their self-interest.

> Private firms, like public agencies, can often be induced to serve the public interest, but not when the public interest is at odds with the firm's private interest. In public/private partnerships, policy coordination often breaks down when differences in mission are ignored [Whetten and Bozeman, 1984, p. 7].

Partnerships are not founded solely on philanthropic motives (Davis, 1986). Collaborative efforts that rely heavily on the goodwill of the private sector and do not recognize that sector's interest in favorable publicity, tax incentives, or profit enhancement are less likely to be sustained (Whetten and Bozeman, 1984).

Global competition creates powerful incentives for collective strategies among private-sector firms to improve competitive advantage. Participation will continue as long as such ventures enhance and do not limit the firms' strategic flexibility (Bresser and Harl, 1986).

In some environmental cases, government agencies or courts are in the position to mandate that the parties enter negotiations. While this may guarantee that parties appear at the table, external mandates do not typically encourage parties to negotiate in good faith (Susskind, Bacow, and Wheeler, 1983).

For parties to take negotiations seriously and search for an integrative outcome, they must believe that their interests are better served by collaborating than by other means. Mandate does not guarantee these beliefs.

Process Factors

In addition to member issues, conveners and mediators can exercise discretion over the process of collaborating. Several process factors can positively influence the chances of success.

Agreement on Scope of Collaboration. It is important that parties know up front the scope of the effort to which they are all committing, since differing expectations can derail the proceedings. Scope includes the general problem domain and the intent of the collaboration (for example, information exchange, drafting recommendations, and so forth). Bingham (1986) describes a collaboration between an educational institution, which was planning a large housing development, and the communities surrounding it. The collaboration fell apart because of differing expectations about its scope. The developer envisioned an information exchange, while the others thought development was contingent on an agreement being struck among all the stakeholders.

Adjusting the scope of a collaboration is part of the problem-setting phase. In some cases, the problem will need to be enlarged or redefined to incorporate the interests of critical stakeholders. The lenders in Urban Heights would not meet to eliminate redlining. They agreed to participate after a redefinition of the problem as "promoting reinvestment in the community" was proposed by the mayor. In other cases, the scope of the presenting problem needs to be delimited. If too many issues are addressed with too few interests represented, the quality of agreements will be threatened. As a pioneering effort, the National Coal Policy Project's scope was too far-reaching. As a result, subsequent policy dialogues have been more limited in scope, more focused, and often involve rotation of stakeholders as different aspects of a general problem domain are addressed.

For example, in the third phase of its Biotechnology Policy Dialogue, as the agenda shifts to international issues and questions about the patenting of animal life, the Keystone Center plans to reconfigure the stakeholder group to reflect these interests (J. Ehrmann, personal communication, May 9, 1988).

Timing. The maturity of an issue can be a critical determinant of stakeholders' readiness to collaborate. An issue's maturity is reflected by where it is on the issues life cycle (Post, 1978; Ewing, 1987). Issues that have not yet reached the point of having attained a measure of national public attention may be premature for collaboration in a national arena. In contrast, issues that have passed the legislative stage may no longer be ripe for collaboration until specific questions of implementation are raised by the agency charged with administering the statute. Timing is important at this stage also. In seeking parties for regulatory negotiations, for example, the issues need to be sufficiently crystallized that groups are publicly aligned with them (Harter, 1986a).

Local issues may also require time to mature so stakeholders can be identified, groups can organize, and data can be gathered. Local officials should be sensitive to the needs for newly formed groups to develop their agenda both privately and publicly before they may be willing to negotiate. Sometimes a critical incident is needed to heighten public attention to a problem and galvanize commitment to solve it.

Careful Management of Process. Conveners and negotiators frequently underestimate the critical role of process in ensuring successful collaboration (Patton, 1981; Wondollek, 1985). Process considerations are frequently overwhelmed by substantive ones. Yet collaborative designs involve incorporating the principles of participation, ownership, and power sharing into stakeholder interactions. Stakeholders assume responsibility for ratifying the process of their deliberations as well as the outcomes.

Process issues must be discussed openly, and agreements should be sought on how the group will conduct itself. Drafting and agreeing on ground rules are an essential step in assuring that the parties accept responsibility for the process. Conferring with the parties about what is going to happen next and who is going to do it ensures that expectations are not mismatched and that the parties retain ownership of everything that happens. Concerns voiced by parties (for example, to the mediator or convener) between meetings need to be addressed by the whole group before proceeding. Even after agreement has been reached, periodic follow-up between designers and implementers of an agreement can prevent withdrawal of support at the eleventh hour of the negotiations.

/ A final process consideration is anticipating change and designing in flexibility.\One major strength of the Newark Collaboration is its permeability to absorbing new participants as the process evolves. When collaborations produce non-self-executing agreements, a crucial transition occurs at the point of implementation./Whenever possible, seating more than one representative from those stakeholders responsible for implementation will greatly facilitate this transition.\

Negotiating in Good Faith. Although conveners have little control over stakeholders' motives and behavior once collaboration is under way, underscoring the importance of good-faith negotiating cannot hurt. Questioning the intentions of other negotiators led to more than one failure in the Bingham (1986) study. Skepticism of mediated negotiations expressed by some environmentalists is partly attributed to their belief that other parties failed to negotiate in good faith—including the refusal to examine pertinent issues and failure to abide by agreements after they were struck (Hayes, 1988).

Conveners and mediators need to be alert to possible or perceived breaches of faith. Often signals are misinterpreted, and parties act in ways that are unwittingly affrontive to other stakeholders. It is important to catch and resolve these misunderstandings when they occur and to maintain a climate in which violations of trust work to the disadvantage of all parties.

Maintaining Good Relationships with Constituencies. Participation by groups that are hastily organized or have little shared history can be particularly problematic if the designated spokesperson does not adequately represent the views of his or her constituency or if the spokesperson is not authorized to bind the group to any agreements reached.

Collaborative designs need to build in mechanisms for participants to confer with and gain the commitment of their constituents before any final agreements are reached. Third parties can play an important role in facilitating the selection of a representative by less organized stakeholders to ensure that their concerns are raised during negotiations. One technique frequently used to improve chances for ratification is for negotiators to coach one another on how to deal with concerns of their back-home constituents. Throughout negotiations, conveners should encourage frequent dissemination of progress to constituents and alert parties to the possibility of renegotiation of agreements to satisfy constituent concerns.

It is important to recognize that even when agreements are reached, unanticipated conflicts may arise during implementation. Provisions should be built into the original agreement for how these subsequent disputes will be addressed (Bingham and Miller, 1984; Carpenter and Kennedy, 1988; Moore, 1986).

Introducing and overseeing a collaborative process requires considerable vigilance on the part of conveners and mediators and perseverance by all participants. Belief in the potential of the process coupled with a realistic appreciation of the possible obstacles is essential to success. Building the necessary process skills to collaborate on critical local as well as global problems is an agenda item for the 1990's. The last chapter elaborates on that challenge.

12

Future Challenges
for the Collaborative Process

One cannot predict the future, one can only invent it.
—Dennis Gabor, 1964

A New Way of Organizing

You cannot open a newspaper today without encountering debate over a prognosis for our global future: Should we believe gloomy prospects about depletion of our natural resources? Can the major powers achieve substantial reduction in nuclear build-up? Is terrorism likely to escalate? How substantial is the threat of AIDS to entire populations, especially in the Third World? What are the probabilities of international monetary collapse? Can our planet continue to tolerate the erosion of our air and water quality? How will we cope with an ever-increasing population on a finite earth?

Questions like these dramatically signal the interconnected web of interdependencies that comprise the fabric of our global society. Yet for most of us these questions have little or no immediate bearing on our everyday lives. None, that is, until some basic premise of our existence is threatened. These interdependencies may become "live" for us, for example, if local water supplies become contaminated or cultural violence flares up in our neighborhood. Even then, we are more likely to construe the problem as violation of one of our inalienable rights rather than as a signal of global interdependence. If we can step back far enough from our individual concerns, however, we may begin to appreciate the intricate ways in which our destinies are wrapped up with those of our neighbors. We may begin to understand that the trade-offs we experience between our desired ends and those of our neighbors, locally, regionally, nationally, and internationally, are symptomatic of the increasingly interconnected world in which we live.

I have argued throughout this book that the fundamental interdependencies that now form the foundation of modern existence compel us to reexamine how we organize to solve problems, locally as well as on a national and international level. The first step in this reexamination requires developing a new metaphor that helps us understand what interdependence means. Schön (1979) talks about the need for generative metaphors that serve as overall frameworks for guilding thought and action. Generative metaphors refocus attention and provide frameworks to guide the necessary change in behavior and values that are needed for adaptation. We need a new metaphor that captures our interdependent relationships.

Replacing the Pioneering Metaphor

For a long time Westerners have operated with a pioneering metaphor. Our culture has stressed individual freedom, entrepreneurship, and an "each man for himself" philosophy (Lodge, 1975; Hofstede, 1981). Until recently we have not needed to search for collaborative solutions, nor have we been trained to do so. As Reich (1983, p. 7) rather bluntly explains:

> The vastness of America's territories enabled generations of Americans to solve social problems by escaping from them, instead of working to change them. So long as the frontier beckoned, the sensible way to settle disputes was not painful negotiation, but simply putting some distance between the disputants.

Surveys comparing attitudes across cultures show that Americans score highest of any country on masculinity and individualism (Hofstede, 1980). We are so steeped in a concept of the person as independent and individualistic that it is easy for us to discount interconnectedness until we come face to face with its consequences (for example, conflict or deadlock).

Now the distances have shrunk, the frontiers have disappeared, and our role as global partners has become undeniable. Gradually, a new metaphor emphasizing dynamic wholeness is beginning to replace the old pioneering one. Dynamic wholeness asserts that the parts of a whole are not distinct elements. They only appear so because of the limits of our ability to empirically observe the connections (Bohm, 1980). Instead, individual parts derive their meaning in relation to other parts, and change occurs as a reconfiguration of the entire set of relationships (Jantsch, 1979).

The notion of dynamic wholeness has profound implications for the way in which we currently understand relations between organizations and groups. Our current values and styles of interacting, which stress independence, need to be complemented with models that stress interdependence and complementarity. And just as old assumptions of independence were institutionalized within specialized organizational forms (namely, bureaucracies and multidivisional corporations), new, more collaborative interorganizational designs based on the principles of dynamic wholeness will be needed for managing in a turbulent world (Perlmutter and Trist, 1986). Gradually we are coming to recognize the limitations inherent in the current mechanisms we use for solving complex problems. They are not suited to managing interdependence; instead, new models of organizing are needed.

Collaboration is proposed as a viable means for organizing across organizations to manage interdependence. Learning to collaborate, however, will require some radical revisions in our thinking and a retooling of our problem-solving abilities. Essentially we need to switch from an image of individual sovereignty over a problem domain in one of shared stewardship.

Shared Stewardship

A steward is someone who actively directs affairs. Stewardship involves managing one's affairs while taking into consideration others' rights and responsibilities. Colllaboration assumes that stakeholders share responsibility for formulating and enacting the future direction of their domain/Shared responsibility entails shared power and requires that stakeholders learn strategies of mutual empowerment that allow them to correlate their behaviors toward mutually desired ends. Shared stewardship implies a more expansive conception of power than is typically in use.

> This assumes a broader conception of power, one where power is defined as the production of intended effects not only unilaterally but also collectively. Power thus becomes catalytic, not commanding, facilitative rather than dominating [Luke, 1984, p. 30].

Collaborative processes unleash this catalytic power and mobilize joint action among the stakeholders. Norman Uphoff has called this generating social energy (Uphoff, 1987).

According to Uphoff (1987), three conditions are necessary to produce social energy. First, ideas about what to do are needed. Second, shared values about how to do it need to be forged. Third, a climate of trust must be fostered. The first two conditions are developed through the process of joint appreciation, which is an essential component of collaboration. Trust is also fostered through collaboration. When these three conditions are met, the potential for creating positive change for all parties is enhanced. The primary advantage of collaboration, then, abides in its transformative potential. Acting together, stakeholders can muster the social energy to introduce desired change.

The process of appreciation deserves further elaboration here. Chapter Ten stressed the idea that the process of collaborating leads to the creation of a negotiated order among the participating organizations. Arriving at a negotiated order requires joint appreciation. An essential notion of appreciation is the power of collective thought to transform existing circumstances. Boje (1982), Smircich (1983), and Bartunek (1984) have described how leaders induce change by introducing new meanings for existing circumstances. This "myth-making" process occurs during collaboration as stakeholders negotiate an image of their

desired future. Myth making involves abandoning existing interpretations and creating new or expanded interpretations for
existing problem domains. Individually, stakeholders are often
constrained from envisioning new possibilities. Their own visions
are only partially formed or are blocked by a sense of individual
powerlessness. Part of the process of myth making involves introducing new language (Boje, 1982; Smircich, 1983) and new
symbols of what is important. Fundamental to this process of
transformation is the idea that "society is made and imagined
and that it can therefore be remade and reimagined" (Unger,
1987, p. 8). A new negotiated order emerges, and stakeholders
begin to invent collective symbols and language to describe the
agreements they reach about the domain. When people share
the fundamental assumptions that undergird their thinking,
they can forge a collective appreciation.

With respect to Uphoff's second point, Vickers (1965) ar-
gues that appreciation also involves valuing. Agreements that incorporate the interests of each stakeholder are based on what it
is that each values. Often people cannot commit to a course of
action because they cannot see how their interests are served.
Building commitment to a course of action collaboratively un-
leashes a latent potential. This potential could not be previously
tapped because it had not been articulated.

In addition to changing our conceptualization of organizing to one of shared stewardship, we need to cultivate or refine
several capacities to collaborate. These are described in the next
section.

Capacities for Collaborating

Five capacities that we as a global society will need to develop
in order to collaborate effectively are:

- channeling conflict constructively
- maximizing joint gains
- reaching agreement about risks
- institutionalizing collaborative processes
- training leaders

Channeling Conflict Constructively

When problems are complex and uncertain, it is predictable that stakeholders will become polarized and conflicts will escalate. Without mechanisms for channeling this conflict, problems fester and positions harden, exacerbating the situation and making solutions even more remote. We need processes that reverse these trends, that acknowledge the potential for conflict, and that expand, rather than reduce, our capacity to act.

Parties facing conflicts of this sort need to seriously weigh the costs of delaying decisions or escalating the conflict compared to the costs of collaborating. Those who fear that their interests will be irreparably compromised by collaboration should make judicious choices about which of the problems they confront are most amenable to collaboration. Critics who challenge the track record so far need to understand that the responsibility of parties in collaboration is not to forego their own interests; they are expected to find ways to protect their interests while respecting those of others. If attempts to collaborate lead only to unsatisfactory compromise, the parties are not precluded from more traditional avenues of handling conflict.

Intergovernmental conflicts and conflicts involving more than one governmental agency appear to be especially amenable to collaboration, since problems that require decisions from multiple agencies are slow to be resolved. Finding an appropriate convener for these problems may pose realistic setbacks to collaborating. Leadership will have to come from agency officials who make a commitment to identifying those disputes in which delays are most harmful to the public interest.

Learning to Maximize Joint Gains

Particularly in the United States, we have a propensity to define solutions for private rather than for public gain (Arndt and Bouton, 1987). Yet unilateral actions in pursuit of private gain are less and less possible. And creative solutions to problems require the knowledge and commitment of stakeholders with diverse perspectives. Integrating the needs and interests of a diverse

population is becoming as critical in the United States as it has
been and continues to be in many countries in Africa, Canada,
Asia, and South America, where different racial and cultural
groups must coexist. Satisfying our individual interests is increasingly possible only in the context of satisfying interests of
others as well.

That means we need to learn to maximize joint gains. To
do so means discovering shared interests and arranging the most
advantageous trade-offs possible among differing interests.

Reaching Agreement About Managing Risks

Countless decisions before township supervisors, local planning
boards, local, state, and federal environmental resource departments, and other agencies that oversee resource utilization involve real or perceived decisions about the allocation of risks.
Virtually every development plan can be challenged because of
its anticipated social or environmental impact. The cleanup of
existing toxic waste dumps epitomizes the difficult risk allocation decisions that must be made. Locating and constructing
sanitary and hazardous waste disposal facilities require difficult
allocation decisions that we in the United States have been para-
lyzed as a nation to confront. We cannot produce wastes indefi-
nitely without making prudent but urgent decisions about waste
disposal.

In many situations, inaction is the least desirable outcome. Moreover, unilateral decisions are either morally or
practically unacceptable. Because of the extremely sensitive nature of these choices, attempts to impose unilateral solutions
that ignore or minimize risks perceived by some stakeholders
are likely to encounter disabling resistance.

> If the historical representative government process im-
> poses a decision upon the electorate prematurely or fails
> to integrate potentially conflicting elements, it can cause
> unnecessary confrontations and polarization. The elector-
> citizen resorts to initiative, referenda, judicial action,
> or recall in order to impose his or her will upon the
> elected body and other groups [Neu, 1988, p. 140].

Experience has shown these processes fail to solve the problems (Harter, 1986b; Susskind and Cruikshank, 1987). Because implementation hinges on stakeholder acceptance of the distribution of gains and losses, and because decisions by individual stakeholders or the courts are often limited in scope, we need other mechanisms for arriving at acceptable risks. What collaboration affords is a process by which such distribution of risks can be negotiated.

On the optimistic side, the lessons from Canada in siting hazardous waste facilities are heartening. Collaborative processes managed at the state level that involve local communities in the search for answers to these problems seem to hold the most promise for tackling these tough issues.

On a more global scale, the recent international treaty on chlorofluorocarbons demonstrates the potential for coming to grips with difficult risk allocation decisions. That agreement, which was signed by forty-eight countries in March 1988, provided for a freeze on production of chlorofluorocarbons, chemicals that deteriorate the earth's ozone layer. According to Richard Benedict, one of the U.S. negotiators and an architect of the treaty, several factors made the treaty possible, including (1) close cooperation between policymakers and scientists; (2) an evolutionary step-by-step process of consensus building; (3) the enlightened self-interest of U.S. chlorofluorocarbon manufacturers, who agreed to a ban; (4) skillful leadership within several constituencies; (5) the absence of blame among industry and environmental organizations in the United States; and (6) a model role by the United Nations Environmental Program, which served as convener for the negotiations (Benedick, 1988).

Generally, the design and conduct of processes that address the allocation of risks will require both institutional forums and skilled leadership. These are discussed further below.

Institutionalizing Collaborative Processes

One of the major limitations to more widespread use of collaboration is the limited availability of forums in which these deliberations can occur. In a limited number of cases, judicial and administrative agencies provide the auspices for convening collaborative negotiations. Nongovernmental organizations such as the Conservation Foundation, the Keystone Center, and the Institute for Resource Management also provide an institutional umbrella for selected policy dialogues. Most collaborations, however, are organized on an ad hoc basis among the parties, perhaps with institutional support from a neutral organization such as a university, a foundation, a mediation service, or even one of the stakeholder groups.

We need institutional commitments to construct forums within and outside existing institutions to encourage experimentation with collaborative solutions. As Reich (1983) pointed out, we have no tradition for bargaining for consensus. From the experience to date, it seems clear that government agencies are in a logical position to initiate collaboration in certain cases. In other cases independent forums under the auspices of the court are appropriate. Private foundations or other neutral third-sector organizations can also play effective roles as conveners and should be encouraged to do so.

In addition to ad hoc arrangements, Bingham (1986, p. 150) identifies several options for the continued provision of mediation services for multiparty disputes. Among them are court referrals and court-sponsored programs; establishment of local, state, or federal mediation services by government agencies; and incorporation of voluntary dispute resolution procedures. All of these options are currently in use on a limited basis.

For example, five states now have statutory procedures that require or recommend a mediation step for the siting of hazardous waste facilities, and at least five states are exploring the use of negotiated rulemaking (Haygood, 1988). In the Massachusetts and Rhode Island statutes, negotiations between the developer and a local assessment committee composed of specific local officials and citizens are required. (For an extensive discussion of the provisions of various state laws regarding negotiations over siting of hazardous facilities, see Bingham and Mealy, 1988.) In 1987 OSHA introduced a new settlement judge procedure that allows for cases to be settled through mediation by a settlement judge if all the parties agree. Numerous other bills at the federal and state levels have incorporated clauses that offer or recommend a mediation option to resolve disagreements arising during administration of a statute.

The key questions regarding institutionalization of collaborative processes revolve around three basic issues: (1) Who has the legitimacy and perceived neutrality to provide auspices for convening and conducting collaborative negotiations? (2) Who will pay for the cost of mediation services if parties desire them? (3) How can concerns about differential or inconsistent application of principles be satisfied if parties in each collaboration are free to adopt their own set of standards (Bureau of National Affairs, 1985; Bingham, 1986)?

The question of the role of government in providing auspices for collaborative negotiations is open for debate. Certainly at the municipal level, officials can play an essential role in "sensing vital issues, involving and empowering affected parties, formulating informed consensus, and enabling implementation of that consensus" (Neu, 1988, p. 140). Sequential steps local officials can take to foster collaborative partnerships with the community are listed in Table 11. The role of the state government in convening and facilitating multiparty negotiations may in part be influenced by the experience of several state-sponsored mediation services that have been operating since 1984 with funding from the National Institute for Dispute Resolution. Designed as trial ventures, these organizations serve as advocates for the use of mediation, provide training and mediation services, and monitor public policy disputes in their states (Haygood, 1988). While these organizations have had varying degrees of involvement in mediating multiparty disputes, one lingering question concerns their ability to remain "neutral," especially if they are chartered under an individual agency (such as a department of environmental protection) or an independent commission (for example, a public utility commission). State mediation services operating under judicial auspices benefit from numerous referrals, but their cases are usually well advanced toward litigation. Other models propose creating offices within the executive branch (for example, the governor's office) or establishing an entirely new state agency (Haygood, 1988).

Table 11.   What Local Officials Can Do to Foster Collaboration.

- identify and focus issues that need to be addressed
- facilitate sharing of information
- act as a convener of divergent opinions and groups
- facilitate development of consensus on the community vision
- ratify the emergent consensus through legislative action
- oversee implementation of programs, policies, and projects resulting from consensus agreements
- maintain support for the vision and actions taken

Adapted from Neu (1988).

Government sponsorship provides a de facto answer to the question of funding. Another model is for parties to hire mediators from national or regional pools such as those that are maintained by the Federal Mediation and Conciliation Service (Bingham, 1986). This does not resolve the questions of who pays for the service or who provides the institutional auspices within which collaboration occurs. Nongovernmental organizations are often able to provide the appropriate institutional home for multiparty collaborations; however, to date financial support to sustain these services has come from foundations and negotiators on a case-by-case basis. For collaborations involving government agencies, funds could be established to contract with designated nongovernmental organizations to provide an institutional forum for collaboration.

Concerns about judicial equity across disputes have only partially been answered. The facts that collaborative processes are not designed as substitutes for any branch of government at any level and that they are voluntary procedures always leave open the option for stakeholders to pursue legal remedies and pursue legal precedents. It also seems plausible that a body of quasi precedents will evolve as parties in one location investigate options that have already proven successful in other similar situations.

A final thought on institutionalization is that the under-organized character of many collaborations and their success in constructively transforming the domain of necessity require the maintenance of open, permeable, and flexible methods of organizing throughout the three phases of collaboration. Nurturing redundancy (Ackoff, 1974) and loose coupling (Weick, 1976) within the domain enhance the prospects for longevity and wider adoption of innovations. This may suggest that continued experimentation with different institutional forums for collaboration is preferable at this time to more standardized arrangements. Ultimately, the demand for collaborative approaches must echo from those who will participate in them. Individual stakeholders must provide the initiative and commitment if collaborative processes are to be effective.

> There is no shortage of knowledge about desirable alternatives to the present social designs and strategies of societies. The greatest task is to create them. Creation can be accomplished only by ordinary people in their ordinary yet threatened life circumstances. Planners, scientists, intellectuals, and others with specialized and more esoteric knowledge and skills can help, but people must make their own futures [Williams, 1982, p. 194].

The objective is to stimulate, not stifle, inquiry among stakeholders.

Training Leaders

A special breed of leaders is also needed if more systematic use of collaboration is to occur. The role of local officials in initiating collaborative processes has already been proposed. Generally, leaders need a vision of what collaboration can accomplish, sensitivity and the ability to develop relationships with diverse stakeholders, and a sense of optimism and process literacy, that is, knowledge of the process tools, both human and organizational, for designing effective collaborations. Cultivating leaders with these special competencies is essential for managing multiparty interdependencies collaboratively.

Reich (1983) summarizes the requisites for meeting the challenge of interdependence as follows:

There is no "best solution" to how the gains and losses
from economic change should be allocated and re-
arranged. . . . We will need leaders who are not afraid to
recognize frankly the political choices that are entailed
in major economic change and who are willing to choreo-
graph openly the bargaining about them. . . . We will
need political institutions capable of generating large
scale compromise and adaptation . . . [and] a national
bargaining arena for allocating the burdens and benefits
of major adjustment strategies. Such an arena would
enable the nation to achieve a broad-based consensus
about adjustment [pp. 267–268, 275–276].

The Potential to Transform Problems

Several examples of collaboration at work around the globe provide reasons for cautious optimism about the prospects for
transforming problems into constructive solutions. Cleveland
(1986, p. 79) cites examples such as European economic integration, cooperative agricultural research institutes, the success
of population limitation in some developing countries, cleanup
of the Mediterranean urged by the United Nations Environmental Programme, and free development in the Pacific Basin as
evidence of a "workable world" for the future.

The numerous examples referenced in this book also provide reason for optimism. Yet the potential for collaboration is
still largely untapped. The list of problems for which collaborative initiatives might prove beneficial is comprehensive. It includes a myriad of local development and land use issues and
environmental issues such as water distribution and preservation,
energy usage, and waste disposal. In the area of health care, issues of cost containment, quality of care, treatment of special
populations, and labor relations are prime candidates for collaboration (Kaye, 1986). The location of affordable housing and
transitional provisions for dealing with plant closings are also
possibilities. The impact of illiteracy and teenage employability
are critical issues in most urban areas. Collaborative processes
for rate making by public utility commissions have met with

some success (O'Leary, 1986). Even controversial topics such as AIDS testing and allocation of liability for Superfund sites are potential candidates for collaborating. And the list goes on.

The real question about collaborating is: Do we have a choice? Given the long list of multiparty problems awaiting resolution, the record of success to date, the potential available, and the dire prospects of irreparable harm to our planet, can we as a global society afford not to search for common ground through collaboration? Robert Redford has framed the issues in terms of a legacy to future generations:

> The world has become too small to allow us to maintain old stances, old-fashioned notions that there is all that space out there—manifest destiny. It's antiquated thinking that we have limitless resources and we don't have to worry—technology will somehow solve all our problems. We are at a point now where we can't afford that attitude any longer. We have to be more thoughtful about our actions. If not, we will be stealing from future generations rather than giving to them. To begin, let us search for the common ground [Redford, 1987, p. 112].

Or, put more positively: Suppose we seriously took up the challenge of crafting a world that aspires to economic stability and fairness, justice and mutual prosperity. Collaboration offers a tool for inventing such a future. Why not test its potential?

References

Abel, R. L. "The Contradictions of Informal Justice." In R. L. Abel (ed.), *The Politics of Informal Justice.* Vol. 1. Orlando, Fla.: Academic Press, 1982.

Ackoff, R. L. *Redesigning the Future.* New York: Wiley, 1974.

Ackoff, R. L. *Creating the Corporate Future.* New York: Wiley, 1981.

Agranoff, R., and Lindsay, V. A. "Intergovernmental Management: Perspectives from Human Services' Problem Solving at the Local Level." *Public Administration Review,* May–June 1983, 227–237.

Aharoni, Y. *The No-Risk Society.* Chatham, N.J.: Chatham House, 1981.

Aldrich, H. "Visionaries and Villains: The Politics of Designing Interorganizational Relations." *Organization and Administration,* 1977, *8* (2 and 3), 23–40.

Alderfer, C. P. "Consulting to Underbounded Systems." In C. P. Alderfer and C. Cooper (eds.), *Advances in Experimental Social Processes, 2.* New York: Wiley, 1979.

Alexander, T. "A Promising Try at Environmental Dente for Coal." *Fortune,* Feb. 13, 1978, 94–102.

Alinsky, S. D. *Rules for Radicals.* New York: Vintage Books, 1971.

Alinsky, S. D. *Reveille for Radicals.* New York: Vintage Books, 1979.

American Productivity Center. *Productivity Perspectives* (Rev. ed.). Houston, Tex.: American Productivity Center, 1982.

American Productivity Center. *Multiple Input Productivity Indexes*. Vol. 6. Houston, Tex.: American Productivity Center, Dec. 1986.

Ansoff, I. "Managing Strategic Surprise by Response to Weak Signals." *California Management Review,* 1975, *18,* 21-33.

Arndt, S. W., and Bouton, L. *Competitiveness: The United States in World Trade.* Washington, D.C.: American Enterprise Institute, 1987.

Ashby, R. *Design for a Brain* (2nd ed.). London: Chapman and Hall, 1960.

Astley, W. G. "Toward an Appreciation of Collective Strategy." *Academy of Management Review,* 1984, *9* (3), 526-535.

Astley, W. G., and Brahm, R. "Organizational Designs for Post-Industrial Strategies: The Role of Interorganizational Collaboration." In C. C. Snow (ed.), *Strategy, Organizational Design and Human Resource Management.* Greenwich, Conn.: JAI Press, 1988.

Astley, W. G., and Fombrun, C. "Collective Strategy: Social Ecology of Organizational Environments." *Academy of Management Review,* 1983, *8* (4), 576-587.

Bachrach, P., and Baratz, M. S. "Decisions and Nondecisions: An Analytical Framework." *American Political Science Review,* 1963, *57,* 641-651.

Bacow, L. S. "The Technical and Judgmental Dimensions of Impact Assessment." *Environmental Impact Assessment Review,* 1980, *1,* 109, 115-120.

Bacow, L. S., and Cohen, B. "Avoiding the Trials of Big Development." *Technology Review,* 1982, 42-44.

Bacow, L. S., and Milkey, J. R. "Overcoming Local Opposition to Hazardous Waste Facilities: The Massachusetts Approach." *Harvard Environmental Law Review,* 1982, *6* (2), 265-305.

Bacow, L. S., and Wheeler, M. *Environmental Dispute Resolution.* New York: Plenum Press, 1984.

Baily, M. N., and Chakrabarti, A. K. *Innovation and the Productivity Crisis.* Washington, D.C.: Brookings Institution, 1988.

Bartunek, J. "Changing Interpretive Schemes and Organizational

Restructuring: The Example of a Religious Order." *Administrative Science Quarterly,* 1984, *29* (3), 355–372.

Bell, D. "Communications Technology—For Better or for Worse." *Harvard Business Review,* 1979, *57* (3), 20–42.

Benedick, R. *An International Success Story: The Chlorofluoro-Carbon Treaty.* Presentation at the Fourth National Conference on Environmental Dispute Resolution, sponsored by the Conservation Foundation, Washington, D.C., June 2–3, 1988.

Benson, J. K. "The Interorganizational Network as a Political Economy." *Administrative Science Quarterly,* 1975, *20,* 229–249.

Berger, R. A. "Private Sector Initiatives in the Reagan Administration." In P. Davis (ed.), *Public-Private Partnerships: Improving Urban Life.* New York: Academy of Political Science, 1986.

Bingham, G. *Resolving Environmental Disputes: A Decade of Experience.* Washington, D.C.: Conservation Foundation, 1986.

Bingham, G., and Mealey, T. *Negotiating Hazardous Waste Facility Siting and Permitting Agreements.* Washington, D.C.: Conservation Foundation, 1988.

Bingham, G., and Miller, D. S. "Prospects for Resolving Hazardous Waste Siting Disputes Through Negotiation." *Natural Resources Lawyer,* 1984, *12* (3), 473–479.

Bohm, D. *Wholeness and the Implicate Order.* London: Routledge and Kegan Paul, 1983.

Boje, D. *Towards a Theory and Praxis of Transorganizational Development: Stakeholder Networks and Their Habitats.* Working Paper 79-6, Behavioral and Organizational Science Study Center, Graduate School of Management, University of California at Los Angeles, February 1982.

Boje, D. M., and Wolfe, T. J. "Transorganization Development: Contributions to Theory and Practice." In H. J. Leavitt, L. R. Pondy, and D. M. Boje (eds.), *Readings in Managerial Psychology* (4th ed.). Chicago: University of Chicago Press, 1988.

Bozeman, B. "Dimensions of 'Publicness.' " In B. Bozeman and J. Straussman (eds.), *New Directions in Public Administration.* Pacific Grove, Calif.: Brooks/Cole, 1984.

Bozeman, B., and Cole, E. "Scientific and Technical Information in Public Management: The Role of Gatekeeping and Channel Preference." *Administration and Society*, 1982, *13* (4), 479-493.

Brazil, W. D. "Special Masters in Complex Cases." *University of Chicago Law Review*, 1986, *53*, 394-423.

Bresser, R. K., and Harl, J. E. "Collective Strategy: Vice or Virtue?" *Academy of Management Review*, 1986, *11* (2), 408-427.

Brooks, H., Liebman, L., and Schellng, C. (eds.). *Public-Private Partnership: New Opportunities for Meeting Social Needs.* Cambridge, Mass.: Ballinger, 1984.

Brown, L. D. "Planned Change in Underorganized Systems." In T. G. Cummings (ed.), *Systems Theory for Organizational Development.* New York: Wiley, 1980.

Brown, L. D. "Leadership Outside Organizational Paradigms: Power in Community Partnerships." In S. Srivastva and Associates (eds.), *Executive Power.* San Francisco: Jossey-Bass, 1986.

Brown, S. M., and Wilson, M. E. "Partnership Models—Three Perspectives." In *Building Partnerships: Business, Industry and Higher Education Working Together.* National Issues in Higher Education, Vol. 22. Kansas State University, 1984.

Brunn, S. D., Johnson, J. H., and Ziegler, D. J. "Final Report on a Social Survey of Three Mile Island Area Residents." East Lansing: Department of Geography, Michigan State University, Aug. 1979.

Bucholtz, E. *Business Environment and Public Policy.* (2nd ed.) Englewood Cliffs, N.J.: Prentice-Hall, 1986.

Bucholtz, E. *Issues of Management and Public Policy—Ethics and Politics.* Paper presented at the Sixth Annual Issues Management Conference, Pennsylvania State University, May 23-25, 1988.

Buckle, L. G., and Thomas-Buckle, S. R. "Placing Environmental Mediation in Context: Lessons from 'Failed' Mediations." *Environmental Impact Assessment Review*, 1986, *6*, 55-70.

Bureau of National Affairs. *Resolving Disputes Without Litigation.* Washington, D.C.: Bureau of National Affairs, 1985.

Bureau of National Affairs. Alternative Dispute Resolution Report, no. 1. Dec. 10, 1987, 327.

Bureau of National Affairs. Alternative Dispute Resolution Report, no. 2. May 12, 1988, 171.

"Can America Compete?" *Business Week*, Apr. 20, 1987, 44–69.

Carpenter, S. L. Presentation at Environmental Mediation Training Workshop, Philadelphia, May 4–6, 1988.

Carpenter, S. L., and Kennedy, W.J.D. *Managing Public Disputes: A Practical Guide to Handling Conflict and Reaching Agreements.* San Francisco: Jossey-Bass, 1988.

Carter, L. J. "Coal: Invoking the 'Rule of Reason' in an Energy-Environment Crisis." *Science,* Oct. 21, 1977, 276–278.

Center for Policy Negotiation, Inc. *Policy Negotiation: An Alternative to Stalemate.* Boston: Center for Policy Negotiation, Inc., 1985.

Center for Public Resources. *A Superfund Multi-Party Site Cost Allocation Procedure.* New York: Center for Public Resources, May 20, 1985.

Center for Public Resources. Pamphlet on mini-trials, 1986.

Chambers, M. "California's Swift, Costly Private Judicial System." *New York Times,* Feb. 24, 1986, A5.

Chevalier, M. *A Wider Range of Perspectives in the Bureaucratic Structure.* Ottawa, Canada: Commission on Bilingualism and Biculturalism, 1966.

Cleveland, H. "The Future of International Governance." Presentation at the 1986 World Future Society Conference, New York. *Vital Speeches of the Day,* July 15, 1986, 78–81.

Colosi, T. "A Core Model of Negotiation." In R. J. Lewicki and J. A. Litterer (eds.), *Negotiation: Readings, Exercises and Cases.* Homewood, Ill.: Irwin, 1985.

Committee for Economic Development, Research and Policy Committee. *Public-Private Partnership: An Opportunity for Urban Communities.* Washington, D.C.: Committee for Economic Development, 1982.

Committee for Economic Development, Research and Policy Committee. *Productivity Policy: Key to the Nation's Economic Future.* New York: Committee for Economic Development, Apr. 1983.

Committee on Interstate and Foreign Commerce, United States House of Representatives. "National Coal Policy Project: Hearings Before the Subcommittee on Energy and Power." Washington, D.C.: U.S. Government Printing Office, 1978.

Cummings, T. G. "Transorganizational Development." In B. Staw and L. Cummings (eds.), *Research in Organizational Behavior*. Vol. 6. Greenwich, Conn.: JAI Press, 1984.

Cyert, R., and March, J. *A Behavioral Theory of the Firm.* Englewood Cliffs, N.J.: Prentice-Hall, 1963.

Dahl, R. A. *Pluralist Democracy in the United States: Conflict and Consent.* Skokie, Ill.: Rand McNally, 1967.

Dahl, R. A. *Dilemmas of Pluralist Democracy.* New Haven, Conn.: Yale University Press, 1982.

Dahl, R. A. *Democracy, Liberty, and Equality.* London: Norwegian University Press, 1986.

Davidson, S. M. "Planning and Coordination of Social Service in Multi-Organizational Contexts." *Social Service Review,* 1976, *50,* 117-137.

Davis, P. "Why Partnerships: Why Now?" In P. Davis (ed.), *Public-Private Partnerships: Improving Urban Life.* New York: Academy of Political Science, 1986.

Davis, K., and Frederick, W. C. *Business and Society: Management, Public Policy, and Ethics* (5th ed.). New York: McGraw-Hill, 1984.

Day, R., and Day, J. V. "A Review of the Current State of Negotiated Order Theory: An Appreciation and a Critique." *The Sociological Quarterly,* 1977, *18,* 126-142.

Dean, J., and Susman, G. I. "Organizing for Manufacturable Design." *Harvard Business Review,* Jan.-Feb. 1989.

Delbecq, A. L. "Contextual Variables Affecting Decision-Making in Program Planning." *Journal of the American Institute for Decision Sciences,* 1974, *5* (4), 726-742.

Deutsch, K. W., and Rieselbach, L. "Recent Trends in Political Theory and Political Philosophy." *Annals of the American Political and Social Science,* 1965, *360,* 151.

Dimaggio, P. J., and Powell, W. W. "The Iron Cage Revisited: Institutional Isomorphism and Collective Rationality in Organizational Fields." *American Sociological Review*, 1983, *48*, 147–160.

Dimancescu, D., and Botkin, J. *The New Alliance: America's R&D Consortia.* Cambridge, Mass.: Ballinger, 1986.

Dispute Resolution Forum. "Regulatory Negotiation: Four Perspectives." Washington, D.C.: National Institute for Dispute Resolution, Jan. 8–11, 1986.

Donnellon, A., Gray, B., and Bougon, M. G. "Communication, Meaning and Organized Action." *Administrative Science Quarterly*, 1986, *31* (1), 43–55.

Downs, G. *Bureaucracy, Innovation and Public Policy.* Lexington, Mass.: Heath, 1976.

Doyle, M. *Collaborative Processes: Strategies for Institution Building.* Paper presented at the Conference on Collaboration and Conflict Resolution in Community Problem Solving: Emerging Trends and Methods, Washington, D.C., Mar. 16, 1988.

Dunlop, J. T. "A Decade of National Experience." In J. M. Rosow (ed.), *Teamwork, Joint Labor Management Programs in America.* New York: Pergamon Press, 1986.

Dunlop, J. T. *Alternative Means of Dispute Resolution in Government.* Working Paper, Harvard University, June 1, 1987.

Dunlop, J. T., and Salter, M. S. "Note on Forums and Governance." Case 0-388-046. Boston: Harvard Business School, 1987.

Dunlop, J. T., Salter, M. S., and Sanabria, S. "A Review of Selected Industrial Governance Forums." Case N9-388-072. Boston: Harvard Business School, 1987.

Edelman, M. "Symbols and Political Quiescence." *American Political Science Review*, 1960, *54*, 695–704.

Edelman, M. *The Symbolic Uses of Politics.* Urbana: University of Illinois Press, 1967.

Elliot, M.L.P. "The Effect of Differing Assessments of Risk in Hazardous Waste Facility Siting Negotiations." In G. Bingham and T. Mealey (eds.), *Negotiating Hazardous Waste Facility Siting and Permitting Agreements.* Washington, D.C.: Conservation Foundation, 1988.

Elsman, M., and the National Institute for Work and Learning. *Industry-Education-Labor Collaboration: An Action Guide for Collaborative Councils.* Report prepared by the Industry-Education-Labor Collaboration Project of the Center for Education and Work. Washington, D.C.: National Institute for Work and Learning, 1981.

Emery, F. E. "Adaptive Systems for Our Future Governance." *National Labour Institute Bulletin,* 1976, *4.* New Delhi, India.

Emery, F. E. *Futures We Are In.* Leiden, The Netherlands: Martinus Nijhoff, 1977.

Emery, F. E., and Emery, M. *A Choice of Futures.* Leiden, The Netherlands: Martinus Nijhoff, 1977.

Emery, F. E., and Emery, M. "Searching: For new directions, in new ways . . . for new times." In J. W. Sutherland (ed.), *Management Handbook for Public Administrators.* New York: Van Nostrand Reinhold, 1978.

Emery, F. E., and Trist, E. L. "The Causal Texture of Organizational Environments." *Human Relations,* 1965, *18,* 21–32.

Emery, F. E., and Trist, E. L. *Towards a Social Ecology.* New York: Plenum Press, 1972.

Ewing, R. P. *Managing the New Bottom Line: Issues of Management for Senior Executives.* Homewood, Ill.: Dow Jones-Irwin, 1987.

Executive Office of the President, Office of Management and Budget. *Managing Federal Assistance in the 1980's.* Washington, D.C.: U.S. Government Printing Office, 1980.

Fiorino, D. J. "Regulatory Negotiation as a Policy Process." *Public Administration Review,* July–Aug. 1988, 20–28.

Fiorino, D. J., and Kirtz, C. "Breaking Down Walls: Negotiated Rulemaking at EPA." *Temple Environmental Law and Technical Journal,* 1985, *4,* 29–40.

Fisher, R. *International Conflict: A Working Guide.* New York: International Peace Academy, 1978.

Fisher, R., and Ury, W. *International Mediation: A Practitioner's Guide.* New York: International Peace Academy, 1978.

Fisher, R., and Ury, W. *Getting to Yes: Negotiating Agreement Without Giving In.* Boston: Houghton Mifflin, 1981.

Foderaro, L. W. "When Development Becomes Divisive." *New York Times*, Apr. 20, 1988, B1, B5.

Folberg, J., and Taylor, A. *Mediation: A Comprehensive Guide to Resolving Conflicts Without Litigation.* San Francisco: Jossey-Bass, 1984.

Fombrun, C. "Strategies for Network Research in Organizations." *Academy of Management Review*, 1982, 7, 280–291.

Fombrun, C. "Structural Dynamics Within and Between Organizations." *Administrative Science Quarterly*, 1986, *31* (3), 403–421.

Fosler, R. S., and Berger, R. (eds.). *Public Private Partnerships in American Cities: Seven Case Studies.* Lexington, Mass.: Lexington Books, 1982.

Fox, J. R. "The National Coal Policy Project (A)." In J. R. Fox (ed.), *Managing Business/Government Relations: Cases and Notes on Business/Government Problems.* Homewood, Ill.: Irwin, 1982a.

Fox, J. R. "Note on the Resolution of Conflicts Involving Business, Government and Special Interest Groups." In J. R. Fox (ed.), *Managing Business/Government Relations: Cases and Notes on Business/Government Problems.* Homewood, Ill.: Irwin, 1982b.

Fraser, D. Speech given at Chautauqua Institute. Chautauqua, New York, July, 1986.

Freeman, R. E. *Strategic Management: A Stakeholder Approach.* Marshfield, Mass.: Pitman, 1984.

Freire, P. *Pedagogy of the Oppressed.* New York: Herder and Herder, 1971.

Friend, J. K., and Jessop, W. N. *Local Government and Strategic Choice.* London: Tavistock, 1969.

Friend, J. K., Power, J. M., and Yewlett, C.J.L. *Public Planning: The Intercorporate Dimension.* London: Tavistock, 1974.

Galanter, M. "Legality and Its Discontents: A Preliminary Assessment of Current Theories of Legalization and Delegalization." In E. Blankenburg, E. Klausa, and H. Rottleuther (eds.), *Alternative Rechtsformen und Alternativen zum Recht.* Opladen, West Germany: Westdeutscher Verlag (Jahrbuch für Rechtssoziologicund Rechtstheorie, Band 6), 1979.

Galaskiewicz, J. "The Structure of Community Organizational Networks." *Social Forces*, 1979, *57*, 1346–64.

Galaskiewicz, J. "Interorganizational Relations." *Annual Review of Sociology*, 1985, *11*, 281–304.

Gamm, L. "An Introduction to Research in Interorganizational Relations (IOR)." *Journal of Voluntary Action Research*, 1981, 18–52.

Gamson, W. A. *The Strategy of Social Protest.* Homewood, Ill.: Dorsey Press, 1975.

Gaventa, J. *Power and Powerlessness: Quiescence and Rebellion in an Appalachian Valley.* Urbana: University of Illinois Press, 1980.

Gellhorn, E. "Too Much Law, Too Many Lawyers, Not Enough Justice." *Wall Street Journal*, June 8, 1984, 28.

Giddens, A. *Central Problems in Social Theory.* Berkeley: University of California Press, 1979.

Gilmore, T., Weiss, H., and Williams, T. *Western Search Conference on the Jail of the Future: A Record of the Session.* Working paper, Management and Behavioral Science Center, The Wharton School, University of Pennsylvania, 1979.

Goffman, E. "The Interaction Order." *American Sociological Review*, 1983, *48*, 1–17.

Goldberg, S., Green, E., and Sander, F. *Dispute Resolution.* Boston: Little, Brown, 1985.

Governor's Task Force on Private Initiatives. Boston, 1982.

Gray, B. "Conditions Facilitating Interorganizational Collaboration." *Human Relations*, 1985, *38* (10), 911–936.

Gray, B. *Negotiations: Arenas for Reconstructing Meaning.* Working paper. Center for Research in Conflict and Negotiation. Pennsylvania State University, University Park, Penn., 1989.

Gray, B. *New York City Partnership Youth Employment Initiative.* Report prepared for the Synergos Institute, New York, N.Y., October 1988.

Gray, B., and Hay, T. M. "Political Limits to Interorganizational Consensus and Change." *Journal of Applied Behavioral Science*, 1986, *22* (2), 95–112.

Green, E. D. "The CPR Legal Program Mini-Trial Handbook."

In Center for Public Resources (ed.), *Corporate Dispute Management.* New York: Bender, 1982.

Green, E. D. "Corporate Alternative Dispute Resolution." *Ohio State Journal on Dispute Resolution,* 1986, *1* (2), 203–297.

Gricar, B. G. "Fostering Collaboration Among Organizations." In H. Meltzer and W. R. Nord (eds.), *Making Organizations Humane and Productive.* New York: Wiley, 1981.

Gricar, B. G., and Baratta, A. J. "Bridging the Information Gap: Radiation Monitoring by Citizens." *Journal of Applied Behavioral Science,* 1983, *19* (1), 35–41.

Gricar, B. G., and Brown, L. D. "Conflict, Power and Organization in a Changing Community." *Human Relations,* 1981, *34,* 877–893.

Gross, J. A., and Greenfield, P. A. "Arbital Value Judgments in Health and Safety Disputes: Management Rights Over Workers' Rights." *Buffalo Law Review,* 1986, *34* (3), 645–691.

Gulliver, P. H. *Disputes and Negotiations.* New York: Academic Press, 1979.

Hall, R. P., Clark, J. P., Giordano, P. C., Johnson, P. V., and Van Roekel, M. "Patterns of Interorganizational Relationships." *Administrative Science Quarterly,* 1977, *22,* 457–74.

Hallisey, B., Sanabria, S., and Salter, M. S. "[TC^2] and the Apparel Industry." Case 0-387-160. Boston: Harvard Business School, 1987.

Hanlon, M. D., and Williams, J. C. "In Jamestown: Labor-Management Committee at Work." *QWL Review,* Summer 1982, *1* (3), 2–8.

Harding, M. E. *The "I" and the "Not-I": A Study in the Development of Consciousness.* Princeton, N.J.: Princeton University Press, 1965.

Harrington, C. B. "Voluntariness, Consent and Coercion in Adjudicating Minor Disputes: The Neighborhood Justice Center." In J. Brigham and D. Brown (eds.), *Policy Implementation: Choosing Between Penalties and Incentives.* Beverly Hills, Calif.: Sage, 1980.

Harris, L., and Cronen, V. E. "A Rules-Based Model for the Analysis and Evaluation of Organizational Communication." *Communication Quarterly,* Winter 1979, 12–28.

Harter, P. J. "Negotiating Regulations: A Cure for Malaise." *Georgetown Law Journal*, 1982, *71* (1), 1–188.

Harter, P. J. "Regulatory Negotiation: An Overview." *Dispute Resolution Forum*, Jan. 1986, 3–4, 11–14.

Hay, T. M. *The National Coal Policy Project: Analysis of One Collaborative Approach to Problem Solving.* Thesis, University Scholars Programs, Division of Organizational Behavior, Pennsylvania State University, June 16, 1983.

Hayes, S. "What's Wrong with Mediation?" *Sylvanian,* Feb.–Mar. 1988, 2.

Haygood, L. V. "Opportunities and Challenges in Providing State-Level Support for the Mediation of Public Disputes." *Resolve,* 1988, *1* (19), 3–10.

Hedberg, B.L.T., Nystrom, P. C., and Starbuck, W. H. *Designing Organizations to Match Tomorrow.* In P. C. Nystrom and W. H. Starbuck (eds.), *Prescriptive Models of Organizations. North-Holland and TIMS Studies in the Management Sciences,* 1977, *5,* 171–181.

Heenan, D. A., and Perlmutter, H. V. *Multinational Organization Development.* Reading, Mass.: Addison-Wesley, 1979.

Heimer, C. "Allocating Information Costs in a Negotiated Information Order: Interorganizational Constraints on Decision Making in Norwegian Oil Insurance." *Administrative Science Quarterly,* 1985, *30,* 395–417.

Hill, W. L., Hitt, M. A., and Hoskisson, R. E. "Declining U.S. Competitiveness: Reflections on a Crisis." *Academy of Management Executive,* 1988, *2* (1), 51–59.

Hirschman, A. O. *Exit, Voice and Loyalty: Responses to Decline in Firms, Organizations and States.* Cambridge, Mass.: Harvard University Press, 1970.

Hofstede, G. *Culture's Consequences: International Differences in Work-Related Values.* Beverly Hills, Calif.: Sage, 1980.

Holusha, J. "Mixing Cultures on the Assembly Line." *New York Times,* June 5, 1988, 1, 8.

Horowitch, M., and Prahalad, C. K. "Managing Multi-Organizational Enterprises: The Emerging Strategic Frontier." *Sloan Management Review,* 1981, *22* (2), 3–16.

Hughes, B. B. *World Futures: A Critical Analysis of Alternatives.* Baltimore, Md.: Johns Hopkins University Press, 1985.

"Industry, Activists Unite on Coal." *Coal Outlook*, Feb. 13, 1978.

Jantsch, E. *The Self-Organizing Universe*. New York: Pergamon Press, 1979.

Johnson, E. W. *Management and Labor: Breaking Away*. Speech presented at DePaul University, Baldwin-Wallace College, and University of Illinois at Chicago, Spring 1988. Detroit, Mich.: General Motors Corporation.

Kaplan, R. E. "Intervention in a Loosely Organized System: An Encounter with Non-Being." *Journal of Applied Behavioral Science*, 1982, *18* (4), 415–432.

Katz, H. *Shifting Gears*. Cambridge, Mass.: MIT Press, 1985.

Kaye, P. E. "Health Care Spotlight: Issues for Dispute Resolution." In *Dispute Resolution: An Open Forum. Proceedings of the Fourteenth Annual Conference*. Washington, D.C.: Society for Professionals in Dispute Resolution, 1986.

Kemeny, J. G. *Report on the President's Commission on the Accident at Three Mile Island*. Washington, D.C.: U.S. Government Printing Office, Oct. 31, 1979.

Kennedy, M., and Goldberg, R. "Migrant Farm Workers in the Midwest." Case 0-586-073. Boston: Harvard Business School, 1985.

Keystone Center, Annual Report. Keystone, Colo.: Keystone Center, 1986.

King, W. R. "Environmental Analysis and Forecasting: The Importance of Strategic Issues." *Journal of Business Strategy*, Winter 1981, *2*, 74.

Kirlin, J. L. *The Political Economy of Fiscal Limits*. Lexington, Mass.: Lexington Books, 1982.

Klein, D. "Some Notes on the Dynamics of Resistance to Change: The Defender Role." In W. Bennis, K. D. Benne, R. Chin, and K. E. Cory (eds.). *The Planning of Change*. New York: Holt, Rinehart, and Winston, 1976.

Kochan, J., Katz, H., and McKersie, R. *The Transformation of American Industrial Relations*. New York: Basic Books, 1987.

Kolb, D. M. *The Mediators*. Cambridge, Mass.: MIT Press, 1983.

Kosnett, J. "Enemies Tour Battle Sites." *Charleston Daily Mail*, September 30, 1977, 2C.

Kriger, M. P. "The Increasing Role of Subsidiary Boards in

MNC's: An empirical study." *Strategic Management Journal,* 1988, *9,* 347–360.

Laumann, E. O., Galaskiewicz, J., and Marsden, P. "Community Structure as Interorganizational Linkages." *Annual Review of Sociology,* 1978, *4,* 455–484.

Lawrence, P., and Lorsch, J. *Organizations and Environment: Managing Differentiation and Integration.* Boston: Harvard University Graduate School of Business, 1967.

Lax, D. A., and Sebenius, J. K. *The Manager as Negotiator.* New York: Free Press, 1986.

Levine, M., and Trachtman, R. *School/Business Partnerships: A Share in New York's Future.* Report prepared for the New York City Partnership, Oct. 25, 1985.

Levine, S., and White, P. E. "Exchange as a Conceptual Framework for the Study of Interorganizational Relations." *Administrative Science Quarterly,* 1961, *5,* 583–601.

Levitan, S. A., and Werneke, D. *Productivity: Problems, Prospects and Policies.* Baltimore, Md.: Johns Hopkins University Press, 1984.

Lichtenberg, F. R., and Siegel, D. *Using Linked Census R&D-LED Data to Analyze the Effect of R&D Investment on Total Factor Productivity Growth.* Columbia University, Jan. 1987.

Lieberman, J. K. *The Litigious Society.* New York: Basic Books, 1983.

Lilly, W., III, and Miller, J. C., III. "The New Social Regulation." *Public Interest,* 1977, *47,* 49–52.

Lodge, G. *The New American Ideology.* New York: Knopf, 1975.

Lorsch, J. "Managing Culture: The Invisible Barrier to Strategic Change." *California Management Review,* 1986, *28* (2), 95–109.

Lowi, T. J. *The End of Liberalism.* New York: Norton, 1969.

Luke, J. S. *Managing Interconnectedness: The Challenge of Shared Power.* Paper presented at the Conference on Shared Power, University of Minnesota, May 10, 1984.

Lund, R. T., and Hansen, J. A. *Keeping America at Work: Strategies for Employing the New Technologies.* New York: Wiley, 1986.

Lundine, S. *The Jamestown Labor Management Committee.* Presentation to the Conference on Collaborative Problem Solving, Synergos Institute, Pocantico Hills, New York, May 10–12, 1987.

Lyall, K. C. "Public-Private Partnerships in the Carter Years." In P. Davis (ed.), *Public-Private Partnerships: Improving Urban Life.* New York: Academy of Political Science, 1986.

McCann, J. E. *Developing Interorganizational Domains: Concepts and Practice.* Unpublished doctoral dissertation, Wharton School, University of Pennsylvania, 1980.

McCann, J. E. "Design Guidelines for Social Problem-Solving Interventions." *Journal of Applied Behavioral Science,* 1983, *19,* 177–189.

McCarthy, J., with Shorett, A. *Negotiating Settlements: A Guide to Environmental Mediation.* New York: American Arbitration Association, 1984.

McCrory, J. P. "Environmental Mediation, Another Piece for the Puzzle." *Vermont Law Review,* 1981, *6* (1), 49–84.

McGovern, F. E. "Toward a Functional Approach for Managing Complex Litigation." *University of Chicago Law Review,* 1986, *53,* 440–493.

McKewen, T. D., and Sloan, A. C. "A Successful Hazardous Waste Landfill Siting—Maryland's Experience." *Site Management and Closure,* 1986, 247–251.

McQuaid-Cook, J. *Yes in My Backyard: Managing Special Wastes in Alberta.* Environment Canada, Eighth Canadian Waste Management Conference, Halifax, Sept. 3–5, 1986. Ottawa: Environment Canada, 29–37.

Manufacturing Studies Board. *Toward a New Era in U.S. Manufacturing.* Washington, D.C.: National Academy Press, 1986.

Mason, R. O., and Mitroff, I. I. *Challenging Strategic Planning Assumptions.* New York: Wiley, 1981.

Mather, L., and Yngvesson, B. "Language, Audience, and the Transformation of Disputes." *Law and Society Review,* 1980–1, *15* (3–4), 775–821.

Mead, M. *Culture and Commitment: The New Relations Between the Generations in the 1970s.* New York: Columbia University Press, 1978.

Meyer, J. M., and Rowan, B. "Institutionalized Organizations:

Formal Structure as Myth and Ceremony." *American Journal of Sociology,* 1977, *83* (2), 340–363.

Meyer, J. W., and Scott, W. R. *Organizational Environments.* Beverly Hills, Calif.: Sage, 1983.

Michael, D. *On Learning to Plan and Planning to Learn.* San Francisco: Jossey-Bass, 1973.

Millstein, I. M., and Katsh, S. M. *The Limits of Corporate Power.* New York: Macmillan, 1981.

Milward, H. B. "Interorganizational Policy Systems and Research on Public Organizations." *Administration and Society,* 1982, *13* (4), 457–478.

Mitroff, I. I. *Business Not as Usual: Rethinking Our Individual, Corporate, and Industrial Strategies for Global Competition.* San Francisco: Jossey-Bass, 1987.

Monthly News. Air Products & Chemicals, Inc., 1978.

Moore, C. W. *The Mediation Process: Practical Strategies for Resolving Conflict.* San Francisco: Jossey-Bass, 1986.

Morgan, G. "Cybernetics and Organization Theory: Epistemology or Technique?" *Human Relations,* 1982, *35* (7), 521–538.

Morgan, G., and Ramirez, R. "Action Learning: A Holographic Metaphor for Guiding Social Change." *Human Relations,* 1984, *37,* 1–28.

Motamedi, K., and Cummings, T. "Transorganizational Development: Developing Relations Among Organizations." In D. D. Warrich (ed.), *Contemporary Organization Development.* Glenview, Ill.: Scott, Foresman, 1984.

Moxon, R. W., and Geringer, J. M. "Multinational Ventures in the Commercial Aircraft Industry." *Columbia Journal of World Business,* 1985, Summer, 55–62.

Mulford, C. L., and Rogers, D. L. "Definitions and Models." In D. L. Rogers and D. A. Whetten (eds.), *Interorganizational Coordination.* Ames: Iowa State University Press, 1982.

Murray, F. X., and Curran, J. C. *The National Coal Policy Project: Interim Report to the Mellon Foundation.* Washington, D.C.: Center for Strategic and International Studies, 1981.

Murray, F. X., and Curran, J. C. *Why They Agreed: A Critique and Analysis of the National Coal Policy.* Washington, D.C.: Center for Strategic and International Studies, 1982.

Naisbett, J. *Megatrends.* New York: Warner, 1982.

National Coal Policy Project: Final Report. Washington, D.C.: Center for Strategic and International Studies, 1981.

National Institute for Work and Learning. *Industry-Education-Labor Collaboration: An Action Guide for Collaborative Councils.* Washington, D.C., 1981.

National Research Council. *Critical Issues for National Urban Policy.* Washington, D.C., 1982.

Nemeth, C. "Bargaining and Reciprocity." *Psychological Bulletin,* 1970, *74,* 297–308.

Neu, C. H., Jr. "Strategic Governance: A Community Integration Process." *National Civic Review,* 1988, 77 (2), 133–142.

A New Partnership to Conserve America's Communities: National Urban Policy. President's Urban and Regional Group Report. Washington, D.C.: U.S. Government Printing Office, Mar. 1978.

New York City Partnership, Inc. *The Partnership Blueprint: Strengthening New York as a World City.* New York: New York City Partnership, 1984.

Ohmae, K. *Triad Power: The Coming Shape of Global Competition.* New York: Free Press, 1985.

O'Leary, M. C. "Negotiated Settlements in Utility Regulation." *Public Utilities Fortnightly,* August 21, 1986, 11–14.

Olson, M. *The Logic of Collective Action: Public Goods and the Theory of Groups.* Cambridge, Mass.: Harvard University Press, 1965.

O'Toole, J. *Declining Innovation: The Failure of Success. A Summary Report of the Seventh Twenty-Year Forecast Project.* Center for Futures Research, Graduate School of Business, University of Southern California, 1983, 1–28.

O'Toole, R., and O'Toole, A. W. Negotiating Interorganizational Orders. *Sociological Quarterly,* 1981, *22* (1), 29–41.

Otterbourg, S. D., and Timpane, M. "Partnerships and Schools." In P. Davis (ed.), *Public-Private Partnerships: Improving Urban Life.* New York: Academy of Political Science, 1986.

Ozbekhan, H. "Planning and Human Action." In P. A. Weiss (ed.), *Hierarchically Organized Systems in Theory and Practice.* New York: Hafner, 1971, 123–230.

Ozbekhan, H. "The Future of Paris: A Systems Study in Strategic Urban Planning." In J. Sutherland (ed.), *Management Handbook for Public Administrators*. New York: Van Nostrand Reinhold, 1979.

Parenti, M. "Power and Pluralism: A View from the Bottom." *Journal of Politics*, 1970, *32*, 501–530.

Patton, L. K. "Problems in Environmental Mediation: Human, Procedural and Substantive." *Environmental Consensus*, Nov. 1981, 7–10.

Peelle, E. "Innovative Process and Inventive Solutions: A Case Study of Local Public Acceptance of a Proposed Nuclear Waste Packaging and Storage Facility." In Rene Dubos Institute for Environmental Management, *Symposium on Land Use Management*. New York: Praeger Press, 1987.

Pennar, K. "The Productivity Paradox." *Business Week*, June 6, 1988, 100–102.

"Pennsylvania MILRITE Council: Three year report." *Partners in Progress*. Harrisburg, Pa., 1983.

Perlmutter, H. V., and Heenan, D. A. "Cooperate to Compete Globally." *Harvard Business Review*, Mar.–Apr. 1986, 136–152.

Perlmutter, H. V., and Trist, E. "Paradigms for Societal Transition." *Human Relations*, 1986, *39* (1), 1–27.

Perritt, H. H., Jr. "Administrative Alternative Dispute Resolution: The Development of Negotiated Rulemaking and Other Processes." *Pepperdine Law Review*, 1987, *14* (4), 863–928.

Perucci, R., and Pilisuk, M. "Leaders and Ruling Elites: The Interorganizational Basis of Community Power." *American Sociological Review*, 1970, *35*, 1040–57.

Peters, T. "Restoring American Competitiveness: Looking for New Models of Organizations." *Academy of Management Executive*, May 1988, *2* (2), 103–110.

Pfeffer, J. "Management as Symbolic Action: The Creation and Maintenance of Organizational Paradigms." In L. L. Cummings and B. M. Staw (eds.), *Research in Organizational Behavior*. Greenwich, Conn.: JAI Press, 1981, *3*, 1–52.

Pfeffer, J., and Salancik, G. *The External Control of Organizations*. New York: Harper and Rowe, 1978.

Post, J. E. *Corporate Behavior and Social Change*. Reston, Va.: Reston, 1978.

Prigogine, I. "Order Through Fluctuation: Self-organization and Social System." In E. Jantsch and C. H. Waddington (eds.), *Evolution and Consciousness: Human Systems in Transition.* Reading, Mass.: Addison-Wesley, 1976.

"A Promising Stab at Environmental Dialogue." *Industry Week,* Jan. 17, 1977, 25-26.

Provan, K. "The Federation as an Interorganizational Linkage Network." *Academy of Management Review,* 1983, *8* (1), 79-89.

Provan, K. G., Beyer, J. M., and Kruytbosch, C. "Environmental Linkages and Power in Resource-Dependence Relations Between Organizations." *Administrative Science Quarterly,* 1980, *25,* 200-225.

Pruitt, D. G., and Lewis, S. A. "The Psychology of Integrative Bargaining." In D. Druckman (ed.), *Negotiations: Social Psychological Perspectives.* Beverly Hills, Calif.: Sage, 1977.

Raiffa, H. *The Art and Science of Negotiation.* Cambridge, Mass.: Harvard University Press, 1982.

Raiffa, H. "Post-Settlement Settlements." *Negotiation Journal,* 1985, *1,* 9-12.

Ramirez, R. "Action Learning: A Strategic Approach for Organizations Facing Turbulent Conditions." *Human Relations,* 1983, *36* (8), 725-742.

Redford, R. "Search for Common Ground." *Harvard Business Review,* May-June 1987, 107-112.

"Regulatory Negotiation: Four Perspectives." *Dispute Resolution Forum,* Jan. 1986, 8-11.

Reich, R. B. "Regulation by Confrontation or Negotiation." *Harvard Business Review,* 1981, *59* (3), 82-93.

Reich, R. B. *The Next American Frontier.* New York: Times Books, 1983.

Richman, R. "Formal Mediation in Intergovernmental Disputes: Municipal Annexation Negotiations in Virginia." *Public Administration Review,* 1985, *45* (4), 510-517.

Riesel, D. "Negotiation and Mediation of Environmental Disputes." *Ohio State Journal on Dispute Resolution,* 1985, *1* (1), 99-111.

Rittel, H. W. J., and Webber, M. W. "Dilemmas in a General Theory of Planning." *Policy Sciences,* 1973, *4,* 155-169.

Rogers, D. L. "Reflections and Synthesis: New Directions." In D. L. Rogers, D. A. Whetten, and Associates, *Interorganizational Coordination*. Ames: Iowa State University Press, 1982.

Rogers, D. L., Whetten, D. A., and Associates. *Interorganizational Coordination*. Ames: Iowa State University Press, 1982.

Rogovin, M. *Three Mile Island. Report to the Commissioners and to the Public*. Washington, D.C.: U.S. Nuclear Regulatory Commission Special Inquiry Group, Jan. 24, 1980.

Rosenau, J. *The Study of Global Interdependence: Essays on the Transnationalization of World Affairs*. New York: Nicholas, 1980.

Rubin, J. Z., and Brown, B. R. *The Social Psychology of Bargaining and Negotiation*. Orlando, Fla.: Academic Press, 1975.

Ruckelshaus, W. D. "Resolving Environmental Disputes." Presentation at the second National Conference on Environmental Dispute Resolution, the Conservation Foundation, Washington, D.C., Oct. 1, 1984.

Sapolsky, H. M. *The Polaris System Development*. Cambridge, Mass.: Harvard University Press, 1972.

Sarason, S. B., and Lorentz, E. *The Challenge of the Resource Exchange Network: From Concept to Action*. San Francisco: Jossey-Bass, 1979.

Saunders, H. H. "We Need a Larger Theory of Negotiation: The Importance of Pre-Negotiating Phases." *Negotiation Journal*, 1985, *1* (3), 249-262.

Schein, E. "Personal Change Through Interpersonal Relationships." In W. G. Bennis, J. Van Maanen, E. H. Schein, and F. I. Steele (eds.), *Essays in Interpersonal Dynamics*. Homewood, Ill.: Dorsey, 1979.

Scherer, F. M. "R&D and Declining Productivity Growth." *American Economic Review*, 1983, *73*, 215-218.

Scherer, F. M. *Innovation and Growth: Schumpeterian Perspectives*. Cambridge, Mass.: MIT Press, 1984.

Schermerhorn, J. R. "Determinants of Interorganizational Cooperation." *Academy of Management Review*, 1975, *18* (4), 846-856.

Schermerhorn, J. R. "Interorganizational Development." *Journal of Management*, 1979, *5*, 21-38.

Schmidt, S. M., and Kochan, T. A. "Interorganizational Relationships: Patterns and Motivations." *Administrative Science Quarterly*, 1977, *22*, 220-234.

Schmitter, P. C. "Still the Century of Corporatism." *Review of Politics*, 1974, *85*, 85-131.

Schön, D. A. "Generative Metaphor: A Perspective on Problem-Setting in Social Policy." In A. Ortony (ed.), *Metaphor and Thought*. Cambridge, England: Cambridge University Press, 1979.

Schön, D. "Framing and Re-Framing the Problems of Cities." In D. Morley, S. Proudfoot, and T. Burns (eds.), *Making Cities Work*. Boulder, Col.: Westview Press, 1980.

Schumaker, P. D. "Policy Responsiveness to Protest Group Demands." *Journal of Politics*, 1975, *37*, 488-521.

Schuster, M. "Models of Cooperation and Change in Union Settings." *Industrial Relations*, 1985, *24* (3), 382-394.

Scobel, D. N. "Business and Labor—From Adversaries to Allies." *Harvard Business Review*, Nov.-Dec. 1982, pp. 129-136.

Scott, W. R., and Meyer, J. W. "Environmental Linkages and Organizational Complexity: Public and Private Schools." In H. M. Levin and T. James (eds.), *Comparing Public and Private Schools*. New York: Falmer Press, 1987.

Scranton, W. W. *Report on the Governor's Commission on Three Mile Island*. Harrisburg: Commonwealth of Pennsylvania, Feb. 26, 1980.

Selznick, P. *Leadership and Administration*. Evanston, Ill.: Row, Peterson, 1957.

Sherif, M. "Superordinate Goals in the Reduction of Intergroup Conflicts." *American Journal of Sociology*, 1958, *63*, 349-358.

Smircich, L. "Organizations as Shared Meaning." In L. R. Pondy, P. Frost, G. Morgan, and T. Dandridge (eds.), *Organizational Symbolism*. Greenwich, Conn.: JAI Press, 1983.

Smith, A. "Commonwealth Cross-Sections: Prenegotiation to Minimize Conflict and to Develop Cooperation." In E. S. Lall (ed.), *Multilateral Negotiation and Mediation: Instruments and Methods*. Elmsford, New York: Pergamon, 1985.

Smith, B.L.R. "Changing Public–Private Sector Relations." *Annals*, 1983, *446*, 149-164.

Smith, K. *Groups in Conflict: Prisons in Disguise."* Dubuque, Iowa: Kendall/Hunt, 1982.

Solomon, J. "To Cut Backlog, an Ohio Court Tries Mediation." *Wall Street Journal,* May 19, 1986.

Stein, A. A. "Conflict and Cohesion." *Journal of Conflict Resolution,* 1976, *20* (1), 143–172.

Stephan, A. *The State and Society: Peru in Comparative Perspective.* Princeton, N.J.: Princeton University Press, 1978.

Stewart, R. B. "The Reformation of American Administrative Law." *Harvard Law Review,* 1975, *88,* 1667, 1790–1802.

Strauss, A. *Negotiations: Varieties, Contexts, Processes, and Social Order.* San Francisco: Jossey-Bass, 1978.

Strauss, A., and Others. "The Hospital and Its Negotiated Order." In E. Freidson (ed.), *The Hospital in Modern Society.* New York: Free Press, 1963.

Strauss, D. *Process Management: Planning the Plan to Do.* Presentation at the Conference on Collaboration and Conflict Resolution in Community Problem Solving: Emerging Trends and Methods, Washington, D.C., March 17, 1988.

Strauss, D., Clark, P., and Susskind, L. *Guidelines to Identify, Manage and Resolve Environmental Disputes.* New York: Research Institute, American Arbitration Association, n.d.

Susskind, L. "Environmental Mediation and the Accountability Problem." *Vermont Law Review,* 1981, *6* (1), 1–47.

Susskind, L. E. "Court-Appointed Masters as Mediators." *Negotiation Journal,* Oct. 1985, 295–300.

Susskind, L. E., Bacow, L., and Wheeler, M. *Resolving Environmental Regulatory Disputes.* Cambridge, Mass.: Schenkman, 1983.

Susskind, L. E., and Cruikshank, J. *Breaking the Impasse.* New York: Basic Books, 1987.

Susskind, L., and McMahon, G. "The Theory and Practice of Negotiated Rulemaking." *Yale Journal on Regulation,* 1985, *3* (1), 133–165.

Susskind, L., and Madigan, D. "New Approaches to Resolving Disputes in the Public Sector." *Justice System Journal,* 1984, *9* (2), 197–203.

Susskind, L., and Ozawa, C. "Mediated Negotiation in the Public Sector." *American Behavioral Scientist,* 1983, *27,* 2.

Taber, T. D., Walsh, J. F., and Cooke, R. A. "Developing a Community-Based Program for Reducing the Social Impact of a Plant Closing." *Journal of Applied Behavioral Science*, 1979, *15* (2), 133–155.

Talbot, A. R. *Settling Things: Six Case Studies in Environmental Mediation*. Washington, D.C.: Conservation Foundation, 1983.

Tinbergen, J. *Reshaping the International Order: A Report to the Club of Rome*. New York: Dutton, 1976.

TMI Support Staff. *Environmental Assessment for Decontamination of the Three Mile Island, Unit 2 Reactor Building Atmosphere*. (NUREG-0662.) Washington, D.C.: Office of Nuclear Regulation, U.S. Nuclear Regulatory Commission, Mar. 1980.

Toffler, A. *The Adaptive Corporation*. New York: McGraw-Hill, 1985.

Tolbert, P., and Zucker, L. G. "Institutional Sources of Change in the Formal Structure of Organizations: The Diffusion of Civil Service Reform, 1800–1935." *Administrative Science Quarterly*, 1983, *23*, 22–39.

Tolbert, P., and Allen, J. B. "Institutionalization and Negotiations in Organizations." In R. Lewicki, M. Bazerman, and B. Sheppard (eds.), *Research on Negotiations, Vol. 2*. Greenwich, Conn.: 1988.

Touval, S., and Zartman, I. W. "Introduction: Mediation in Theory." In S. Touval and I. W. Zartman (eds.), *International Mediation in Theory and Practice*. Boulder, Colo.: Westview Press, 1985.

Trist, E. L. "A Concept of Organizational Ecology." *Australian Journal of Management*, 1977, *2*, 162–175.

Trist, E. L. "Referent Organizations and the Development of Interorganizational Domains." *Human Relations*, 1983, *36* (3), 247–268.

Trist, E. L. "Intervention Strategies in Interorganizational Domains." In R. Tannenbaum, R. Marguiles, and F. Massarik (eds.), *Human Systems Development*. San Francisco: Jossey-Bass, 1985.

Truman, D. *The Governmental Process*. New York: Knopf, 1975.

Unger, R. M. *Social Theory: Its Situation and Its Task.* Cambridge, England: Cambridge University Press, 1987.

Uphoff, N. *Drawing on Social Energy in Project Implementation: A Learning Process Experience in Sri Lanka.* Paper presented at the American Society for Public Administration Meetings, Boston, March 1987.

"Use of Mini-Trial Seeks to Ease Burden of Corporate Litigation." *Washington Post,* Oct. 13, 1985.

Van Bever, D. "HBS Focuses Microscope on General Electric CEO." *Harbor News,* Nov. 2, 1987, *51* (25), 1, 5.

Van de Ven, A. H., Emmett, D. C., and Koenig, R., Jr. "Theoretical and Conceptual Issues in Interorganizational Theory." In A. R. Negandhi (ed.), *Interorganizational Theory.* Kent, Ohio: Kent State University Press, 1975.

Van de Ven, A. H., and Walker, G. "The Dynamics of Interorganizational Coordination." *Administrative Science Quarterly,* 1984, *29* (4), 598–621.

Van de Ven, A. H., Walker, G., and Liston, J. "Coordination Patterns Within an Inter-Organizational Network." *Human Relations,* 1979, *32,* 19–35.

Vickers, Sir G. *The Art of Judgment.* London: Chapman and Hall, 1965.

Vickers, Sir G. *Value Systems and Social Process.* London: Tavistock/New York: Basic Books, 1968.

Waddock, S. *Public-Private Partnership in Boston: An Urban Case Study.* Working paper. Boston: School of Management, Boston College, 1986.

Walton, R. E. *Interpersonal Peacemaking: Confrontations and Third-Party Consultation.* Reading, Mass.: Addison-Wesley, 1969.

Walton, R. E. "Third-Party Roles in Interdepartmental Conflict." In W. W. Burke and H. A. Hornstein (eds.), *The Social Technology of Organization Development.* La Jolla, Calif.: University Associates, 1972.

Wamsley, G., and Zald, M. "The Environments of Public Managers: Managing Turbulence." In W. Eddy (ed.), *Handbook of Organization Management.* New York: Marcel Dekker, 1983.

Warren, R. L. "The Interorganizational Field as a Focus for Investigation." *Administrative Science Quarterly,* 1967, *12,* 396–419.

Warren, R., Rose, S., and Bergunder, A. *The Structure of Urban Reform.* Lexington, Mass.: Heath, 1974.

Weick, K. "Educational Organizations as Loosely Coupled Systems." *Administrative Science Quarterly,* 1977, *21,* 1–19.

Wessel, M. R. *The Rule of Reason: A New Approach to Corporate Litigation.* Reading, Mass.: Addison-Wesley, 1976.

"Where Do Industry and Ecology Meet?" *Coal Outlook,* Oct. 10, 1977.

Whetten, D. A., and Aldrich, H. "Organization Set Size and Diversity: Links Between People-Processing Organizations and Their Environments." *Administration and Society,* 1979, *11,* 251–282.

Whetten, D. A., and Bozeman, B. *Policy Coordination and Interorganizational Relations: Some Guidelines for Sharing Power.* Paper presented at the Conference on Shared Power, Humphrey Institute and School of Management, University of Minnesota, May 10, 1984.

Whetten, D. A., and Leung, T. K. "The Instrumental Value of Interorganizational Relations: Antecedents and Consequences of Linkage Formation." *Academy of Management Journal,* 1979, *22,* 325–44.

Wildavsky, A. *Speaking Trust to Power—The Art and Craft of Policy Analysis.* Boston: Little, Brown, 1979.

Williams, T. A. *Learning to Manage Our Futures.* New York: Wiley, 1982.

Wilson, G. K. "Why Is There No Corporatism in the United States?" In G. Lembruch and P. C. Schmitter (eds.), *Patterns of Corporatist Policy-Making.* Beverly Hills, Calif.: Sage, 1982.

Wondolleck, J. "The Importance of Process in Resolving Environmental Disputes." *Environmental Impact Assessment Review,* 1985, *5,* 341–356.

Woodcock, L. "A Negotiator's Advice to Lawyers." University of Michigan Law School, *Quadrangle Notes,* 1982, *27,* 28–30.

Wright, D. S. "Managing the Intergovernmental Scene: The

Changing Dramas of Federalism, Intergovernmental Relations and Intergovernmental Management." In W. G. Eddy (ed.), *Handbook of Organization Management.* New York: Marcel Dekker, 1983.

Young, O. "Intermediaries: Additional Thoughts on Third Parties." *Journal of Conflict Resolution,* 1972, *16* (1), 51-65.

Zartman, W., and Berman, M. R. *The Practical Negotiator.* New York: Yale University Press, 1982.

Ziegler, H. *Pluralism, Corporatism and Confucianism.* Philadelphia: Temple University Press, 1988.

Zucker, L. G. "The Role of Institutionalization in Cultural Persistence." *American Sociological Review,* 1977, *41,* 726-743.

Zucker, L. G. "Organizations as Institutions." In S. B. Bacharach (ed.), *Research in the Sociology of Organizations,* Vol. 2. Greenwich, Conn.: JAI Press, 1983.

Name Index

Subject Index